Fore

M000075981

For more than 90 years, the Gospel Advocate Company has published annually a year's worth of lessons for Bible study. Originally called *Elam's Notes* because E.A. Elam was the author, the title later changed to *Teacher's Annual Lesson Commentary* and then to *Companion*. This 2014–2015 edition offers several improvements in this highly useful class tool.

Additions to the weekly lessons include a reproducible planning outline (see page 10), enabling the teacher to make detailed preparation for each lesson. A second important feature is an essay titled "How to Study *Companion* and *Foundations*" (see page 8). These practical tips should equip the teacher with practices and procedures for class preparation and presentation. The truly conscientious teacher will want to make every effort to present each Bible lesson with all the skills and emphasis possible. No Bible class should suffer from poor or inadequate preparation on the part of the teacher or student.

Also included in this new *Companion* is a schedule for daily Bible reading (see page 270). Following this plan will make it possible for each student to read through the Bible in a year's time and thus aid one's growth "in the grace and knowledge of our Lord and Savior Jesus Christ" (2 Peter 3:18).

The topics covered for 2014-2015 offer a renewed emphasis on basic biblical doctrines and practices for life. The four quarters are based on the overall theme "God's Plan for Us." In detailing that plan, the lessons will deal with these general topics: fall – "This We Believe"; winter – "This We Teach"; spring – "This We Do"; summer – "This We Recognize." The topics are all Bible fundamentals with lessons designed to further one's depth of understanding and appreciation. This is a study of God's Word, and it must be presented with depth and thoroughness, for each soul matters.

These lessons have been written and edited by well-trained and committed Christian teachers and are offered with full confidence in the soundness of each lesson and in the value of each for the lives of individual children of God. May God bless you in your year of study.

– *The Editors*

This We Believe
Fall Quarter

Some truths are so essential that each person must be grounded in those principles. This quarter presents the importance of the Word, inspiration, basic history, salvation, the Christ and the church. These we believe.

Companion 2014-2015
ANNUAL LESSON COMMENTARY

GOD'S PLAN
for Us

FALL

This We Believe

WINTER

This We Teach

SPRING

This We Do

SUMMER

This We Recognize

Published by Gospel Advocate Co.
1006 Elm Hill Pike, Nashville, TN 37210
www.gospeladvocate.com

ISBN: 978-0-89225-636-5

This We Teach
Winter Quarter

Building on the foundational truths studied last quarter, these studies now turn to some basic doctrines held and taught in the church for all Christians. These include the oneness of the church, the Holy Spirit, authority, grace, faith, obedience, repentance, confession and baptism. These we teach.

This We Do
Spring Quarter

With this quarter's emphasis on worship and our participation in it, these in-depth studies enable us to re-examine concepts and practices we have studied before, but now we seek to renew our emphasis on each one. These we do.

This We Recognize
Summer Quarter

These lessons will focus on fellowship, preaching, teaching and serving; at the same time, we must understand church structure; anticipate the return of Jesus; and give serious thought to judgment, heaven and hell. These we recognize.

How to Study *Companion* and *Foundations*

Your desire for a more uniform and biblically oriented study guide for adult Bible class curriculum has led you to *Companion* and *Foundations*. These suggestions will enrich the preparation, teaching, receptivity and appropriate application of this biblical material in your Bible class.

Long-Range and Ongoing Preparation

Companion, a yearly commentary intended to supplement Gospel Advocate's adult and teen quarterlies, contains 52 lessons.

- Place 52 file folders in a filing cabinet or box. Label the files with the 52 lesson titles and the corresponding dates. Place in each file materials that are appropriate for that subject. This will assure you a wealth of resources to use in your teaching ministry in addition to the commentary and quarterlies. Also encourage your students to look for materials that will enrich their participation in the lesson discussions.

- Copy the table of contents before each new quarter, and keep a copy near the place where you do most of your reading and studying. This will help you recognize if something you are reading might be appropriate to incorporate in a future lesson.

- Subscribe to the *Gospel Advocate* magazine. As a teacher, this material will enrich your Bible lessons.

- Glance through the commentary, getting in your mind an overview of the material. Write down what you hope to accomplish in class for the week, quarter and year. What are your immediate and long-range objectives?

Lesson Preparation and Teaching Methods

- Resolve that your lessons will be true to the Scriptures, interesting and not always limited to a question/answer method.

- Employ various methods such as analysis of the Scriptures, discussions, problem solving, reports, lectures, allusions to real situations and role-play.

- Present biblical, historical and present-day illustrations that enlighten the class about the subject being taught.

- When appropriate, give research assignments. Encourage student participation.

Planning Your Weekly Lesson

Keeping the class objectives in mind, start concentrating on the immediate lesson. Prayerfully invest an average of one hour each day in studying and preparing for Sunday's lesson. Here are some suggestions:

Monday: Prayerfully study the Bible lessons presented in *Foundations.* Begin by reading the Scripture text; then read the lesson straight through to get the overall gist and feel of it. Capitalize on what aspects really piqued your interest. Now study the lesson more thoroughly, and answer the questions. Mark the scriptures, sentences and paragraphs that contain answers to the questions. Start jotting down what will help Sunday's lesson to be scriptural, interesting, relevant, practical and helpful.

Tuesday: Prayerfully invest one hour studying the lesson in *Companion.* Make note of scriptures and remarks from that chapter that will enhance the lesson in the student book.

Wednesday: Throughout the day, reflect upon what you have studied. Prayerfully keep the lesson text, your students, and the class environment in mind as you prepare for the lesson. Aim to make the lessons understandable, challenging and applicable so the students leave with something practical and livable.

Thursday: Take one hour to combine ideas from both books, additional scriptures, commentaries and historical and present-day resources for Sunday's lesson. Always be aware of how you can give each lesson an evangelistic slant.

Friday: It is now time to refine the material you have researched. Spend one hour in prayer and study as you organize your thoughts for Sunday's lesson. Divide the lesson not only into main thoughts but also into time segments. It's not always possible or practical to stick with this plan, but doing so helps the lesson progress in an orderly manner and often prevents getting sidetracked. Of course, each class session will be different, and it is imperative to remember that the students' spiritual needs are more important than a rigid outline.

Saturday: Meditate upon the lesson, and visualize how you plan to present it and involve your students. Decide on the type of assignments that will be given for next week's lesson, and write these down to share with your students. By now, you are excited and looking forward to tomorrow, when you and the students will explore God's truths together.

Sunday: Rise early, and find a quiet place to invest one hour in prayer and meditation as you get ready for your class and your lesson. Arrive at the church building at least 30 minutes before the appointed meeting time. Greet the students as they arrive. Present the lesson in truth and love to the best of your ability. When you do this, God will be glorified, your students will be blessed, and you will be motivated to start praying and preparing for next Sunday's lesson.

Finally, remember you have a classroom of souls, each one worth more than the world (Matthew 16:26), and you are sharing a gospel with them that is the power of God to salvation (Romans 1:16)!

These ideas for studying *Companion* and *Foundations* were garnered from an article by Burnice Wesbrooks, reprinted from the July 2001 issue of *Gospel Advocate.*

Planning Outline

Objectives

What are my overall class objectives?

What are my objectives for this lesson?

Introduction

How will I introduce the lesson?

Lesson Topics

What are my main points? How will I present them?

1

2

3

Application

How can I make the lesson relevant/practical?

Next Week

What type of assignment will I give the students for next week?

This We Believe
Fall Quarter

Some truths are so essential that each person must be grounded in those principles. This quarter presents the importance of the Word, inspiration, basic history, salvation, the Christ and the church. These we believe.

Lesson 1 • Week of Sept. 7, 2014

The Reality of God

Job 38:1-11

[1] Then the LORD answered Job out of the whirlwind, and said:

[2] "Who is this who darkens counsel By words without knowledge?

[3] Now prepare yourself like a man; I will question you, and you shall answer Me.

[4] "Where were you when I laid the foundations of the earth? Tell Me, if you have understanding.

[5] Who determined its measurements? Surely you know! Or who stretched the line upon it?

[6] To what were its foundations fastened? Or who laid its cornerstone,

[7] When the morning stars sang together, And all the sons of God shouted for joy?

[8] "Or who shut in the sea with doors, When it burst forth and issued from the womb;

[9] When I made the clouds its garment, And thick darkness its swaddling band;

[10] When I fixed My limit for it, And set bars and doors;

[11] When I said, 'This far you may come, but no farther, And here your proud waves must stop!' "

Psalm 8:1-9

[1] O LORD, our Lord, How excellent is Your name in all the earth, Who have set Your glory above the heavens!

[2] Out of the mouth of babes and nursing infants You have ordained strength, Because of Your enemies, That You may silence the enemy and the avenger.

[3] When I consider Your heavens, the work of Your fingers, The moon and the stars, which You have ordained,

[4] What is man that You are mindful of him, And the son of man that You visit him?

5 For You have made him a little lower than the angels, And You have crowned him with glory and honor.

6 You have made him to have dominion over the works of Your hands; You have put all things under his feet,

7 All sheep and oxen – Even the beasts of the field,

8 The birds of the air, And the fish of the sea That pass through the paths of the seas.

9 O LORD, our Lord, How excellent is Your name in all the earth!

Psalm 139:7-14

7 Where can I go from Your Spirit? Or where can I flee from Your presence?

8 If I ascend into heaven, You are there; If I make my bed in hell, behold, You are there.

9 If I take the wings of the morning, And dwell in the uttermost parts of the sea,

10 Even there Your hand shall lead me, And Your right hand shall hold me.

11 If I say, "Surely the darkness shall fall on me," Even the night shall be light about me;

12 Indeed, the darkness shall not hide from You, But the night shines as the day; The darkness and the light are both alike to You.

13 For You formed my inward parts; You covered me in my mother's womb.

14 I will praise You, for I am fearfully and wonderfully made; Marvelous are Your works, And that my soul knows very well.

Introduction

Whether ancient or modern, people have believed and continue to believe that a universal power, intelligent and eternal, underlies the order and beauty of the world we know. That intelligence or power is by definition God. Atheists were unheard of in the ancient world. Those spawned since the 18th-century Enlightenment continue to be small in number. Christians are hardly distinctive because they believe God exists; people everywhere do. Their distinctiveness lies in their understanding of God. It begins with a conviction that God has entered into the world of men and women in order to speak. The reality of God is more, much more, than the lazy reflection of a middle-aged man observing the night sky. God did not "leave Himself without witness" (Acts 14:17) in the material creation, but what people can know of God from observing the world is limited. To know God requires that there be a voice.

The God Christians worship has done more than leave His fingerprints on the universe; He has spoken. He has injected the human family with His infinity through the limiting medium of language. If it is true, as Christians believe, that

God has spoken, the implications are far reaching. First, it means humankind has confronted authority. The changing landscape of the cosmos is not random. Second, the stuff of the universe is finite. A Creator brought it into being at a point in time. It is proceeding toward an end. Third, to be human is meaningful. Men and women are made "in the image of God" (Genesis 1:27). Morality is objectively rooted in the being of God. Right and wrong mean something.

The battleground where Christians struggle to disarm chaotic "principalities and powers" (Colossians 2:15) that deceive and spread misery to the human family is in the Bible. God has interacted in time with people He has called. Following that, He has communicated by means of His Spirit in order to see that a record of words instruct succeeding generations. Within the pages of the Bible, God declares the fact that He exists and describes who He is. The Bible is a tangible link between God's mighty deeds and the moving kaleidoscope of the present world where people make moral and religious choices. The Bible is the place where the reality of God unfolds.

God the Creator (Job 38:1-11)

When confronted with suffering, the patriarch Job did not throw up his hands and embrace non-belief. Atheism was no option, but Job did summon up the boldness to challenge God. Before tragedy struck, Job and his friends had been on the same page. They agreed that God granted abundance and healthy families to those who offered sacrifice and homage to Him.

But in an instant Job's world turned topsy-turvy. His wealth and health were gone. He sat on an ash heap, scraped his boils with a potsherd and chafed at the rebuke of a nagging wife (Job 2:7-10). When Job's friends arrived, they gave voice to the same belief he had always embraced. God was just. Job's only recourse, they said, was to confess his offenses against God and to plead for forgiveness. As the man of integrity he was, Job refused to manipulate God by saying what he believed to be a lie. He had done nothing to offend God; his suffering had no reason behind it. God had been unjust. To the consternation of his friends, Job gave voice to his complaint. He begged God just to leave him alone (7:16-17). Job was in the right, but what did it matter? God's power guaranteed He would prevail (9:1-12). God had acted arbitrarily; justice held no sway in the affairs of men (12:18-25; 19:7-8). Job pleaded with God to confront him face to face (23:1-7).

In time, Job received what he wanted. God spoke to him, but as is normally the case, confrontation was on God's terms. Instead of addressing the issues Job raised, God challenged the patriarch's credentials to practice law before an eternal tribunal. When men choose to indict God, they do well to consider the platform from which they speak. From the whirlwind God spoke, from the chaos of a world tainted by sin, inconsistency and self-serving greed. So you want to be my equal, God said. Were you there when I laid the foundations of the universe? Where are your credentials? Tainted with sin as they are, men and women do well to come to God's presence with humility and faith. His ways are beyond human understanding. The just live by faith. And with these words, the complaint of Job ends.

God and Man (Psalm 8:1-9)

When confronted with the holiness and otherness of God, we sometimes cringe in fear, stammer in ignorance, bask in His lovingkindness, or simply praise. Comparison between the approach of Job to God and that of the psalmist does not result in the pronouncement that one is right and one is wrong. Both were in faith; both from the heart. Job's conviction that God was at work in human affairs was similar to that of the psalmist, but the questions of the two and their response to what they experienced were considerably different. Most of us at various points in our lives have stood in the shoes of each.

Moments of awe may strike us when we stand in the presence of magnificent landscapes or creep upon us in the most ordinary settings. For the psalmist, the night sky evoked awe, and the awe in turn evoked praise. The moon and the stars excited his imagination. In other circumstances it might have been the sun or storm clouds, lightning and rain. The wonders of the created world can settle upon us in settings as varied as the sight of valleys and streams from a mountaintop to the feel of a breeze against the cheek in the quietness of one's back yard.

For the moment, the psalmist pushes the ugliness of the world out of his mind; he gives no thought to the ash heap where Job sat. The ugliness, tears and random accidents of the world are still there; but for all the gloom that might have clouded his mind, he was aware evil had not crowded out the beauty and symmetry of creation. The psalmist's mind turned to humankind. Nothing can be said of God without implications for those created in His image. Nothing can be said of what it means to be human without reflection on God. God sets human power, armies and wisdom at nothing; from the mouth of babes, He manifests strength. Given the frailty and sin of the human family, why should the Creator of stars and galaxies bother with them? Neither the psalmist nor we can explain it. We bask only in His glory and love. For reasons known only to Him, He has visited us. He has made us "a little lower than angels" (Psalm 8:5); He has given us dominion over the works of His hands (v. 6). The Christian can add, when sin and death seemed to be gaining the upper hand, He gave us a Savior and Lord.

God's Presence (Psalm 139:7-14)

Jonah was not alone in the desire to escape God's presence, nor was he alone in discovering the futility of his efforts. God is limited to no point in space; He needs no intelligence agency to let Him know what is happening. "You know my sitting down and my rising up," the psalmist confessed. "You understand my thought afar off" (Psalm 139:2). The one Creator is both omniscient and omnipresent. The psalmist knew there was no corner of creation where he could go and shut God out. God's being permeates all from heaven above to the grave below.

God's omnipresence is both comforting and disconcerting. The comfort follows on the heels of His love. Astronauts whirling about in space and scientists in deep sea submarines are in the presence of God. Anyone who thinks that sin removes him from the care of God is mistaken. His love never fails. Whether it is jubilation or despair, God's presence attends the fluctuation of daily affairs.

The disconcerting aspect of God's omnipresence is that nothing anyone does escapes Him. An old hymn reminds worshipers, "There's an eye watching you." We will hope that morality and goodness spring from higher motives than fear of a celestial spy program, but many could profit from reflecting on the Judge before whom every knee will bow (Romans 14:10), the God who searches the hearts of men and women and knows their ways (Jeremiah 17:10).

Conclusion

Idolatry wears faces in the modern world at once more blatant and more subtle than ancient people could have imaged. Idolatry in its varied forms is men and women worshiping themselves. In the past people formed gods in wood and stone; in the modern world they worship themselves more openly. Whether "secularism" or "scientism" or some other thing, when people dismiss God from their lives, it is the old idolatry with a new name. The mystery of existence guarantees that all of us, in one form or another, adopt religious faith.

The Bible has no systematic treatment of reasons to believe in God. Genesis opens with no theoretical evaluation of monotheism. The reality of God is self-evident. To argue for the existence of God is like arguing that our senses put us in touch with a real world out there, beyond us. It is like arguing that people must breathe and eat in order to live. The reality of God is a truth from which life unfolds, not a theorem that requires proof.

Questions

1. How much can people know about God by observing the natural world?
2. Where can a person read God's self-revelation in words?
3. What would Job and his friends have agreed on before tragedy struck Job?
4. From where did God speak when He confronted Job?
5. How did Job answer when God put questions to him?
6. From what source did the psalmist declare that God decreed power and strength?
7. As the psalmist pondered the night sky, what question filled his mind?
8. Over what has God given mankind domination?
9. From what did the psalmist find himself unable to escape?
10. Who did the psalmist say had formed him in the womb of his mother?

Discussion Starters

1. What were some of the complaints Job brought against God in the course of the discussions with his friends? Do Christians sometimes ask similar things?
2. What did the questions God put to Job have to do with Job's questioning of God and with Job's pleas that God confront him?
3. What do the words "omniscience" and "omnipresence" mean? How does the psalmist apply them to God?
4. How is God's omnipresence both encouraging and disconcerting for Christians? Is fear of God's all-knowing ways a good motivation for righteous living?

The Inspired Word

Psalm 119:89-104

89 Forever, O LORD, Your word is settled in heaven.

90 Your faithfulness endures to all generations; You established the earth, and it abides.

91 They continue this day according to Your ordinances, For all are Your servants.

92 Unless Your law had been my delight, I would then have perished in my affliction.

93 I will never forget Your precepts, For by them You have given me life.

94 I am Yours, save me; For I have sought Your precepts.

95 The wicked wait for me to destroy me, But I will consider Your testimonies.

96 I have seen the consummation of all perfection, But Your commandment is exceedingly broad.

97 Oh, how I love Your law! It is my meditation all the day.

98 You, through Your commandments, make me wiser than my enemies; For they are ever with me.

99 I have more understanding than all my teachers, For Your testimonies are my meditation.

100 I understand more than the ancients, Because I keep Your precepts.

101 I have restrained my feet from every evil way, That I may keep Your word.

102 I have not departed from Your judgments, For You Yourself have taught me.

103 How sweet are Your words to my taste, Sweeter than honey to my mouth!

104 Through Your precepts I get understanding; Therefore I hate every false way.

2 Timothy 3:16-17

16 All Scripture is given by inspiration of God, and is profitable for doctrine, for reproof, for correction, for instruction in righteousness,

17 that the man of God may be complete, thoroughly equipped for every good work.

2 Peter 1:19-21

19 And so we have the prophetic word confirmed, which you do well to heed as a light that shines in a dark place, until the day dawns and the morning star rises in your hearts;

20 knowing this first, that no prophecy of Scripture is of any private interpretation,

21 for prophecy never came by the will of man, but holy men of God spoke as they were moved by the Holy Spirit.

Introduction

The caricature of a guru sitting on a mountain top claiming divine wisdom has a long history. The mountain top is optional, but those who claim to have a personal link with the supernatural, who appeal to experiences to support knowledge about the future or to dictate the way devotees are to behave were hardly rare in the ancient world; neither are they rare in the modern one. Motives, no doubt, vary, but it is a matter of observation that many turn claims to an inside track with the divine into material wealth for themselves. Paul was putting distance between himself and such mediums when he wrote, "For we are not, as so many, peddling the word of God; but as of sincerity, but as from God, we speak in the sight of God in Christ" (2 Corinthians 2:17).

God's messengers, whether prophets, apostles or other inspired men, tended to encounter competition. False prophets (2 Peter 2:1) and false apostles (2 Corinthians 11:13) appeared in short order. To help His people distinguish between those who had a divinely inspired message and those whose claims were unsupported, God gave signs through His spokesmen in order to confirm the truth of what they said. Moses told Israel that when a prophet's words did not come to pass the Lord had not sent him (Deuteronomy 18:22). Paul reminded readers that they had seen the signs of an apostle (2 Corinthians 12:12). The Word once confirmed by miraculous signs (Hebrews 2:3-4) moved from oral to written form. When the New Testament had come into being, the miracles had served their purpose. God never intended miracles to be a part of the long-term life of His church. The written Word "once for all delivered to the saints" (Jude 3) was and continues to be a monument of God's self-revelation.

After the affirmation that God exists, nothing is of more fundamental importance to the Christian family than what He has spoken. Christians believe that the 66 books of the Bible are inclusively and exclusively the authoritative Word God has revealed. In matters of religious faith and morality, the Bible is the only book of its kind. Scripture carefully defined and with established limits is essential if Christians are to be under authority. The words of Scripture are the place where Christians go for guidance. Just as no other god stands as a peer to the God of heaven (Isaiah 45:6-7), nothing else competes with the Bible as the place where God has made known His authoritative will.

God's Word (Psalm 119:89-104)

On the eve of Israel's entering the Promised Land, Moses gathered the people and rehearsed their blessings. These people were God's chosen. The

Lord had guided them through 40 long years of wandering in the wilderness, and as occasion demanded, He had given victory in battle. Before them lay a land flowing with milk and honey. It was the inheritance God had given them. Material blessings were many, but Moses said that none of them compared to this: God had given Israel a law. Their idolatrous neighbors, the lawgiver said, would look at Israel and say, "Surely this great nation is a wise and understanding people" (Deuteronomy 4:6). It was not the land, not victory in battle, not material wealth that made Israel great. The measure of the nation's greatness was in the law. "And what great nation is there," Moses asked, "that has such statutes and righteous judgment as are in all this law?" (v. 8).

Throughout Israel's history, God's self-revelation to prophets and wise men built on the law given through Moses. The longest of the psalms, the longest book of the Bible, is entirely given over to the praise of the law. Psalm 119 is carefully and artistically arranged in order to teach Israel to reflect on and even to revel in the blessings God had given His people when He revealed a law to guide them. The psalm is an elaborate acrostic. Its 176 verses are a multiple of 22 and 8. The Hebrew alphabet has 22 letters; eight lines of the psalm begin with the successive letters. The equivalent in English would be for eight lines to begin with letters from "a" to "z." Verses 89 through 96 of Psalm 119 have eight lines beginning with the Hebrew letter *lamed* (l) and verses 97 through 104 with the letter *mem* (m). Every verse of the psalm draws attention to the blessing God gave Israel because He had spoken. None passes without mention of "word," "faithfulness," "ordinances," "law," "precepts," "testimonies," "commandment," or some other near equivalent. Modern Christians may think of law as restrictive; the psalmist thought of praise.

The author of the psalm felt no need to argue that God had become involved in the affairs of men. The divine origin of the law had been hammered out in experiences of life. The God of law was also the God who established the earth and brought joy to the hearts of His people. The law was no frightening restriction of freedom; it occasioned no wringing of hands or dread. Experience, wisdom and reflection resulted in exuberant praise, "Oh, how I love Your law!" the psalmist wrote. "It is my meditation all the day" (Psalm 119:97). The law blessed by restraining wayward feet from evil, by giving meaning and direction to life that otherwise would be aimless, bleak and cold. The godly learned by experience that God's law was "sweeter than honey" (v. 103); it was a beam of light guiding the path to life.

Inspired by God (2 Timothy 3:16-17)

The ordered life revealed from God stands in contrast to the chaotic evil of lawless men. Timothy was not alone in the requirement that he make a choice. He could give his ear to men who "grow worse and worse, deceiving and being deceived" (2 Timothy 3:13), or he could listen to wisdom from above. He had learned the Holy Scriptures on the knees of his grandmother, Lois, and his mother, Eunice (1:5). The Old Testament had been the first Scripture Timothy had learned, but from Paul and other inspired men he had taken in the gospel,

God's grace revealed through Jesus Christ. Paul, Timothy, Peter and other Christians were conscious that the Holy Spirit was contributing to the store of Scripture through the writings of apostles (1 Corinthians 2:13; 2 Peter 3:16).

For Paul, Scripture was about God's authority in human affairs. Whether it was about doctrine or morality, Scripture was God's expressing His will for His people. If reproof was necessary, if a brother or sister needed to repent and set a new course for life, Scripture set the parameters. Neither salvation by grace nor a life of faith (Ephesians 2:8) meant that law had been eliminated from the Christian vocabulary (1 Corinthians 9:21; Galatians 6:2). God's authority grows out of His fatherhood and His love. Yielding to God's authority is not like a prisoner who yields to his jailer. Through Scripture a Christian comes to know God. Trust and obedience flow from knowledge, and it all flows from His self-revelation in Scripture.

Written by Holy Men of God (2 Peter 1:19-21)

The disciples of Jesus were slow in coming to the understanding that He was the Christ, the Son of God. Nothing was more important to their education than the events that took place on the Mount of Transfiguration (Matthew 17:1-9). Peter reflected on the significance of the voice he and others heard "on the holy mountain" in his second letter (2 Peter 1:18). He continued, "And so we have the prophetic word confirmed" (v. 19). He did not specify whether the events on the mountain confirmed the testimony of Scripture or the testimony of Scripture confirmed the truth of what the apostles heard on the holy mountain. In either case, God's testimony that Jesus was His Son was all the more reason for Christians to heed the teachings of the Bible. In this life, until the day of the Lord's return, Scripture shines like a light, giving guidance in a dark world.

"The prophetic word" is a shortened way to refer to the entirety of Scripture, the law, the prophets and the wisdom writings. Peter declared that no part of the Bible had come at the initiative of men. It was not the product of a human interpretation of events. The 1984 New International Version's rendition, "No prophecy of Scripture came about by the prophet's own interpretation" (2 Peter 1:20) captures the sense well. Scripture, Peter said, came into being when "holy men of God spoke as they were moved by the Holy Spirit" (v. 21). The testimony of the Spirit is a guarantee that those things recorded in the Bible are accurate and complete. Scripture can be trusted to guide the church in its confession of faith and its way of life.

Conclusion

Without an authoritative revelation from God, the darkness of idolatry is the only recourse for humankind. If God has not spoken, in matters of religion and morality people are left to their own devices; they decide for themselves what they want their god or gods to be. One opinion is as good as another; no arbiter exists. An atheist can point to no logical reason for the adoption of whatever moral compass he chooses. A compass requires an external force. A moral compass without God is a meaningless, whirling mechanism. A moral compass is impossible without a religious compass. Over a period of about 1,500 years, God endowed a few of His servants with His Spirit and caused them to put in writing a record of Himself and His ways. The result is the Old and the New Testaments. The reality of God is certain; He has spoken and He continues to speak through His Word. Like Paul, the Christian declares, "I believed and therefore I spoke" (2 Corinthians 4:13).

Questions

1. What did God do so that hearers could distinguish between messengers who were from God and pretenders who served themselves?
2. What is the subject matter of Psalm 119?
3. What literary device used in Psalm 119 demonstrates the thought and artistic structure the psalmist put into its composition?
4. What did the psalmist say the precepts of God had given him?
5. In what ways did the psalmist manifest his love for the law God had given?
6. From whom had Timothy learned the Scriptures from the time he was a child?
7. For what type of instruction did Paul say that Scripture was profitable?
8. How and where did Peter say that God's prophetic word shone?
9. What did Peter mean when he wrote that Scripture was of no "private interpretation" (2 Peter 1:20)?
10. Who moved and inspired holy men of God to put God's revelation in written form?

Discussion Starters

1. Why is a written record of God's self-revelation a necessity if Christians are to have a religious and moral compass?
2. Why did Israel and why ought Christians consider God's laws and His self-revelation the greatest of all their blessings?
3. Why was it important for Paul to put distance between himself and false teachers? What lessons ought Christians to learn from Paul's example?
4. How can a Christian demonstrate that Scripture "given by inspiration of God" (2 Timothy 3:16) includes the New Testament even though Timothy had learned only the Old Testament as a child?

Reading God's Word

Luke 10:25-28

25 And behold, a certain lawyer stood up and tested Him, saying, "Teacher, what shall I do to inherit eternal life?"

26 He said to him, "What is written in the law? What is your reading of it?"

27 So he answered and said, " 'You shall love the LORD your God with all your heart, with all your soul, with all your strength, and with all your mind,' and 'your neighbor as yourself.' "

28 And He said to him, "You have answered rightly; do this and you will live."

Acts 8:30-35

30 So Philip ran to him, and heard him reading the prophet Isaiah, and said, "Do you understand what you are reading?"

31 And he said, "How can I, unless someone guides me?" And he asked Philip to come up and sit with him.

32 The place in the Scripture which he read was this: "He was led as a sheep to the slaughter; And as a lamb before its shearer is silent, So He opened not His mouth.

33 In His humiliation His justice was taken away, And who will declare His generation? For His life is taken from the earth."

34 So the eunuch answered Philip and said, "I ask you, of whom does the prophet say this, of himself or of some other man?"

35 Then Philip opened his mouth, and beginning at this Scripture, preached Jesus to him.

1 Timothy 4:13-16

13 Till I come, give attention to reading, to exhortation, to doctrine.

14 Do not neglect the gift that is in you, which was given to you by prophecy with the laying on of the hands of the eldership.

15 Meditate on these things; give yourself entirely to them, that your progress may be evident to all.

16 Take heed to yourself and to the doctrine. Continue in them, for in doing this you will save both yourself and those who hear you.

Introduction

In comparison to the modern world, written words were scarce in the Greco-Roman culture of the first century. Some 1,500 years would pass before the impact of the printing press would be felt in Western Europe. Ancient people knew writing from personal letters, hand-copied documents or official decrees chiseled into stone. Oral words from trusted messengers tended to be more reliable than a letter. Written documents were easily forged, and many people read poorly or not at all. It was no afterthought when the Jerusalem church composed a letter concerning the imposition of the Law on Gentile converts and decided to send two witnesses with the letter (Acts 15:22). The written word was reinforced by oral testimony.

Imagine a church, perhaps the one at Philippi, gathering in the courtyard of one of the more well-to-do members. If they had used the modern calendar, the year would have been ca. A.D. 64. Christians had gathered early on the first day of the week for song, prayer and mutual exhortation. A full day's work lay ahead of them. A highlight of the gathering would have been their common breaking of bread and sipping of wine in remembrance of God's Son who had died for their sins. Assembly was always anticipated with joy, but on this particular Lord's Day the small assembly of saints was more excited than normal. Word had spread that a letter from Paul had arrived. It was almost like having him present. One of their number stood before the church and read aloud the words from the apostle. The public reading would be the only contact most Christians had with the letter. In months and years to come, the letter would be read and reread scores of times before the church. Reading in the New Testament period was almost exclusively reading aloud. The Greek word translated "reading" normally means to read aloud.

A letter from Paul meant that his personal words could be transported across distance and time, but the written word served purposes the first readers and hearers could have appreciated only dimly. The Jews had gathered law, prophecy and wisdom into an inspired collection of books that were authoritative for doctrine and behavior. The church under the guidance of the Spirit would do the same. Christians recognized that words written by inspired men for specific occasions were of universal significance. Documents inspired by the Spirit were gathered into the New Testament as gospels, history and letters. A canon came into being and with it new importance was given to reading. In order to guide the church, inspired documents have to be read. The New Testament itself testifies to the importance of reading Scripture.

Reading for Content (Luke 10:25-28)

When a lawyer came to Jesus with the question, "What shall I do to inherit eternal life?" (Luke 10:25), He directed him to the written word. Before the lawyer could expect the Bible to speak to his personal situation and before he could expect it to arouse him to more fervent devotion or intense feelings, the lawyer needed to know what the Bible said. He needed to know content. Knowing what the Bible says is fundamental; a person cannot apply what he or she does not know. Gaining personal guidance from the Bible is a slow process requiring a lifetime of meditation. People commonly come to the Bible with preexistent expectations only to be disappointed when they read what it says. Ten minutes of random reading is not likely to be a fix for whatever personal crisis plagues a person at the moment. The believer invests time well when he learns what a Pharisee believed or what a publican did. One does well to locate Corinth on a map and trace the missionary journeys of Paul. In the end Christians must ask how Scripture speaks to their personal situations, but content must at least be the beginning point.

After Jesus referred the lawyer to the content of the Bible, he answered his own question. Jewish rabbis generally agreed that love for the Lord (Deuteronomy 6:5) and love for one's neighbor (Leviticus 19:18) were the greatest commands of the Law. In a different context, Jesus Himself cited the same two passages (Matthew 22:37-39; Mark 12:30-31) to a lawyer/scribe. It was not enough for the lawyer to cite Scripture. Jesus told him, "Do this and you will live" (Luke 10:28). The two passages the lawyer cited were not merely correct answers to be given on a quiz. Jesus challenged him to apply the passages by relating perhaps the best-known story in the Bible, the parable of the good Samaritan. God intended for His Word to be laid up in the heart as a guide for life, but the first thing that Jesus and the lawyer needed to know was the Bible's content.

Reading for Understanding (Acts 8:30-35)

After the martyrdom of Stephen (Acts 7:58-60), Jewish authorities launched a severe persecution that drove many believers from Jerusalem. Among those scattered was Philip, an evangelist (Acts 21:8) and one of the seven who had been appointed to serve the table of Grecian widows (Acts 6:5). Philip appears to be the first who preached the gospel to the Samaritans although Jesus had worked briefly in one of their villages (John 4:39-42). After converting many Samaritans to Christ, Philip was directed by an angel to go to the south, to a desert road running between Jerusalem and the old Philistine city of Gaza (Acts 8:26). An Ethiopian official was traveling the road, returning from Jerusalem on the way to his homeland far to the south. At the Spirit's prodding, Philip approached the official's chariot and heard him reading from the prophet Isaiah.

The Ethiopian was a powerful man, treasurer in the court of the nation's queen Candace, a generic term akin to a pharaoh in Egypt or an emperor in Rome. The treasurer was reading aloud; when he was close enough, Philip recognized the words of Isaiah. Philip asked the man whether he understood what he was reading (Acts 8:30). Implicitly the evangelist asserted that reading was profitable only when accompanied by understanding. The answer of the Ethiopian is a model for those who want the Bible to guide their lives. He responded to Philip's question with one of his own, "How can I, unless someone guides me?" (v. 31).

The Bible reader needs to be careful about whom he asks to guide him, and he needs to be cautious to evaluate what others teach, but in the end Christians need to learn from one another. Others will have insights into Bible doctrine and accurate understanding of the historical and geographical background against which the stories of the Bible unfold. It would be foolish to fail to profit from the study of those who have devoted lifetimes to research. Philip knew more about the Bible, more about the prophecy of Isaiah than the Ethiopian. The queen's treasurer wanted to learn from the evangelist. The Ethiopian had been reading from the prophecy of the suffering servant of the Lord recorded in Isaiah 53. Philip began from that scripture and taught him about the Christ (Acts 8:35).

Reading for Growth (1 Timothy 4:13-16)

When Paul wrote his first letter to Timothy, death was only a few years away. The apostle had no way of knowing when he would be arrested and publicly executed, but he could read the signs. He had a record of imprisonment, and suspicion of Christians in official Roman circles was gaining in strength. Timothy and others who shared the Great Commission (Matthew 28:18-20) had been able to lean on Paul and other inspired men for guidance, but the time was approaching when the generation of Spirit-endowed men would have no further time on earth. Timothy and his peers would need to take up the mantle of the gospel on their own. They would have to fall back on the Old Testament scriptures and on whatever writings of New Testament apostles and prophets they had available (John 14:26). Growth in love, knowledge and godliness would require their reading and their thoughtful assimilation of the written word.

Paul instructed Timothy to give attention to reading. No doubt, the apostle intended for his protégé to read the Old Testament carefully, but he wanted him to read more. Several of Paul's letters were being circulated (2 Peter 3:14-16), and the gospels were in the early stages of composition. It was incumbent upon Timothy to read for his personal growth and edification, but reading was not entirely for personal enrichment. As an evangelist, Timothy was responsible first to allow himself to be guided and then to guide the church in "sound doctrine" (1 Timothy 1:9-10; Titus 1:9). Every Christian is to be a Bible reader and a Bible student, but an evangelist who is supported financially so that he can give his full-time efforts to study and teaching has a special duty. Elders had laid hands on Timothy to ordain and commission his work (Acts 4:14).

Conclusion

People sometimes read the Bible in the way old timers used to take a dose of castor oil. They gritted their teeth and let it slip down with little idea of what it was for or whether it did any good. Having learned that Bible reading is profitable, Christians may open the Bible to a random passage, read a chapter or so and lay it down having little knowledge of what they had just read. If someone were to ask them, they would have difficulty in putting what they had read in their own words. Sometimes people read as a duty but understand little. In order for reading to be profitable it needs to be first for content and then for understanding and finally for growth. Without all three, there is likely to be no increase of faith, no repentance from sin, no moral uprightness and no fervor of love.

Questions

1. Who asked Jesus the question, "What shall I do to inherit eternal life?"
2. How did Jesus respond to the question asked about inheriting eternal life?
3. If a person is to inherit eternal life, obedience to what two commandments is essential?
4. How was reading in the New Testament period different from what modern people usually think of as reading?
5. Where does Philip first appear in Acts? How is he identified later in Acts?
6. Between what two cities was the Ethiopian treasurer traveling when Philip met him?
7. From where in the Bible was the Ethiopian reading when Philip joined him?
8. To what other two things did Paul advise Timothy to give attention along with his reading?
9. How had Timothy received gifts that Paul urged him not to neglect?
10. Who did Paul tell Timothy that he would save by giving proper attention to "the doctrine"?

Discussion Starters

1. How has the invention of the printing press changed the way modern people think about the Word of God? How did most ancient Christians experience the Word?
2. How does the written word in contrast to the oral word make God's authority over the church more effective?
3. What type of balance ought Christians to maintain between individual, private reading and interpretation of the Bible and seeking guidance from others?
4. Why is the responsibility for Bible study greater for a full-time evangelist than for others? Can or should Christians turn over their personal Bible study to a preacher?

Early Hebrew History

Acts 7:2-16

2 And he said, "Brethren and fathers, listen: The God of glory appeared to our father Abraham when he was in Mesopotamia, before he dwelt in Haran,

3 "and said to him, 'Get out of your country and from your relatives, and come to a land that I will show you.'

4 "Then he came out of the land of the Chaldeans and dwelt in Haran. And from there, when his father was dead, He moved him to this land in which you now dwell.

5 "And God gave him no inheritance in it, not even enough to set his foot on. But even when Abraham had no child, He promised to give it to him for a possession and to his descendants after him.

6 "But God spoke in this way: that his descendants would dwell in a foreign land, and that they would bring them into bondage and oppress them four hundred years.

7 'And the nation to whom they will be in bondage I will judge,' said God, 'and after that they shall come out and serve Me in this place.'

8 "Then He gave him the covenant of circumcision; and so Abraham begot Isaac and circumcised him on the eighth day; and Isaac begot Jacob, and Jacob begot the twelve patriarchs.

9 "And the patriarchs, becoming envious, sold Joseph into Egypt. But God was with him

10 "and delivered him out of all his troubles, and gave him favor and wisdom in the presence of Pharaoh, king of Egypt; and he made him governor over Egypt and all his house.

11 "Now a famine and great trouble came over all the land of Egypt and Canaan, and our fathers found no sustenance.

12 "But when Jacob heard that there was grain in Egypt, he sent out our fathers first.

13 "And the second time Joseph was made known to his brothers, and Joseph's family became known to the Pharaoh.

14 "Then Joseph sent and called his father Jacob and all his relatives to him, seventy-five people.

15 "So Jacob went down to Egypt; and he died, he and our fathers.

16 "And they were carried back to Shechem and laid in the tomb that Abraham bought for a sum of money from the sons of Hamor, the father of Shechem."

20 "At this time Moses was born, and was well pleasing to God; and he was brought up in his father's house for three months.

21 "But when he was set out, Pharaoh's daughter took him away and brought him up as her own son.

22 "And Moses was learned in all the wisdom of the Egyptians, and was mighty in words and deeds.

23 "Now when he was forty years old, it came into his heart to visit his brethren, the children of Israel.

24 "And seeing one of them suffer wrong, he defended and avenged him who was oppressed, and struck down the Egyptian.

25 "For he supposed that his brethren would have understood that God would deliver them by his hand, but they did not understand.

26 "And the next day he appeared to two of them as they were fighting, and tried to reconcile them, saying, 'Men, you are brethren; why do you wrong one another?'

27 "But he who did his neighbor wrong pushed him away, saying, 'Who made you a ruler and a judge over us?

28 'Do you want to kill me as you did the Egyptian yesterday?'

29 "Then, at this saying, Moses fled and became a dweller in the land of Midian, where he had two sons.

30 "And when forty years had passed, an Angel of the Lord appeared to him in a flame of fire in a bush, in the wilderness of Mount Sinai.

31 "When Moses saw it, he marveled at the sight; and as he drew near to observe, the voice of the Lord came to him,

32 "saying, 'I am the God of your fathers – the God of Abraham, the God of Isaac, and the God of Jacob.' And Moses trembled and dared not look.

33 Then the LORD said to him, 'Take your sandals off your feet, for the place where you stand is holy ground.

34 'I have surely seen the oppression of My people who are in Egypt; I have heard their groaning and have come down to deliver them. And now come, I will send you to Egypt.' "

Introduction

The wonderful acts of God encountered in the New Testament were built on a history that stretches back to the beginning of time. Jesus Christ introduced no new God to the world and no new concept of God. He did offer new revelation about the God who had spoken in the past through the patriarchs, Moses and the prophets. "No one knows the Son," He said, "except the Father. Nor does anyone know the Father except the Son" (Matthew 11:27; cf. John 17:25).

In the course of the Bible, revelation about God progresses. God revealed Himself to Abraham in ways Noah had not known. Moses knew more about

God than Abraham, and Isaiah, more than Moses. God revealed Himself – His purposes, His holiness and His kingdom – through Jesus Christ to a degree He had revealed to no one else. For Paul two events bracketed God's interaction with humankind: (1) the sin of Adam and (2) the payment for sin by the second Adam, Jesus of Nazareth (Romans 5:14-15). The progress of events in the Old Testament is a necessary backdrop for those who want to know the child of Mary. The things written there, Paul said, are "for our admonition" (1 Corinthians 10:11).

When the church was still in its infancy, gospel preachers introduced people to Christ by rehearsing the events that led to the coming of the Son of God. The sermon by Stephen (Acts 7), the first recorded Christian martyr, illustrates how the Old Testament leads to the New Testament. It further illustrates why Christians in every age do well when they are acquainted with the God who revealed Himself to Abraham, Jacob, Moses and countless others. Stephen first entered the record of Acts when the Jerusalem church selected him to attend to the needs of the Grecian widows (6:1-5), but in addition to being a servant of the poor Stephen showed himself to be a notable advocate for the gospel of Christ.

Abraham (Acts 7:2-8)

After the flood, the chronology of biblical events is difficult to follow. The genealogies of Genesis 10-11 likely are summaries, listing only pivotal players. Hundreds, perhaps thousands, of years passed after the flood before the sacred record came to rest on the father of the faithful (Romans 4:3), a man known at first as Abram. The Jewish people called him "father" (Matthew 3:9), but he is equally the father of those who own Jesus Christ as Lord (Romans 2:29).

When Abram was a young man his father Terah was patriarch of the clan. They lived in a pocket of civilization in the lower reaches of Mesopotamia, in the city of Ur on the Euphrates River. Genesis offers a bare record of the years-long trek of the family toward their ultimate destination to Canaan. Terah, guided by God's appearance to his son Abram, led the clan northwest, up the Euphrates Valley to the important city of Haran where Terah died (Genesis 11:31-32). In short order Abram, now 75 years old, left part of the clan behind while he, his wife Sarai and his nephew Lot set out for Canaan, the land that was to provide the backdrop for the unfolding of God's promises. It would be a journey beset with hostile tribes and long stretches of desert. Famine could never be far away. The patriarch leaned on his faith and set out to do God's bidding.

Abraham entered the Promised Land as a sojourner, a vagabond moving from place to place. He had no children, but God promised his descendants would be in numbers like the stars of the sky. He claimed no square foot of land as his own, but God said his descendants would claim all of Canaan as their inheritance. God's promises were far away. Before they were realized, those descended from Abraham and Sarah would spend 400 years as slaves in Egypt, but God would judge their captors and bring them back to Canaan. The promises must have seemed remote when Abraham led the band across the Jordan and set foot in Canaan for the first time somewhere in the vicinity of Shechem (Genesis 12:6). It was no light thing when Genesis said of the patriarch that he believed God, and

and it was "accounted to him for righteousness" (15:6). Some 2,000 years after Abraham became a sojourner in Canaan, Stephen stood in Jerusalem and proclaimed to offspring of the patriarch that the promises of God had been realized. God had sent His Son, the redeemer for Israel and Savior of the human race.

Jacob (Acts 7:9-16)

Some 25 years passed after Abraham and Sarah set out from Haran before their faith was realized (cf. Genesis 12:4; 21:5). According to God's promise, He gave them a son they named Isaac. Isaac's son Jacob became father to 12 sons, who produced the millions of Egypt. The story of Israel's sojourn in Egypt began with hatred, betrayal and treachery. The Bible makes no attempt to sugarcoat the event. Jacob's favored son was Joseph, son of his favored wife Rachel. Moved by jealousy, 10 of Jacob's sons hatched a plot, first to kill Joseph and then, when opportunity presented itself, to sell him to a band of slave traders. By God's providence, the darling of Jacob became the property of an Egyptian official named Potiphar. Unknown to Joseph or his brothers, God was at work providing for the preservation and eventual choosing of a people to be His heritage (45:7).

Through a series of events under the umbrella of God's providence, Joseph languished in prison, was befriended by his jailer, and interpreted the dreams of Pharaoh's officials. When Pharaoh had dreams of his own, an official of the king remembered Joseph. After interpreting the dream of Pharaoh and showing himself to be an able administrator, Joseph became powerful in Egypt.

When the clan in Canaan faced starvation by famine, Joseph arranged for his family to come to Egypt. When Jacob died, they took his body back to Canaan, where he was buried in the tomb Abraham had bought from Ephron the Hittite (Genesis 50:13). The Egyptians mummified the body of Joseph and kept it in Egypt until the Israelites could bury his body in a field his father had purchased in the vicinity of Shechem (Joshua 24:32). Beginning with only 75 in number, Israel multiplied in Egypt during the centuries that followed the death of Joseph. They became a slave people more than a million strong. Chafing under the whip, they provided manpower for the building of cities and digging of canals in their adopted land. Israel in Egypt, their deliverance by God's mighty hand, the giving of the Law, and the conquest of Canaan are essential parts of the story leading up to the time when the "Word became flesh and dwelt among us" (John 1:14).

Moses (Acts 7:20-34)

The Jews never grew tired of telling their story. Fathers and mothers told sons and daughters of the birth of the baby Moses, a story Sunday school teachers continue to tell little ones today. Threatened with death, the baby's sister set him afloat in the Nile where he was rescued by the daughter of Pharaoh. Stephen told the story to Jews as if they had never heard it before. Moses spent the first 40 years of his life among the ruling elite of Egypt, became learned in their ways and acclaimed for his deeds. Stephen, not Exodus, divided the life of Moses into three 40-year segments. The second 40 years of the lawgiver's life passed while he tended sheep in Midian, far to the east of Egypt.

When he was 80 years old (Acts 7:23, 30), Moses met God on Mount Sinai, also called Horeb, "the mountain of God" (Exodus 3:1). God commissioned him to return to Egypt and lead Israel into the desert to offer sacrifices. In the weeks and months that followed, Moses confronted the most powerful nation on earth with the judgment of God. Resistance to God on the part of Pharaoh and the Egyptians resulted in the desolation of the land. The story Stephen told the ruling council of the Jews had been ground into the consciousness of Israel for a thousand generations. The newness of Stephen's message was that the coming of Moses as deliverer and lawgiver was preliminary to the coming of Jesus Christ, Son of God, Redeemer of the human race.

Conclusion

Communities of people draw their sense of common purpose from shared ideals and dreams. Whether the community is a nation, civic club or sports team, ideals and dreams arise out of a community's history. The church of Christ is a community of people who share a long and noble history stretching back nearly 4,000 years to the time when God called Abraham from Ur. The love inspired in Christians, the zeal to obey God, and the hope to live with Him eternally arise out of God's revelation of Himself to patriarchs, lawgivers, prophets and wise men. The final chapter of the story begins with a child born in Bethlehem and a rugged preacher who prepared the way for His preaching. Christians who fail to know the earlier chapters of the story deny themselves of their birthright.

Questions

1. To what duty was Stephen assigned when he first appears in Acts?
2. Before whom was Stephen speaking in Acts 7?
3. Where was Abraham when God told him to leave his homeland?
4. Where is Haran, the city where Abraham's father Terah died?
5. What did God promise Abraham about his descendants?
6. In what foreign land were the descendants of Abraham in bondage?
7. What did the family of Jacob come to Egypt to buy?
8. How many members of the family of Jacob first settled in Egypt?
9. Where did Moses spend the first 40 years of his life? the second 40 years?
10. What is an alternative name for Mt. Sinai, where God appeared to Moses?

Discussion Starters

1. What two events did Paul understand to bracket human history? Why are the two events of such importance?
2. Why should Christians study God's self-revelation in the Old Testament?
3. Why is the history of a people important for them when they define their hope, ideals and aspirations?
4. Into what three periods did Stephen divide the life of Moses? Which of the three does the Old Testament describe in greatest detail? Why?

Later Hebrew History

Acts 13:21-41

21 "And afterward they asked for a king; so God gave them Saul the son of Kish, a man of the tribe of Benjamin, for forty years.

22 "And when He had removed him, He raised up for them David as king, to whom also He gave testimony and said, 'I have found David the son of Jesse, a man after My own heart, who will do all My will.'

23 "From this man's seed, according to the promise, God raised up for Israel a Savior – Jesus –

24 "after John had first preached, before His coming, the baptism of repentance to all the people of Israel.

25 "And as John was finishing his course, he said, 'Who do you think I am? I am not He. But behold, there comes One after me, the sandals of whose feet I am not worthy to loose.'

26 "Men and brethren, sons of the family of Abraham, and those among you who fear God, to you the word of this salvation has been sent.

27 "For those who dwell in Jerusalem, and their rulers, because they did not know Him, nor even the voices of the Prophets which are read every Sabbath, have fulfilled them in condemning Him.

28 "And though they found no cause for death in Him, they asked Pilate that He should be put to death.

29 "Now when they had fulfilled all that was written concerning Him, they took Him down from the tree and laid Him in a tomb.

30 "But God raised Him from the dead.

31 "He was seen for many days by those who came up with Him from Galilee to Jerusalem, who are His witnesses to the people.

32 "And we declare to you glad tidings – that promise which was made to the fathers.

33 "God has fulfilled this for us their children, in that He has raised up Jesus. As it is also written in the second Psalm: 'You are My Son, Today I have begotten You.'

34 "And that He raised Him from the dead, no more to return to corruption, He has spoken thus: 'I will give you the sure mercies of David.'

35 "Therefore He also says in another Psalm: 'You will not allow Your Holy One to see corruption.'

36 "For David, after he had served his own generation by the will of God, fell asleep, was buried with his fathers, and saw corruption;

37 "but He whom God raised up saw no corruption.

38 "Therefore let it be known to you, brethren, that through this Man is preached to you the forgiveness of sins;

39 "and by Him everyone who believes is justified from all things from which you could not be justified by the law of Moses.

40 "Beware therefore, lest what has been spoken in the prophets come upon you:

41 'Behold, you despisers, Marvel and perish! For I work a work in your days, A work which you will by no means believe, Though one were to declare it to you.' "

Introduction

From the time of Moses, thoughtful Israelites struggled to reconcile two seemingly inconsistent things. First, the one universal God they worshiped was the Creator of all the human family. Second, God had chosen them, a limited portion of mankind. Why? What was special about Israel? Why had the universal God chosen a peculiar people like themselves? Deuteronomy dealt with the questions mostly in negations. It was not because Israel was more powerful, wiser or more numerous that God had chosen them (Deuteronomy 7:7). It was not because they had worshiped Him faithfully or served him wholeheartedly. Why then?

Moses himself seemed to wrestle with the questions. To Yahweh belonged heaven, earth and all that was in it (Deuteronomy 10:14). Yet the lawgiver wrote, "The Lord your God has chosen you to be a people for Himself, a special treasure above all the peoples on the face of the earth" (7:6). The Old Testament never resolves the tension between God's universality and His particularity, between His creating and loving all humankind and His apparent partiality for Israel.

Only after the coming of Christ did it become clear that Hebrew history fit into a larger framework. God chose Israel, gave them a law, and fashioned them in preparation for a universal message. Paul wrote, "For there is no partiality with God" (Romans 2:11). Peter said, "In truth I perceive that God shows no partiality" (Acts 10:34). The message of Paul and other preachers was that the mystery of God's peculiar choice for ethnic Israel had at last been resolved. The history of Israel fit into the framework of God's plan to save the human race. Hebrew history began with Abraham. With the coming of John the Baptist, the death of Jesus Christ, and the birth of the church an era ended. The mystery of Gentile inclusion was unveiled (Ephesians 3:3-6). Ethnic Israel might continue or not depending on the accidents of history, but God's peculiar relationship with the offspring of Abraham was over.

It was not as though God rejected Israel. Rather, by His grace He offered salvation as a gift to Jew and Gentile alike. The transition from God being over Israel to God being over all mankind was difficult for those who had been accustomed to favored status. Paul's sermon in the synagogue at Pisidian Antioch illustrates the unveiling of the mystery of God in the last days (Hebrews 1:2). The apostle sought to persuade his people that the gift of

God for Jew and Gentile was infinitely better than the favored status Jews had enjoyed in the past. It was better even for the Jews.

John the Baptizer (Acts 13:21-25)

Barnabas and Saul had begun their missionary tour from Antioch in Syria, but by the time they reached Pisidian Antioch, Saul had become Paul and was clearly the leader of the two. Greek rulers by the name of Antiochus had founded several cities around the northeastern corner of the Mediterranean some 300 years before the arrival of the missionaries. They had named them Antioch after themselves. The Antioch in the southwestern portion of the Roman province of Galatia was near a region to its west known as Pisidia. Paul and Barnabas likely chose the city because they knew a portion of the population was Jewish. On the Sabbath, the missionaries joined worshipers in the synagogue. When the synagogue rulers asked their guests to speak, Paul stepped forward. His sermon was brief (Acts 13:16-41).

Like Stephen before him, Paul rehearsed for his countrymen the history of their people. He began with God's leading Israel from Egypt, giving them the Promised Land and appointing kings over them. Only in Paul's sermon is Saul son of Kish said to have ruled for 40 years (see 1 Samuel 13:1 and the marginal note NASB). The apostle rushed on to David, "a man after My own heart," God had said (Acts 13:22). From David's seed, Paul said, God raised up a Savior. The name Jesus itself meant Savior. In time Paul would make it clear that the Savior had come to redeem Jew and Gentile, but for the moment, here in the synagogue, the apostle focused on Israel.

The appearance of John the Baptist had signaled a singular event for the nation of Israel and for the human race. John had prepared the way, baptizing in the wilderness, calling on Israel to repent and produce fruits of righteousness. Some had thought that John might have been the long promised Messiah, Israel's anointed king (Luke 3:15-16; John 1:20). The baptizer had made it clear that his mission was to make the path straight for the One who would follow him. To John was the task of nudging open the door for a universal message of salvation and for drawing the curtain closed on what appeared to be God's partiality for the Jewish race.

Jesus (Acts 13:26-31)

At the beginning of his sermon Paul had addressed his audience, "Men of Israel, and you who fear God" (Acts 13:16). As his sermon progressed, he proclaimed "the word of this salvation" (v. 26) to those outside the net of ethnic Israel. His proclamation was for the "sons of the family of Abraham, and those among you who fear God" (v. 26). Those who lived in Jerusalem and their rulers had fulfilled the words of God's prophets by condemning the Son of God. They had gone so far as to insist that Pilate, the Roman governor, put Him to death.

The death of Christ was both an extension of Hebrew history and something radically new. The story that had begun with Abraham had continued with God's calling the nation from Egypt and giving the people a law. Neither

Abraham nor Moses had seen how God's work with them fit into God's plan of redemption. In ages past, God's plan had been unclear; in the death of Jesus and the coming of the Spirit the mystery was unveiled (Ephesians 3:3-6). When they crucified the Son of God, the Jews and their leaders had rebelled against God and fulfilled what the prophets had foretold.

When Paul said that they "took Him down from the tree" (Acts 13:29) he did not use the ordinary Greek word for a living tree. The word he chose usually refers to something made of wood, perhaps a plank, a club or a pole. New Testament authors use the word for the cross where Jesus was crucified. In the Greek Old Testament the same word was used for the rough timber on which a criminal might be impaled. For good reason the Law had said, "Cursed is everyone who hangs on a tree" (Galatians 3:13; Deuteronomy 21:23). Jesus bore the curse for human sin when He died on a rough plank of wood. When He was taken down from the "tree" (Acts 13:29), they buried Him, but God would not allow Him to remain in the tomb. God proclaimed Jesus the Christ by raising Him from the dead (Romans 1:4), a resurrection attested to by witnesses who had been with Him from the beginning of His ministry in Galilee.

The Gospel (Acts 13:32-41)

Many Jews understood the gospel to imply that God had rejected them, children of Abraham though they were. Paul labored to help his countrymen understand that the inclusion of Gentiles into the family of God meant no rejection of Israel any more than the birth of a child means rejection for older children. It did, however, mean that the Jews no longer had a privileged status. With no partiality God chose the obedient to be saved regardless of their wealth, their ethnicity or their sex (Galatians 3:28). Jews had an advantage over Gentiles only in that they had a long acquaintance with God and His promises. In his sermon at Pisidian Antioch, Paul cited some of the same psalms Peter had cited on Pentecost. Because they knew the Old Testament, Jews had evidence that Jesus was the Christ that many Gentiles would not have appreciated. The apostle labored to demonstrate that what the Psalms foretold could not apply to David. David had died like all men, and his body had decayed.

The conclusion of Paul's sermon was that the Christ of God had not come to be a warrior king; He had come to save humankind from sin. The apostle found it necessary to compare the gospel to the Law of Moses. Forgiveness under the Law was an impossibility. The weight of guilt only accumulated. Jesus was the fulfillment of the Law, a blessing for Jews and Gentiles alike. He would sanctify all those who came to Him through faith in the cross of Christ.

Conclusion

Those who believe that God continues to have a special plan for the redemption of the Jews misunderstand God's universal, impartial love for the entire human family. Many conservative denominations donate large sums of money and ground a considerable portion of their doctrine on the belief that Jews must return to Israel and literal sacrifice be restored in a rebuilt temple before the Lord returns. To understand God's impartiality requires Christians to reject any notion that God will literally reign for 1,000 years on earth from the city of Jerusalem. With no millennium, all ideas of a rapture, a battle of Armageddon, restoration of temple sacrifice and other such accoutrements to millennialism are to be dismissed. God worked redemption for humanity by preparing Israel as the people through whom His Son would come as Savior of the world.

Questions

1. Who was Paul's traveling companion when he arrived at Pisidian Antioch?
2. Where is Pisidian Antioch in relationship to Antioch of Syria? Locate both cities on a Bible-times map.
3. What was the tribe of origin for Saul, Israel's first king?
4. What testimony did God give to David, the son of Jesse?
5. What had John the Baptist proclaimed before the ministry of Jesus began?
6. What two things did Paul say the inhabitants of Jerusalem and their leaders had failed to recognize (Acts 13:27)?
7. Whom did the Jews of Jerusalem call on for help so that they might put Jesus to death?
8. What evidence did Paul offer to the Jews at Antioch that Jesus had been bodily raised from the dead?
9. What Old Testament passage did Paul cite in Acts 13?
10. In light of all that he had said, what did Paul say that he was able to declare to the Jews of Antioch?

Discussion Starters

1. Why would the people of Israel have had difficulty reconciling their understanding of God and His choice of them to be His peculiar people?
2. Why did Hebrew history come to an end in the New Testament period? What did the end of Hebrew history signal for the universal human family?
3. Was God partial to the Jewish people before the coming of Christ? In what sense was He partial, and what was the end of the partiality to be?
4. Why do doctrines about a rapture, a millennium, a battle of Armageddon and such require one to believe that God continues to show partiality to ethnic Israel?

God's Plan to Save Man

John 3:14-17

14 "And as Moses lifted up the serpent in the wilderness, even so must the Son of Man be lifted up,

15 "that whoever believes in Him should not perish but have eternal life.

16 "For God so loved the world that He gave His only begotten Son, that whoever believes in Him should not perish but have everlasting life.

17 "For God did not send His Son into the world to condemn the world, but that the world through Him might be saved."

Romans 5:6-11

6 For when we were still without strength, in due time Christ died for the ungodly.

7 For scarcely for a righteous man will one die; yet perhaps for a good man someone would even dare to die.

8 But God demonstrates His own love toward us, in that while we were still sinners, Christ died for us.

9 Much more then, having now been justified by His blood, we shall be saved from wrath through Him.

10 For if when we were enemies we were reconciled to God through the death of His Son, much more, having been reconciled, we shall be saved by His life.

11 And not only that, but we also rejoice in God through our Lord Jesus Christ, through whom we have now received the reconciliation.

Hebrews 10:19-25

19 Therefore, brethren, having boldness to enter the Holiest by the blood of Jesus,

20 by a new and living way which He consecrated for us, through the veil, that is, His flesh,

21 and having a High Priest over the house of God,

22 let us draw near with a true heart in full assurance of faith, having our hearts sprinkled from an evil conscience and our bodies washed with pure water.

23 Let us hold fast the confession of our hope without wavering, for He who promised is faithful.

24 And let us consider one another in order to stir up love and good works,

25 not forsaking the assembling of ourselves together, as is the manner of some, but exhorting one another, and so much the more as you see the Day approaching.

Introduction

The beginning of the relationship between God the Creator and man the creature is recorded in the first chapters of Genesis. From the perspective of the creature, it is a story about the pride and rebellion that engulfed Adam and Eve and their descendants. From the perspective of the Creator, it is a story of grace. The plan of God to save His creation is the outworking of His grace. Salvation is a meaningful subject only in the context of sin and grace.

The unanswered questions are numerous. Why did God create moral beings who could choose to obey or to rebel, to do good or evil? A believer may cite biblical passages to support a conclusion that God created us as an outpouring of His love, but it is a proposition never stated explicitly in the Bible. An unbeliever will ask what kind of love creates foreknowing the misery and suffering that will inflict the race. The questions are not only numerous, but they are also complex and confusing. God Himself warned that the relationship between God and humankind includes matters knowable only to the Divine (Deuteronomy 29:29; Isaiah 55:8-9). Speculation aside, this much is certain: Sin and suffering are woven into human experience.

Sin drove a wedge between the Creator and the creature. For God to reward men and women in their sin would have tainted His holiness. He could have vindicated Himself by banishing them to oblivion. God chose instead a path for reconciliation. He acted freely to save. He determined to pay the price for sin Himself. Moved by grace, He worked through Abraham and his offspring to bring the world to the point when His Son took on human flesh and in the flesh condemned sin (Galatians 4:4; Romans 8:3).

God Gave His Son (John 3:14-17)

While interacting with His people between Abraham and the coming of John the Baptist, in various ways God foreshadowed the event that would mean the saving of Adam's race. The coming of the Christ was the driving force behind God's choosing Israel and giving them His law. While the young nation was on its way to Canaan, God impressed on the people that suffering resulted from sin and that He by His grace saved in spite of sin. At one point, when the sin of the people was particularly bad, God sent fiery serpents among them and many died (Numbers 21:6). When Israel repented and begged for relief, God told Moses to set up a bronze serpent on a pole. Whoever looked on the bronze serpent was healed (v. 9).

More than a thousand years later, Jesus told His generation that the bronze serpent set up by Moses had been a type of Himself. God had foreshadowed the grace He would display when the Son of Man was lifted up from the earth (John 3:14-15). In one sense the lifting up of Jesus was to be literal. He was lifted up on the cross, but the words can be used in another sense. A person is lifted up by honor, praise or acclamation. In John's Gospel "lifted up" seems to be used in a double sense. Jesus was lifted up when He was crucified, but the humiliation of the cross was at the same time His exaltation. It was a paradox embraced by Paul. "For though He was crucified in weakness," the apostle was to write, "yet He lives by the power of God. For we also are weak in Him, but we shall live with Him by the power of God toward you" (2 Corinthians 13:4). The defeat of Jesus on the cross was His triumph and His glorification (John 8:28; 12:23, 32; 13:31-32).

God's plan to save man has been driven from the beginning by His love. All people are sons and daughters of God, but Jesus was a Son in that He partook of the Divinity of God. "The Word was God" and "the Word became flesh," John wrote (John 1:1, 14). No law, no degree of human obedience, results in salvation (Acts 13:38-39). God saves by grace through faith in Jesus Christ (Ephesians 2:8), but grace is not cheap; faith is not without response. Faith that saves expresses itself in obedience (Romans 1:5; 16:26). The world had been judged by its sin. In sin it had been condemned. Jesus came to save the lost, to open the path of life for the human family. Judgment and condemnation were for those who rejected the Son (John 9:39).

Christ Died for Us (Romans 5:6-11)

"Vicarious atonement" is not a phrase found verbatim in the Bible, but it is a concept that lies near the heart of God's plan to save. Atonement is peculiarly an English word, coined to express the removal of sin as a barrier between the Creator and the created. Bible students combined at+one+ment to express the removal of barriers. The King James Version used the word "atonement" in the New Testament only once (Romans 5:11). Some translations do not use it in the New Testament at all; others use it rarely. "Atonement" is a common word in the Old Testament, especially in the Law; especially in Leviticus. In the New Testament, the operative word that incorporates and goes beyond atonement is "reconciliation." The translators of the New King James Version chose reconciliation instead of atonement in Romans 5:11.

A thing done vicariously is done through the experiences of another. Thus, vicarious atonement expresses what happened on the cross. Jesus paid the price for our sins; He paid it all. Because of the vicarious atonement of Jesus, sinners may be reconciled to God through faith and obedience. Paul wrote that the atoning work of Christ was done for sinners when they were helpless (Romans 5:6). After that he explained the marvels of the love that caused God to allow His Son to die. Not only did Jesus die to pay the price for sin, but He lives at God's right hand. Through His intercession, reconciliation continues.

The link between John 3:16 and Romans 5:8 is God's love. Like the Israelites in the wilderness, the redeemed and reconciled turn a puzzled face to God and ask, "Why? What is the source of His love? Why did Jesus die to reconcile us when the entire course of the human race had been set on sin and rebellion?" Paul's answer is no different from the answer Moses gave to Israel. He has loved us because that is who He is. The reconciled sinner's part is to bask in His love, not to question it.

"Let Us" (Hebrews 10:19-25)

The doctrine of God's grace has not been compromised when authors of the New Testament insist that those who are saved by faith must obey God in order to be reconciled to Him. After sin entered the world and men and women had become enemies of God, He took the initiative and planned for reconciliation. His plan came to fruition when Jesus died sinlessly and affected vicarious atonement and reconciliation with the Father. Beginning from there, some theologians have built a doctrine that claims God in the eternal past has predestined some to be saved and others lost. It is said that nothing people do has a bearing on their being saved or lost. Obedience is irrelevant; God's choice solely determines who is saved and who is lost. This abstract doctrine of God's sovereignty runs up against reality in the Bible itself.

After the author of Hebrews had detailed God's work of grace in offering His Son as a sinless High Priest, as a sacrifice for sins (Hebrews 10:10), the sacred writer continued, "Let us draw near" (v. 22), "Let us hold fast the confession" (v. 23) and "Let us consider one another in order to stir up love and good works" (v. 24). Because the Lord paid the price for sin, those who hear the gospel must go on to obedience if they are to be saved. Obedience to God is not the price sinners must pay in order to be saved; it is their response by faith because they have been saved. The faith that saves is a faith that obeys.

Conclusion

To know God's plan for reconciliation between Himself and people is depressing and shameful, but it is also exhilarating and hopeful. It is depressing because sin is embedded in our lives. "There is none righteous," Paul wrote, "no, not one" (Romans 3:10). It is exhilarating because God so loved us that He gave His only begotten Son to save us from sin. After the sin of Adam and Eve, the world languished in misery. The only hope to brighten the horizon was a dimly understood promise that God would send a Son descended from David. In Jesus of Nazareth, the promise was realized. Paul called Him a second Adam (1 Corinthians 15:45). The fleshly father of the race introduced sin and death; the Son of God came as our brother and our king. He paid the price for sin and returned hope and life to the race of Adam.

The story of redemption and reconciliation ends neither with the cross nor with the resurrection. The resurrected Son has returned to heaven where He reigns at God's right hand making intercession for a people who remain in the thralls of sin (Hebrews 7:25). In His own time, He will come again. When He does, God's plan of salvation will have entered its final act. Until He comes, Christians live in the middle time, the time between His first coming and His second. They live as communities of people, sharing fellowship with one another and fellowship with Him (1 John 1:3).

Questions

1. What brought about the breach in the relationship between God and humankind?
2. Why did God plan for reconciliation between Himself and mankind?
3. What did Moses lift up in the wilderness that foreshadowed the crucifixion of Christ?
4. What has God promised for those who put their faith in the Son of Man?
5. What did God's love for the human family cause him to give to the world?
6. What is the broad word used in the New Testament that incorporates the meaning of atonement?
7. What important New Testament word links John 3:16 and Romans 5:8?
8. Before Christ paid the price for sin, what existed between God and man that resulted in their separation?
9. What is the source of Christian boldness when approaching God in His holiness?
10. With what disposition did the author of Hebrews say that Christians were to "draw near" to God?

Discussion Starters

1. How did the cross contribute to the exaltation of Jesus and His glorification? What lessons should Christians learn about weakness and victory?
2. Was Jesus in the flesh human or divine? Which did He need to be in order to pay the price for human sin? Why?
3. What is the meaning of "vicarious atonement"? Is the phrase an appropriate designation for what took place on the cross? Explain.
4. Because salvation is by God's grace, what role do works play in a person being saved? Do good works result in merit for salvation? Why?

Salvation Foreshadowed Among the Patriarchs

Galatians 3:6-9

6 ... just as Abraham "believed God, and it was accounted to him for righteousness."

7 Therefore know that only those who are of faith are sons of Abraham.

8 And the Scripture, foreseeing that God would justify the Gentiles by faith, preached the gospel to Abraham beforehand, saying, "In you all the nations shall be blessed."

9 So then those who are of faith are blessed with believing Abraham.

Hebrews 2:14-18

14 Inasmuch then as the children have partaken of flesh and blood, He Himself likewise shared in the same, that through death He might destroy him who had the power of death, that is, the devil,

15 and release those who through fear of death were all their lifetime subject to bondage.

16 For indeed He does not give aid to angels, but He does give aid to the seed of Abraham.

17 Therefore, in all things He had to be made like His brethren, that He might be a merciful and faithful High Priest in things pertaining to God, to make propitiation for the sins of the people.

18 For in that He Himself has suffered, being tempted, He is able to aid those who are tempted.

Hebrews 10:1-4

1 For the law, having a shadow of the good things to come, and not the very image of the things, can never with these same sacrifices, which they offer continually year by year, make those who approach perfect.

2 For then would they not have ceased to be offered? For the worshipers, once purified, would have had no more consciousness of sins.

3 But in those sacrifices there is a reminder of sins every year.

4 For it is not possible that the blood of bulls and goats could take away sins.

1 Peter 1:18-21

18 ... knowing that you were not redeemed with corruptible things, like silver or gold, from your aimless conduct received by tradition from your fathers,

19 but with the precious blood of Christ, as of a lamb without blemish and without spot.

20 He indeed was foreordained before the foundation of the world, but was manifest in these last times for you

21 who through Him believe in God, who raised Him from the dead and gave Him glory, so that your faith and hope are in God.

Introduction

Promises have a great deal to do with God's self-revelation. The covenants between God and His people were often accompanied by events whose impacts would be felt for centuries. With the covenants came promises. The descendants of Noah would fill the earth (Genesis 9:8-9); the offspring of Abraham would inherit Canaan (17:5-8); David's sons would rule forever (2 Samuel 7:8, 12-16). Promises sustained Israel in the face of hardships and buoyed the nation up when it faced annihilation, but something grander, more momentous, more universal than national survival crept into the psyche of Israel as God's promises stretched across centuries.

In time it became clearer to prophets and wise men that God was giving voice to a promise that transcended Israel. God had said that all the families of the earth would be blessed by Abraham's seed (Genesis 12:1-3). Of David and his descendants God declared, "I will be his Father, and he shall be My son" (2 Samuel 7:14). The prophets put flesh on the promise. "Unto us a Son is given," Isaiah wrote, "And the government will be upon His shoulder. And His name will be called Wonderful, Counselor, Mighty God, Everlasting Father, Prince of Peace" (Isaiah 9:6). Through Jeremiah God said, "I will make a new covenant with the house of Israel" (Jeremiah 31:31). The Lord added, "I will put My law in their minds, and write it on their hearts" (v. 33).

God's promise was that He would send a Messiah, an Anointed One whose mission would embrace Israel and extend to humankind. Often the promise was explicit, but more than words secured God's design for Adam's race that He was working out through Israel. The promise was woven into the history, the rituals and habits of Israel. From macro features of Israel's religion and government such as the high priesthood or the kingship to micro incidents such as the crossing of the Red Sea (1 Corinthians 10:1-4) or the setting up of a bronze serpent to which the dying might look and be cured (John 3:14) – in events great and small God foreshadowed what was coming. In the promise of a new King and His Kingdom, God prepared a people for the greatest event the world would ever experience, for the appearing of the Son of God in the flesh.

A Promise (Galatians 3:6-9)

The long shadow of the Christ that stretched back through time to the sin of Adam and Eve, through the call of Abraham and the Law of Moses, was of decisive importance during the transition from God's favoritism for ethnic Israel to universal salvation in the kingdom of God. The first Christians were Jews or Jewish proselytes, but it soon became apparent that Christians were more than a new sect of Judaism. In Cornelius and among the believers in Antioch of Syria, Gentiles became Christians without adopting Jewish rituals. Paul and Barnabas traveled among cities in the southern portion of the Roman province of Galatia and preached the gospel to Jews and Gentiles. The missionaries did not require Gentiles to be circumcised or to accept other ceremonial features of the Law of Moses. Christianity was to be no mere extension of Judaism.

The preaching of Paul and others aroused controversy in the church still made up in large measure by Jewish believers. Some of them radically disagreed with Paul. They followed Paul into churches of Galatia and insisted that Gentile believers submit to the Law of Moses in order to be saved (Acts 15:1). Galatian Christians were confused. Some sided with Paul, some against him. The apostle wrote the Galatian letter in response to the controversy. He defended the truth of what he preached by drawing on Genesis to demonstrate that God through Abraham had foreshadowed the gospel of Christ.

Paul pointed his readers to a time while Abraham was fairly new in Canaan and had no children. God spoke with him in a vision while Abraham was an old man, past childbearing age. He was confused by God's promise that his descendants were to inherit the land. God would bless all nations through them. How could it happen? The patriarch had no children. He proposed that descendants of his servant Eliezer be his heirs, but God said, "No." Abraham had no way of understanding how God was going to bring it about, but Genesis records, "And he believed in the Lord, and He accounted it to him for righteousness" (Genesis 15:6). The righteousness based on faith that God accounted for Abraham foreshadowed the gospel preached by Paul. Gentiles were to be saved like faithful Abraham because of their faith. God's promise to Abraham was fulfilled when Jesus died for the sins of mankind.

A Provision (Hebrews 2:14-18; 10:1-4)

In both Hebrew (the language of the Old Testament) and Greek (the language of the New Testament) words translated "sacrifice" literally mean "slaughter," "butcher" or the like. They are bloody words of knife and death. When the Bible was translated into English in the late 16th and early 17th centuries, blood offerings were things of the past. English had no equivalent words. Translators resorted to a word of Latin origin, *sacrificium*, meaning "a sacred gift." "Sacrifice" was the best they could do, but the bloody aspect of the Hebrew and Greek words was lost.

The dedication of animals to the gods and their slaughter were common practices among Israel's neighbors, but commonly pagans imagined the fat of beasts to be food for deities. God transformed the concept. For Israel blood sacrifices became bound up with making atonement for sin. The slaughter of animals was a reminder that breaking God's law was no casual affair. For Israel, burnt offerings caused confession and repentance to happen. Israel sometimes became fixated on the form and ritual of sacrifice and took them to be ends in themselves, but ideally the slaughter and offering of animals reminded the community of Israel that sin had consequences. Israel enjoyed fellowship with God only because of His grace.

The author of Hebrews appealed to priestly sacrifice and temple ritual to help believers appreciate the magnitude of the gift offered to God when Jesus died for sin. Unlike the goats and bulls offered in the court of tabernacle or temple, Jesus shared in the flesh and blood of those He came to save. The sacrifices of priests in the Old Testament foreshadowed the payment for sin made by Jesus. His blood did what the blood of bulls and goats could not do (Hebrews 10:4). Jesus destroyed "him who had the power of death" (2:14) and became a faithful and merciful High Priest.

A Purpose (1 Peter 1:18-21)

Peter declared that God foreordained redemption from sin "before the foundation of the world" (1 Peter 1:20). He purposed to save; it was no afterthought. Christians are inclined to associate salvation and redemption with the return of the Lord, judgment and life in the age to come. They tend to neglect the meaning of the terms for this life. Peter did not tell his readers that they would be redeemed in the future but that they had been redeemed for the present. Already Christians were saved; already they had been purchased by the blood of the Lamb. The plea of the apostle is that believers live in such a way as to reflect the holy people God has made them to be (vv. 15-16). By His grace, God has saved and redeemed a people. Believers are to live like the redeemed, like the reconciled people God has made them to be.

God's purpose has been to fashion a people to wear His name, to be redeemed from sin and to reflect His holiness. He has decreed that the saints purify their souls "in obeying the truth" (1 Peter 1:22). The path to salvation entails believing the truth, but the truth is also to be obeyed. The truth is both a confession and a way of life. Peter wanted his readers to know that the way of life they had begun in Christ was a radical move. It was being born again. The apostle associated sanctification, obedience, the blood of Christ and the new birth in the opening words of his letter (vv. 2-4). He closed his thought by returning to the themes (vv. 22-23). Faith and truth are more than abstractions to be embraced. When a sinner acts on his faith, repents and is baptized into Christ, spiritually he is born anew. Peter's words coupled with Jesus' conversation with Nicodemus (John 3:5; cf. Titus 3:5) draw an unmistakable association between baptism and new birth.

Conclusion

When Christians make the transition from Malachi to Matthew they follow a continuation of the Old Testament story. No radical break appears in the seam. The same God speaks; holiness and moral uprightness persist. In Christ, promises are fulfilled, mysteries are unveiled and shadows become substance. No new understanding of God appeared when Jesus proclaimed the kingdom of God. On the other hand, when Jesus came, something entirely new appeared – something radically new. The discontinuities between the New Testament and the Old Testament ought not to drown out the continuities, but neither should the reverse occur. Jesus fulfilled prophecy embedded in direct predictions, and He revealed Himself in the foreshadowing of Old Testament types. At the same time Jesus redeemed a people and brought hope to a hopeless landscape. He revealed the God of creation by His words and deeds as people had never known Him before. In the patriarchs and prophets of the Old Testament, Christians find God's promises. They discover the provision God has made for reconciliation between Himself and the human family. In the foreshadowing of the Old Testament is the unfolding of God's purposes so that "the day dawns and the morning star rises in your hearts" (2 Peter 1:19).

Questions

1. What are some of the promises God made to people prominent in the Old Testament?
2. What was the most important promise God made as Old Testament history unfolded?
3. What did Abraham do that God accounted it to him for righteousness (Galatians 3:6)?
4. How did Paul define the "sons of Abraham" (Galatians 3:7), i.e., what is characteristic of the sons of Abraham?
5. What controversy erupted in Galatian churches that caused Paul to write a letter to them?
6. In what was it necessary for Jesus to share in order for Him to destroy the power of death?
7. What is the meaning of the Latin root from which the English word "sacrifice" is derived?
8. What did the sacrifices remind worshipers about on a yearly basis?
9. With what did Peter say that Christians had been redeemed?
10. How had Peter's readers purified their souls?

Discussion Starters

1. What are some of the great and small ways the Old Testament foreshadowed the person and the mission of Christ?
2. If the sacrifices prescribed by the Law could not take away sin, what was their purpose? Why are they meaningful for Christians?
3. What was Peter referencing when he reminded his readers that they had been "born again"? Where in the New Testament does one read of the new birth?
4. How does the New Testament make a radical break with the Old Testament but at the same time maintain a firm continuity with the Old Testament?

Salvation Foreshadowed in the Law of Moses

Galatians 3:23-25

23 But before faith came, we were kept under guard by the law, kept for the faith which would afterward be revealed.

24 Therefore the law was our tutor to bring us to Christ, that we might be justified by faith.

25 But after faith has come, we are no longer under a tutor.

Hebrews 4:14-16

14 Seeing then that we have a great High Priest who has passed through the heavens, Jesus the Son of God, let us hold fast our confession.

15 For we do not have a High Priest who cannot sympathize with our weaknesses, but was in all points tempted as we are, yet without sin.

16 Let us therefore come boldly to the throne of grace, that we may obtain mercy and find grace to help in time of need.

Hebrews 9:11-15

11 But Christ came as High Priest of the good things to come, with the greater and more perfect tabernacle not made with hands, that is, not of this creation.

12 Not with the blood of goats and calves, but with His own blood He entered the Most Holy Place once for all, having obtained eternal redemption.

13 For if the blood of bulls and goats and the ashes of a heifer, sprinkling the unclean, sanctifies for the purifying of the flesh,

14 how much more shall the blood of Christ, who through the eternal Spirit offered Himself without spot to God, cleanse your conscience from dead works to serve the living God?

15 And for this reason He is the Mediator of the new covenant, by means of death, for the redemption of the transgressions under the first covenant, that those who are called may receive the promise of the eternal inheritance.

Hebrews 12:22-24

22 But you have come to Mount Zion and to the city of the living God, the heavenly Jerusalem, to an innumerable company of angels,

23 to the general assembly and church of the firstborn who are registered in heaven, to God the Judge of all, to the spirits of just men made perfect,

24 to Jesus the Mediator of the new covenant, and to the blood of sprinkling that speaks better things than that of Abel.

Introduction

For the people of Israel, revelation began with the Law. In the New Testament period, Jews called the first five books of the Old Testament "the Pentateuch," a combination of the Greek *pente*, meaning "five," and *teuchoi*, the scrolls on which the Law was written. The five books were Jewish law, Torah, though Hebrew scholars will argue that "law" and Torah are not quite the same. Torah, they say, is a broader word, something like "instruction." Jewish scholars in the middle ages counted 613 laws in the Pentateuch, but laws were a bare smattering of all God revealed in the five books. In addition to laws, Torah guided and inspired Israel with stories, songs, genealogies and epics. The Pentateuch was the mine from which Israelites dug the jewels that defined their relationship to God and to one another.

Among other things, the Pentateuch foreshadowed the redemption that was to come for Israel and humankind. God made tantalizing promises that were interpreted differently by the teachers and wise men of Israel. What did God mean when He said that all nations would be blessed by Abraham's seed? Had the promise changed when one interprets as the footnote of the English Standard Version has, "By you all families of the earth shall bless themselves" (Genesis 12:3)? Was the promise given to Moses to raise up a Prophet (Deuteronomy 18:18) an extension of the one He made to Abraham? If God's statements in the Law about Israel's future roused uncertainty, the foreshadowing in types called forth yet more discussion. It was not until the revelation of the New Testament that Christians came to understand, for example, that Israel's high priest foreshadowed Christ (Hebrews 7:26) or that Israel's crossing the Red Sea was a type of Christian baptism (1 Corinthians 10:1-4).

To say that salvation is foreshadowed in the Law is to say that the coming of the Son of God to redeem the human family from sin is foreshadowed in the Law. Authors of the New Testament open Christian eyes to the subtleties and precision of the Law of Moses as it unfolds God's revelation concerning the coming of the Christ of God.

The Purpose of the Law (Galatians 3:23-25)

From its earliest days, the church has struggled to define the way the Old Testament generally and the Law of Moses in particular informs and instructs Christians. On the one hand, the Old Testament is Scripture, "profitable for doctrine, for reproof, for correction, for instruction in righteousness" (2 Timothy 3:16), but on the other hand Christians are under no constraints to obey ceremonial aspects of the Law that define ethnic Judaism (Galatians 5:1). Because churches of Christ have insisted that none of the Law is binding on believers, they have been falsely accused of not believing in the Old Testament. Generally they have affirmed the value of teachings and examples in the Old Testament but have rejected the popular notion that the Law can be divided neatly into a ceremonial portion that Christians can ignore and a moral portion that they are to obey. The New Covenant is on a different order than was the Old Covenant.

Paul asked, "What purpose then does the law serve?" (Galatians 3:19). Although the promises were primary, he maintains that the law was necessary in order for men to feel the weight of sin (v. 22). The people God chose and led from Egypt were "kept under guard by the law" (v. 23); it was a temporary arrangement until the way of life through faith should afterward be revealed. As one scholarly study observes, "[N]owhere in the Old Testament is it suggested that anyone was saved by keeping the Law. Rather the Law was God's gift to Israel." [1]

Drawing on a custom that was familiar to himself and his readers, Paul said that the Law was a *paidagogos* "to bring us to Christ" (Galatians 3:24). The translations reflect the difficulty in finding a reasonably English equivalent. The King James Version rendered it "schoolmaster." The New King James Version and the New American Standard Bible have "tutor." Others go with "guardian" (ESV) or "disciplinarian" (NRSV). The 1984 New International Version resorts to a phrase, "So the law was put in charge to lead us to Christ." The word draws on the ways of a rich man who wanted to discipline his son. He might appoint a slave who would get his charge to school and see that he did his assignments. The slave was a *paidagogos*. If the young man neglected his work, the slave would beat him. He was not the teacher, but he was in charge of the progress of the manners and learning of the rich man's son. Paul found a *paidagogos* to be a helpful illustration of the way the Law foreshadowed salvation in Christ. The Law guided and when necessary disciplined God's people, but it was never an end in itself. Salvation was by faith, and once faith had been realized, God's people were no longer under a *paidagogos*.

Our Great High Priest
(Hebrews 4:14-16; 9:11-15)

In none of the letters to which Paul attaches his name is Jesus said to be High Priest; in Hebrews it is a theme to which the author returns several times. Jesus lived in the flesh "like His brethren" and thus became "a merciful and faithful High Priest" (Hebrews 2:17). The author takes up the subject again in 4:14-16. Before he is done, he will have turned to Genesis 14:18-20 and Psalm 110:4 to argue that the priesthood of Jesus had been foreshadowed first in Melchizedek and then more precisely in the high priesthood of Aaron.

Both prophets and priests in the Old Testament stood between the people and God. The direction of priestly service was upward. Priests took the offerings of the people and presented them to God according to rituals prescribed in the Law. The direction of a prophet's ministry was downward. Moses spoke of a Prophet who would come after him who would declare all that God commanded (Deuteronomy 18:18; Acts 3:22-23). God revealed messages to the prophet which he heralded to the people. The ideals of priestly and of prophetic office each in its own way foreshadowed the work of the Son of God.

The High Priesthood of Jesus is superior to that of Aaron and his descendants on several counts. First, when Christians come to God through Him they can be sure that He understands their weaknesses. Jesus "was in all points tempted as we are" (Hebrews 4:15). Second, Christians pray to no God who stands aloof in celestial realms unacquainted with the grime of life. Job indicted God with questions, "Do You have eyes of flesh? Or do You see as man sees? Are Your days like the days of a mortal man?" (Job 10:4-5). The patriarch thought God could not appreciate what he suffered; Jesus has forever silenced the complaint. Third, Jesus serves as High Priest in the courts of heaven itself (Hebrews 9:11). Fourth, Jesus has offered his own flesh as a sacrifice. Unlike the priests of the Old Covenant, He gave Himself as the payment for sins.

Our Mediator (Hebrews 12:22-24)

The author of Hebrews likely referred to his readers' conversions when he said that they had "come to Mount Zion" (Hebrews 12:22). Zion first appears in the Bible as a Jebusite fortification. Valleys to the east, west and south provided natural protection, but David and his men gained entrance through a water shaft and brought the stronghold under his rule (2 Samuel 5:7-8). Originally Zion designated the projection of land to the south of Mount Moriah where Solomon built the temple (2 Chronicles 3:1). Over time the name Zion prevailed for the area immediately west of the Kidron Valley including the Temple Mount (Psalm 78:68-69). Then, by metonymy, Zion came to stand for Jerusalem in its entirety (e.g., Isaiah 30:19).

By human appearance, Jerusalem or Zion was a material city like any other, but because of its spiritual importance, the place foreshadowed heavenly realities. Zion in the New Testament becomes synonymous with "the Jerusalem above" (Galatians 4:26; cf. Revelation 21:2) and Christian fellowship an extension of heavenly realms (1 John 1:3). To belong to Christ is to share in the "church of the firstborn," to have one's name "registered in heaven" (Hebrews 12:22-23). In the New Jerusalem where Christians have their fellowship, the Son of God is mediator. Having offered His blood, He is able to represent men and women with all their frailties and to plead their case before God's judgment bar.

Conclusion

The people and the institutions of the Old Testament foreshadowed the work of Christ, the promises He extends, and the makeup of His church. But even in these things we have not exhausted Old Testament foreshadowing. Individual believers find strength to overcome temptations and courage to face challenges through countless instances where biblical characters, events and places foreshadow their own lives. In Esau who sold his birthright for a bowl of stew (Genesis 25:34), in Peter's searching question, "Lord, to whom shall we go?" (John 6:68), and in myriads of places in-between, Christians see themselves in the words and choices of biblical characters. In the foreshadowing, they find occasion for reflection; they find inspiration to pursue noble and good things. "The people of God are still a pilgrim people, treading the 'highways to Zion,' but by virtue of His sure promise they have already arrived there in spirit." [2]

Questions

1. What name did Jews from the New Testament period give to the first five books in the Old Testament?
2. By what did Paul say we were "kept under guard" before faith came?
3. By what did Paul say Christians were justified when the Law brought us to Christ?
4. What did Paul say Christians had become through faith in Christ?
5. Because Christians have a great High Priest who has passed through the heavens, what did the Hebrews author urge them to do?
6. Why can the Christian's High Priest sympathize with the temptations he or she faces?
7. With what attitude or disposition can Christians come before the throne of grace?
8. With what has the Christian's High Priest entered the Most Holy Place?
9. When one becomes a Christian, to what did the Hebrews author say that he or she had come?
10. Of what is Christ the believer's mediator?

Discussion Starters

1. Why is "law" an inadequate designation for the first five books of the Old Testament? Give examples of things in them that are not laws as ordinarily defined.
2. What are some examples where Christ, His church or the way of salvation is foreshadowed in the Law of Moses?
3. What is the meaning of the Greek word *paidagogos*, translated "schoolmaster" in the King James Version? How does it illustrate the way the Law leads to Christ?
4. What is "Zion" in the Old Testament? How does Zion foreshadow Christian experience and Christian hope?

The Coming of the Christ, Part 1

Isaiah 7:14

14 Therefore the Lord Himself will give you a sign: Behold, the virgin shall conceive and bear a Son, and shall call His name Immanuel.

Isaiah 53:4-6

4 Surely He has borne our griefs And carried our sorrows; Yet we esteemed Him stricken, Smitten by God, and afflicted.

5 But He was wounded for our transgressions, He was bruised for our iniquities; The chastisement for our peace was upon Him, And by His stripes we are healed.

6 All we like sheep have gone astray; We have turned, every one, to his own way; And the LORD has laid on Him the iniquity of us all.

Matthew 1:20-23

20 But while he thought about these things, behold, an angel of the Lord appeared to him in a dream, saying, "Joseph, son of David, do not be afraid to take to you Mary your wife, for that which is conceived in her is of the Holy Spirit.

21 "And she will bring forth a Son, and you shall call His name JESUS, for He will save His people from their sins."

22 So all this was done that it might be fulfilled which was spoken by the Lord through the prophet, saying:

23 "Behold, the virgin shall be with child, and bear a Son, and they shall call His name Immanuel," which is translated, "God with us."

Galatians 4:4-7

4 But when the fullness of the time had come, God sent forth His Son, born of a woman, born under the law,

5 to redeem those who were under the law, that we might receive the adoption as sons.

6 And because you are sons, God has sent forth the Spirit of His Son into your hearts, crying out, "Abba, Father!"

7 Therefore you are no longer a slave but a son, and if a son, then an heir of God through Christ.

John 2:11

11 This beginning of signs Jesus did in Cana of Galilee, and manifested His glory; and His disciples believed in Him.

John 20:30-31

30 And truly Jesus did many other signs in the presence of His disciples, which are not written in this book;

31 but these are written that you may believe that Jesus is the Christ, the Son of God, and that believing you may have life in His name.

Introduction

The Christian confession begins and ends with the confidence that in Jesus of Nazareth something absolutely unique in the annals of humankind took place. The incarnation of the Son of God was so unexpected that even those closest to Jesus had difficulty recognizing who He was. In Matthew, Jesus manifested Himself as a teacher who spoke with authority. He followed His teachings with miracles that testified of God's approval. His priorities and practices met with stiff resistance from religious leaders. The disciples were perplexed when He asked them, "Who do men say that I, the Son of Man, am?" (Matthew 16:13). Right through the crucifixion and resurrection, they did not understand the significance of what was happening before their eyes. How could they? Nothing like it had ever happened.

After the Holy Spirit had been poured out on the apostles on Pentecost, they came to understand that the man who had walked with them in the flesh had been the incarnate Son of God. Enlightened as they were by the Spirit, the apostles proclaimed that nothing can be right between men and God until they put their trust and faith in the Teacher from Nazareth. Without faith it is impossible to please God (Hebrews 11:6). Still, faith is not easy. Great faith requires great effort. Easy belief is like seed on shallow ground. It springs up quickly and then dies for lack of root (Matthew 13:20-21). The greatness of one's faith is not measured by how many ridiculous things he or she can believe before breakfast each day. Seeds of great faith are sown in reason.

Before, during and after the coming of Christ, God has given abundant reasons to reinforce the confidence of those inclined to be skeptical about claims that the Carpenter from Nazareth was God manifest in the flesh. The evidence and the reasoning have not and will not satisfy everyone, but what God has provided is sufficient for those who look into the mystery of existence, who probe the blackness of sin and who reach for a life with religious and moral directions. Reason and faith are not enemies, not opposites. In Christ an examined life is a life of promise and hope.

The Virgin Birth (Isaiah 7:14; Matthew 1:20-23; Galatians 4:4-7)

Faith treads a narrow path between the knowable and the unknowable. How it can be that the Divine became a man is in the realm of the unknowable. What is knowable is the event itself. God began the story of His Son with a virgin birth. That much is a matter of record. Not only did God announce the coming of His Son with an event unique in human history, but He also proclaimed what He was going to do centuries in advance. To call an event in advance is evidence for planning and purpose. A poor billiards player may make an amazing shot by accident, but if he calls a shot that includes banks off cushions and combinations with neutral balls, it inspires confidence that he knows what he is doing. Before the coming of Christ, God announced what He was going to do.

The story began with a young couple. They were not wealthy; their immediate families were undistinguished. Before they came together as husband and wife, Mary, the bride-to-be, discovered she was pregnant (Matthew 1:18). Joseph, her espoused, thought it best to put the matter discreetly behind him. God had other plans. An angel appeared to Joseph in a dream and told him that Mary's child had been fathered by the Holy Spirit. The child would be remarkable. He would "save His people from their sins" (v. 21). The birth of the child would fulfill the prophecy of Isaiah. Deliverance had been the prophet's subject when he told Ahaz, king of Judah, that a virgin would have a child. The child's name would be Immanuel, meaning "God with us" (v. 23). Beginning with His birth of a virgin, all generations would see evidence that Mary's child was the Christ.

The Gospels give Christians four different perspectives on the words and deeds of Jesus, but it is left for the Holy Spirit through Paul to set forth the significance of the events in clear, succinct words. Jesus was born in a world carefully prepared for His birth. It was, in Paul's words, "when the fullness of the time had come" that Jesus appeared in Judea (Galatians 4:4). The Law governed the Jewish people when He came, but His mission was to "redeem those who were under the law" (v. 5). Jesus came to inaugurate a new covenant between God and His people. He came to give freedom. By the infusion of His Spirit, the saved find strength to live godly. Because He has paid the price for sin, they hope for eternal life.

The Suffering Servant (Isaiah 53:4-6)

From a purely literary perspective, it is difficult to find any place in the Old or the New Testament that speaks of the mission of Jesus with the emotion and beauty of Isaiah 53. Although scholars differ about precise beginning and ending points, most point to four passages in Isaiah where the Messiah appears as a "suffering servant" (Isaiah 42:1-4; 49:1-6; 50:4-9; 52:13–53:12). The last is the longest and the most intense. Its description is unparalleled. Many Jews who were contemporaries of Jesus expected a warrior Messiah who would lead an army and set Himself up as a king like David. At one point some 5,000 men attempted to make Jesus king over them by force (John 6:10, 15). Then as elsewhere, the Lord refused the way of arms and chose the way of the cross (18:36).

When the apostles spoke to Jewish audiences, a large part of their burden was to orient hearers to a different type of Christ than they expected. Nowhere is this clearer than during the stay of Paul, Timothy and Silas at Thessalonica. The missionaries speaking in the synagogues offered evidence that "the Christ had to suffer and rise again from the dead." From there they sought to persuade them that Jesus, crucified as a criminal in Jerusalem, was the Christ (Acts 17:3).

Acts offers no evidence that Paul cited Isaiah 53 at Thessalonica, but the prophecy comes up elsewhere. When Philip approached the chariot of the Ethiopian eunuch, he found the Queen's treasurer reading from Isaiah 53:7-8,

"He was led as a sheep to the slaughter" (Acts 8:32-33). Philip "beginning at this Scripture, preached Jesus to him" (v. 35). Peter drew on the words of Isaiah to help his readers understand what happened on the cross: "By whose stripes you were healed," the apostle wrote (1 Peter 2:24).

That the Son of God took human flesh in the form of a suffering servant has far-ranging implications. Paul wrote, "For though He was crucified in weakness, yet He lives by the power of God. For we also are weak in Him, but we shall live with Him by the power of God toward you" (2 Corinthians 13:4). The people of Christ, like the Christ Himself, are to be a people who are mild and gentle, who know the ways of peace and goodness (Galatians 5:22-23).

Signs and Miracles (John 2:11; 20:30-31)

During the years when Jesus' ministry was ongoing and during the apostolic age that followed, miracles and signs were door openers for the gospel. They bore witness to truths spoken. Greek has no word with the same connotations as "miracle." General words meaning "powers" or "wonders" sometimes are defined as miracles by the contexts where they appear. In John's gospel, the Greek word translated "miracle" literally means "sign." The miracles of Jesus and, for that matter, miracles performed throughout the apostolic age were signs that pointed beyond themselves. They testified that God's authority lay behind the words spoken.

The first of Jesus' signs was at a wedding His mother wanted Him to attend. The miracle averted no great tragedy; it delivered no leper from his shame and no blind man from his helplessness. The first sign Jesus did helped a family avoid embarrassment. That appears to be all until we come to the end of the account. Because of what He did, the disciples are nudged in the direction of faith. In the deed Jesus manifested His glory. Because of it, "His disciples believed in Him" (John 2:11).

John records seven of Jesus' signs: (1) the water to wine (John 2:1-11), (2) the nobleman's son (4:46-54), (3) the lame man at Bethesda (5:1-15), (4) feeding the 5,000 (6:1-13), (5) walking on water (6:15-20), (6) the blind man at Siloam (9:1-11), and (7) the raising of Lazarus (11:38-44). Of course, Jesus' own resurrection should be added to these. Many more miracles are in the first three gospels, but of those recorded in John, only the feeding of the 5,000 and the walking on water are in the other accounts. When John is near the end of his story, he assures readers that he has been selective in the miracles he records. Many others occurred, but the few he described were sufficient to demonstrate God's testimony that Jesus was all He had claimed to be.

Conclusion

By means of prophetic predictions, by means of signs and wonders, by means of His resurrection from the dead, God bore witness to His Son. The testimony was so compelling that the circle around Jesus, the apostles in particular, laid down their lives in order to proclaim Him to a waiting world. The crucifixion of Jesus was not the death of an ordinary criminal. His death and the resurrection that followed provided a final seal of approval that God placed on His life. The evidence has stood the test of more than 2,000 years. In the person of Jesus of Nazareth, God has become manifest among us.

Questions

1. What name did Isaiah give the child he prophesied about who would be born of a virgin?
2. How did Joseph learn that his espoused bride was with child through the Holy Spirit?
3. What did Paul say that God sent His Son to do for those born under the Law?
4. What did Paul say the Spirit in the hearts of Christians cried out?
5. What are the passages in Isaiah that prophesy of Christ as a "suffering servant"?
6. What are at least two places in the New Testament where authors associate the cross of Christ with the suffering servant of Isaiah 53?
7. Why does Isaiah say that the suffering servant he described would be wounded and bruised?
8. What is the word that John's gospel uses for the miracles of Jesus?
9. How many of Jesus' miracles are described by John? Name them.
10. Why did John say he had recorded the signs done by Jesus?

Discussion Starters

1. Why is it important for those lost in sin to ask questions and to satisfy themselves that Jesus was the Son of God who died for their sins?
2. What practical implications do Christians perceive that the Christ was crucified in weakness? How is one to be strong in weakness?
3. What was the purpose of miracles done by Christ and the apostles that followed Him? What is the implication for the perpetuation of the miraculous in the church?
4. Why was it difficult for the disciples of Jesus to understand that He was the Son of God? How has God testified to ancient and modern people about Jesus?

The Coming of the Christ, Part 2

Matthew 20:17-19

17 Now Jesus, going up to Jerusalem, took the twelve disciples aside on the road and said to them,

18 "Behold, we are going up to Jerusalem, and the Son of Man will be betrayed to the chief priests and to the scribes; and they will condemn Him to death,

19 "and deliver Him to the Gentiles to mock and to scourge and to crucify. And the third day He will rise again."

John 12:46-50

46 "I have come as a light into the world, that whoever believes in Me should not abide in darkness.

47 "And if anyone hears My words and does not believe, I do not judge him; for I did not come to judge the world but to save the world.

48 "He who rejects Me, and does not receive My words, has that which judges him – the word that I have spoken will judge him in the last day.

49 "For I have not spoken on My own authority; but the Father who sent Me gave Me a command, what I should say and what I should speak.

50 "And I know that His command is everlasting life. Therefore, whatever I speak, just as the Father has told Me, so I speak."

1 Corinthians 15:1-8

1 Moreover, brethren, I declare to you the gospel which I preached to you, which also you received and in which you stand,

2 by which also you are saved, if you hold fast that word which I preached to you – unless you believed in vain.

3 For I delivered to you first of all that which I also received: that Christ died for our sins according to the Scriptures,

4 and that He was buried, and that He rose again the third day according to the Scriptures,

5 and that He was seen by Cephas, then by the twelve.

6 After that He was seen by over five hundred brethren at once, of whom the greater part remain to the present, but some have fallen asleep.

7 After that He was seen by James, then by all the apostles.

8 Then last of all He was seen by me also, as by one born out of due time.

Introduction

Belief that Jesus is the Christ has something of a threefold aspect. First, Christians believe in a past event. More than 2,000 years ago, a man appeared in real time who was God manifest in the flesh. Had we been there, we could have seen him heal a leper or walk on the waters of Galilee. Jesus lived as surely as did Julius Caesar or George Washington. Second, Christians have a real, vital relationship to God in the present. They believe He lives now and reigns at God's right hand. The second tier of faith is important when a child lies gasping for air or when a marriage appears to be on the verge of collapse. When we feel uncertain and alone, helpless and afraid, it is not so much the Man who lived in Galilee to whom we turn as it is the Man who rules over human affairs and makes intercession for us. Third, Christian faith is about hope for the future. The world is moving toward a purposeful end. Christ will return. Judgment and eternity are before us. Of course, the Galilean who lived more than 2,000 years ago, the King at God's right hand, and the Lord who will come again are the same. The three ways Christians relate to Christ – past event, living presence and future hope – are interwoven, but each brings up its own questions. The varied experiences of life cause Christians to think about the Savior and Lord sometimes in one way, sometimes in another.

Faith begins with a historical confidence. All is built on quicksand unless the Galilean said and did what Scripture affirms of Him. The miraculous, of which prophecy is a part, is God's testimony in time to the incarnation of His Son. Having put down a peg secured in historical events, faith is ready to move on to the Christ who reigns and to the Lord who is coming again. The historical event of Jesus recorded in the gospels was a step in God's plan for Him to come a second time for judgment and eternity. The coming of Christ as an event in human history has implications not only for the affirmation of faith but also for Christian trust in the sovereign rule of God and the Christian hope for life in the New Jerusalem.

Jesus' Prediction (Matthew 20:17-19)

The first two-thirds of Matthew's gospel are driven by the question, "What are we to think of this man?" Only the demons knew for sure. "What have we to do with You, Jesus, You Son of God?" they cried out (Matthew 8:29). Jesus' enemies attribute the miraculous signs they could not deny to the power of Beelzebul (Beelzebub NKJV), the ruler of the demons (12:24). The crowds, including the disciples, did not know what to think. They had difficulty conceiving the possibility that their Teacher was Immanuel, "God with us" (1:23). It is difficult for any of us to open our minds to something absolutely different from anything we have ever experienced.

Two events were pivotal for the disciples as they grew in self-awareness about Jesus: (1) the retreat to Caesarea Philippi (Matthew 16:13ff.) and (2) events on the Mount of Transfiguration (17:1ff.). Not to be overlooked is the fact that Jesus followed the confession of Peter at Caesarea Philippi by telling the disciples that death awaited Him at Jerusalem (16:21). Following the Transfiguration, He repeated the warning (17:22-23). On the way to Jerusalem for His final Passover, He told them a third time of His coming death (20:17-19). The request of James and John for high office in the kingdom demonstrates how thoroughly they failed to listen to the words of Jesus (vv. 20-24).

The path to glory for Jesus was the crucifixion, not that of a worldly empire. Jesus came to redeem men from sin, not to lead armies. All that He said and did was preparatory for the cross. With the end in sight Jesus asked, "Shall I not drink the cup which My Father has given Me?" (John 18:11). Jesus offered up His sinless life as a payment for sin. His offering entailed His being betrayed, spat on, mocked, scourged and crucified. The Christian faith is that something of ultimate significance in the relationship between God and man happened when Jesus suffered. Before His coming, men stood before God as enemies; after He paid the price, peace and reconciliation reigned.

Jesus' Promise (John 12:46-50)

The public ministry of Jesus comes to a conclusion in the final part of John 12. Beginning with chapter 13, His words are directed mostly to the inner circle of the disciples. The crucifixion is close at hand. Great themes of the gospel find a final expression in John 12:46-50. Jesus is "a light into the world" that is enveloped "in darkness" (v. 46). By believing in the Son and obeying His words, disciples will find favor with God when He judges the world. The authority of the Son proceeds from the Father. To have faith in Jesus is to have faith in God.

What are we to make of the declaration, "I did not come to judge the world" (John 12:47)? Elsewhere the Lord said that the Father "has committed all judgment to the Son" (5:22), and "I have many things to say and to judge concerning you" (8:26). The same tension appears in the admonition of Jesus to the disciples, "Judge not" (Matthew 7:1), which He followed by urging them to judge teachers by their fruits (v. 20). Unless Christians make careful judgments, moral ambiguity and chaos reign, but God has not given indiscriminate judgment even to the faithful. Only God is qualified to render judgments of eternal significance.

When Jesus spoke of Himself as judge, He drew on a range of meaning the word may have. The Lord did not take on flesh with a contingent plan to abandon the human family should He decide they were unworthy. The guilt of humankind was certain. In Eden and through the intervening centuries after, people passed judgment on themselves by turning their backs on God's grace. Jesus did not come to judge men to be rebellious. That question had been answered. He came to save. The New King James Version translates the same Greek word "to judge" in John 12:47 that it renders "to condemn" in 3:17, but the sense is the same. The mission of the Son of God was to open the door for everlasting life by living sinlessly and offering Himself as a payment for sin. He did not come to take life away. None of that changes the certainty that He will come again on the last day. At that time, every soul will be judged by Him (John 5:28-29; 2 Corinthians 5:10).

Jesus' Resurrection (1 Corinthians 15:1-8)

To a church plagued with controversy, Paul set the base line for Christian confession like this: (1) Jesus died for our sins, (2) He was buried, (3) on the third day God raised Him from the dead (1 Corinthians 15:3-4). All of this, Paul said, was in fulfillment of what the prophets had said of the Christ. It was all right with Paul for skeptics to ask questions as hard as they wished. God knew that Thomas would not be the last to doubt personal testimonies (John 20:25). He multiplied the appearances of the risen Lord; Paul was able to bury doubts under an abundance of testimony, but even he did not mention some of the appearances of the risen Christ recorded in the gospels. The Lord had appeared to Cephas, Paul's preferred name for Peter. After that, He was seen by the twelve. James saw him as did all the apostles. Paul alone has recorded that Jesus appeared to some 500 disciples at one time, possibly an appearance in Galilee. The important thing was that some of them were still alive. They could be questioned. If human testimony can establish anything, the crucified Christ, dead on the cross and placed in a tomb, had risen bodily. The resurrected Lord had been seen in the flesh; He had talked with His followers and instructed them about the kingdom of God (Acts 1:3). To conclude his argument, Paul declared that finally the Lord had appeared to him personally. Likely he was referring to his call on the road to Damascus (9:4-5).

The resurrection of Jesus was evidence that all who were in the grave would come forth (John 5:28-29). In a sense, that universal resurrection of the human race had already begun, for Jesus, Paul said, "has become the firstfruits of those who have fallen asleep" (15:20). A firstfruit implies that the full harvest is to follow. As Jesus rose bodily from the dead, so shall every man and woman be raised. The Christian hope rests on the assurance that Jesus was the Christ and that He died for sins. God bore witness to Him by raising Him from the dead (Romans 1:4).

Conclusion

When the resurrected Jesus met with His disciples on a mountain in Galilee, He told them to "make disciples of all the nations" (Matthew 28:18-20). They were to teach that converts were to obey all that Jesus had commanded. The process of making disciples then and now begins with telling the story of Jesus of Nazareth. Peter said that He was a man whom God anointed with the Holy Spirit and with power, a man who "went about doing good and healing all who were oppressed by the devil" (Acts 10:38). He died on a Roman cross, bearing the sins of humanity. On the third day, God raised Him from the dead. The story begins with Jesus, Son of God. It works backward to the preparation God made for His appearance in the calling of Abraham and the giving of Canaan to his descendants. It will end when He comes again in glory. The story goes through many changes between the first Adam and the Second. But through it all, Jesus is "the Alpha and the Omega, the Beginning and the End" (Revelation 1:8) of redemption and peace with God.

Questions

1. What has God used to testify to men that Jesus was and is the promised Christ, Savior and Redeemer?
2. As the story of Jesus begins in Matthew, who knows for sure that He is the Son of God?
3. With what two pivotal events did the disciples grow in their realization that Jesus was the Son of God?
4. After Peter's confession of Jesus at Caesarea Philippi, what did Jesus reveal to the disciples about what was to happen in Jerusalem?
5. To whom did Jesus say that He would be betrayed?
6. Who would mock and scourge Jesus before He was turned over to be crucified?
7. What did Jesus say that He had come to be to a world engulfed in darkness?
8. To whom did Paul say that Jesus had appeared after His resurrection from the dead?
9. To how many brethren had Jesus appeared at one time?
10. Who had been the last to whom the resurrected Jesus appeared?

Discussion Starters

1. In what ways do Christians look to the past, the present and the future when they consider their faith in Christ?
2. Why does the New Testament speak of Jesus as Judge when He said that He had not come to judge but to save? In what sense are Christians forbidden to judge?
3. What three things did Paul say were of first importance in his preaching? Why are those three matters primary?
4. Why did Paul say of Jesus that He was "the firstfruits" of those risen from the dead? Why is it important for Christians that Jesus was raised bodily?

Lesson 11 • Week of Nov. 16, 2014

The Identity of the Church

Matthew 16:13-19

13 When Jesus came into the region of Caesarea Philippi, He asked His disciples, saying, "Who do men say that I, the Son of Man, am?"

14 So they said, "Some say John the Baptist, some Elijah, and others Jeremiah or one of the prophets."

15 He said to them, "But who do you say that I am?"

16 Simon Peter answered and said, "You are the Christ, the Son of the living God."

17 Jesus answered and said to him, "Blessed are you, Simon Bar-Jonah, for flesh and blood has not revealed this to you, but My Father who is in heaven.

18 "And I also say to you that you are Peter, and on this rock I will build My church, and the gates of Hades shall not prevail against it.

19 "And I will give you the keys of the kingdom of heaven, and whatever you bind on earth will be bound in heaven, and whatever you loose on earth will be loosed in heaven."

Acts 2:41-47

41 Then those who gladly received his word were baptized; and that day about three thousand souls were added to them.

42 And they continued steadfastly in the apostles' doctrine and fellowship, in the breaking of bread, and in prayers.

43 Then fear came upon every soul, and many wonders and signs were done through the apostles.

44 Now all who believed were together, and had all things in common,

45 and sold their possessions and goods, and divided them among all, as anyone had need.

46 So continuing daily with one accord in the temple, and breaking bread from house to house, they ate their food with gladness and simplicity of heart,

47 praising God and having favor with all the people. And the Lord added to the church daily those who were being saved.

Ephesians 1:22-23

22 And He put all things under His feet, and gave Him to be head over all things to the church,

23 which is His body, the fullness of Him who fills all in all.

10 ... to the intent that now the manifold wisdom of God might be made known by the church to the principalities and powers in the heavenly places,

11 according to the eternal purpose which He accomplished in Christ Jesus our Lord,

12 in whom we have boldness and access with confidence through faith in Him.

Introduction

The word "church" occurs only three times in the Gospels, in Matthew 16:18 and in 18:17 twice. Instead of calling the people who belong to Him "the church," in Matthew Jesus normally called them "the kingdom of heaven" or in Mark and Luke "the kingdom of God" (compare, for example, Matthew 13:11 with Mark 4:11 and Luke 8:10). In the person of Jesus, the kingdom of God manifested itself. Jesus could say to those who rejected Him, "But if I cast out demons by the Spirit of God [and He clearly did], surely the kingdom of God has come upon you" (Matthew 12:28). Still, leading up to the cross, the full measure of the kingdom Jesus was to rule lay in the future. In the future tense the Lord said to Peter, "I will give you the keys of the kingdom" (16:19). In the presence of Jesus, the disciples anticipated a kingdom yet to come (Mark 9:1).

On the first Pentecost after the resurrection, Peter announced the terms of salvation (Acts 2:38), and for the first time people were reconciled to God, which is to say they were added to the kingdom. The King James and New King James versions add the word "church" for clarity in Acts 2:47, but they could just as well have translated, "And the Lord added to the kingdom daily those who were being saved." The first occurrence of the Greek word for church is in Acts 5:11. After that "church" becomes the common designation for the people who belong to Christ. By comparison, references to "the kingdom of God" in Acts and the letters are infrequent. "Church" implies congregations assembled where believers enjoyed fellowship and worked together guided by evangelists, teachers and elders (Ephesians 4:11). Churches are communities of believers who together make up the kingdom of God.

In order to support previously determined doctrinal stances, some try to make a distinction between "church" and "kingdom of God" in the New Testament. Jesus came to build His church (Matthew 16:18), and those who belong to Him are in "the kingdom of the Son of His love" (Colossians 1:13). Those who are saved by the blood of the Lamb are the church of Christ, and they constitute the kingdom of God. Subtle nuances in the way church and kingdom of God appear in the New Testament do not erase the fact that the terms are synonymous.

Christ the Builder (Matthew 16:13-19)

When Jesus took His disciples north of Galilee to the regions around Caesarea Philippi, He set the stage for a turning point in His ministry. The world was slow to recognize what God was doing in Jesus. Before the trek to Caesarea, demons had confessed Him to be the "Son of God" (Matthew 8:29). John the Baptist had misgivings about His being the Christ (11:2-3). Confusion reigned. In response to miracles crowds asked, "Could this be the Son of David?" (12:23). After He had come to them walking on water and had rescued Peter from the waves, those in the boat had gone to their knees. "Truly You are the Son of God," they had said (14:33). But when the excitement had passed, even those closest to Jesus did not know what to make of Him. They had never seen or heard anything like Him before. He was not what they had expected the Christ to be.

Jesus retreated with His disciples in the vicinity of a Greek temple dedicated to Pan, Greek god of wild creatures. At a quiet moment and to His friends, Jesus posed a crucial question: What are people saying about Me? No common opinion prevailed, the disciples said. Even the disciples may have had different opinions. The first question by Jesus was a prelude for the second, "But who do you say that I am?" (Matthew 16:15). Peter may have broken an awkward silence. He did not hesitate to say what he thought. Those who believed Jesus to be John the Baptist risen from the dead or Elijah or Jeremiah were wrong. Jesus was not one of the prophets at all. "You are the Christ," the Galilean fisherman said, "the Son of the Living God" (v. 16). Peter lifted the speculation to an entirely new level.

The disciples were discovering what Jesus wanted them to discover. Peter was right. Jesus told him that his confession would prove to be a blessing for himself and for the world. Peter had received no revelation from God that the others had not, but Peter recognized the implications of what he had seen. Jesus told the apostle that the confession he had made was to be the bedrock on which He would build His church (Matthew 16:18). It would be an aggressive, victorious church. The gates of hell would not be able to fend off its onslaughts. Because Peter was an apostle, Jesus said that to him would be given the "keys of the kingdom" (v. 19). The message Peter proclaimed would turn the lock that had barred men and women from God. Jesus spoke of the kingdom of God and the church in the same breath. To give Peter the keys to one was to give him keys to the other. The Holy Spirit would so endow the apostle that what he spoke would have the authority of God. What Peter bound or loosed on earth would be bound or loosed in heaven (v. 19). It was a promise Jesus was to repeat to all the apostles (18:18).

Christ the Sustainer (Acts 2:41-47)

After Peter made use of "the keys of the kingdom" on the first Pentecost after the resurrection, some 3,000 embraced the gospel, repented of their sins and were baptized into Christ (Acts 2:41). Answering the question, "What shall we do?" (v. 37) was an essential step, but the apostles soon learned that their responsibilities continued beyond the baptizing of the lost. New Christians needed to grow in faith. Believers had yet to become communities of faith. The apostles had much to do before the kingdom of God emerged as an effective force in the world, but the Lord did not leave them without resources. Through the Holy Spirit, Christ guided and sustained believers by means of apostolic teaching (John 14:26). Jesus empowered His people to do what He commanded by means of the Holy Spirit, which had been given to them when they were baptized into Christ (Acts 2:38). A crucial element in the Spirit's work was the word spoken by apostles and teachers. Paul was later to write of "the sword of the Spirit, which is the word of God" (Ephesians 6:17).

The sustaining work of Christ entailed the worship and fellowship of believers. Through the spoken word, Christians grew in their understanding of what they were to believe and how they were to behave. The worship of the church included observing the Lord's Supper and prayers. The Lord works through "the breaking of the bread" as He works through baptism. In baptism He takes away sins; in the Lord's Supper He builds up and empowers the saved. Paul said that in the cup and the bread believers communed or shared in the blood and body of Christ (1 Corinthians 10:16). By means of prayer, the Word, the Lord's Supper, and the indwelling Spirit, and through the fellowship of a community who share spiritual and material needs, Christ sustains and builds up His people.

Christ the Head
(Ephesians 1:22-23; 3:10-12)

For a community of people to pursue purposeful goals and do worthwhile things, leadership is crucial. When Paul used the metaphor of Christ as head of His church, leadership was the subject. Christ is the authority from which the doctrine, the worship, the hope, and the behavior of the church flow. As the head of one's physical body is the nerve center from which the whole functions as a unit, Christ is the head who gives unity to Christians spread across time and space. He exercises His headship by means of the words recorded in Scripture. The church knows how He is to be praised and what kind of lives they are to live because He has spoken in His Word.

Headship implies authority, but that isn't all. The head of a business enterprise, of a governmental entity or of a family ought to seek the best interests of those who look to him or her for leadership. Christ is the fountainhead of the church; He is the source from which its ideals and purposes find expression. Because He is the firstfruit of those to be raised from the dead (1 Corinthians 15:20), He is the Christian's hope. He has become head of the church by modeling the life He wants His people to live and by giving His life in order for them to be saved (1 Peter 2:21, 24).

Conclusion

In the modern world, questions about the identity of the church arise from the background of a divided denominational world. Christians confront two sets of facts they find hard to balance. First, Christ made it clear that He wanted His people to be united, one flock following one shepherd (John 17:20-21). Yet believers are confronted with hundreds of denominations each with their own creeds and governance. How can a Christian be a member of the church Christ built, practice unity among believers, and still be a part of one denomination to the exclusion of others? How is one to identify the church Christ built? Answers are not easy. The sincere believer will look to Christ and to the words of Scripture for guidance. Each must be his or her own interpreter, but at the same time each must have the humility to learn from brothers and sisters. The church Christ built will look to Him as builder, sustainer and head. In its government, its doctrine, its worship, its way of life, its hope and promise the church of Christ will be guided by the Lord. When a sinner obeys Christ, when he or she believes, repents, confesses and is baptized, the Lord adds him to His church. If the church adheres to the way of the Lord, a believer is only a Christian. Nothing necessitates his being a member of a denomination under human direction.

Questions

1. Of the four Gospels, which of them uses the word "church"? What is the context for the occurrences?
2. What is the phrase Matthew normally uses where "kingdom of God" appears in Mark and Luke?
3. Where had Jesus gone with the disciples when He asked them who men were saying He was?
4. How did Peter respond when Jesus asked the disciples who they thought He was?
5. Upon what did Jesus tell Peter and the other disciples He would build His church?
6. What did Jesus say that He was going to give Peter?
7. What did the people do who gladly received Peter's sermon on Pentecost?
8. What does Acts say believers did after thousands obeyed the gospel on Pentecost?
9. After saying that the church is the body of Christ, what does Paul say that Jesus is to the body?
10. By what has God decreed that His manifold wisdom be made known to powers in heavenly places?

Discussion Starters

1. Through what means did Jesus sustain and build up the church that came into being after Peter's sermon? Does He use the same means today? Explain.
2. In addition to being memorials, how do baptism and the Lord's Supper function in the church to sustain God's people?
3. In view of the multitude of denominational bodies, why is it important for Christians to know the identifying marks of the church Christ has built?
4. Why did Paul use the metaphor of a head and the body in order to illustrate the relationship of Christ to His church?

Descriptions of the Church

Romans 12:4-5

4 For as we have many members in one body, but all the members do not have the same function,

5 so we, being many, are one body in Christ, and individually members of one another.

1 Corinthians 3:5-11

5 Who then is Paul, and who is Apollos, but ministers through whom you believed, as the Lord gave to each one?

6 I planted, Apollos watered, but God gave the increase.

7 So then neither he who plants is anything, nor he who waters, but God who gives the increase.

8 Now he who plants and he who waters are one, and each one will receive his own reward according to his own labor.

9 For we are God's fellow workers; you are God's field, you are God's building.

10 According to the grace of God which was given to me, as a wise master builder I have laid the foundation, and another builds on it. But let each one take heed how he builds on it.

11 For no other foundation can anyone lay than that which is laid, which is Jesus Christ.

Ephesians 3:14-15

14 For this reason I bow my knees to the Father of our Lord Jesus Christ,

15 from whom the whole family in heaven and earth is named,

Colossians 1:13-14

13 He has delivered us from the power of darkness and conveyed us into the kingdom of the Son of His love,

14 in whom we have redemption through His blood, the forgiveness of sins.

1 Timothy 3:14-15

14 These things I write to you, though I hope to come to you shortly;

15 but if I am delayed, I write so that you may know how you ought to conduct yourself in the house of God, which is the church of the living God, the pillar and ground of the truth.

Introduction

Common to speech everywhere, whatever the language or the time, is the use of figurative expressions. Specialists sort out dozens of ways that people speak figuratively, but among the most common are metaphors and similes. A simile employs "like" or "as" in order to make a comparison. Jesus used a simile when He said, "The kingdom of heaven is like a mustard seed" (Matthew 13:31). A metaphor serves the same function as a simile but expresses the idea more strongly. When Jesus said, "I am the door of the sheep" (John 10:7) or Paul wrote that Jesus is "head over all things to the church" (Ephesians 1:22), each was using a metaphor.

At least two problems arise when a speaker or an author uses figurative language. First, illustrations teach in a roundabout way. Paul could have said that Jesus has authority over His church instead of saying that He is the head. Direct speech would save the reader a step in interpretation. Second, figures of speech may be confusing. One of the proverbs, for example, reads, "Do not remove the ancient landmark" (Proverbs 22:28). Does it forbid the removal of memorial stones set up to commemorate past events? Does the proverb call on people to be respectful of what their fathers and mothers have done? Perhaps, but ancient people often marked the boundaries of fields with large stones. Perhaps the proverb forbids thievery. The adage, no doubt, made sense to the people who used it, but the figure of speech may be lost on modern people. We come back to the question: Why use figurative language?

Metaphors and similes involve a risk, but the ability of the figures of speech to give power and color to language makes the risk worthwhile. Jesus could have said, "I am the source from which My disciples learn how to produce good deeds." Instead, He said, "I am the vine, you are the branches" (John 15:5). The first expression is anemic and bland compared to the second. Figures of speech stir the minds and memories of those who hear. Hearers make associations and in the process reach conclusions on their own. Through the use of metaphors, teachers do more than tell students what to think; they stir them to think.

Paul, like other biblical authors, used metaphors to stir thoughts and emotions. Some of his most memorable figures of speech are ones he applied to the church. Because he used metaphors, Christians are awakened to the nuances of what God wants the church, the kingdom of God, to be.

Body (Romans 12:4-5)

The use of metaphor often requires no explanation. Associations may be self-evident. The church is obviously not a literal body, but in significant ways it functions like a literal body. First, a literal body is made up of many parts. The arm is essential, but the work of the arm can be effective only if the legs work. In addition, the body offers support for the arm that usually goes unnoticed. The liver, lungs, stomach and kidneys do their work with no conscious effort by the arm. Similarly, the church has many members, parts that depend on each other. No one is effective working alone.

Second, a literal body is one entity. It is many parts; it is a single whole. Paul makes the point that each member of the church, like each part of the body, contributes to the well-being of all. Each finds its reward in the health of the whole. None seeks its own independent glory. In order for the church to be one body, all its parts must be coordinated. The body needs a head, a brain that assigns tasks to the visible and hidden parts. Christ functions to define the worship, work and manner of life of the church in a way similar to the way the head gives direction to the physical body.

Building (1 Corinthians 3:5-11)

Paul drew on experiences and objects from everyday life, things readily understood, in order that his readers might appreciate God's design for them as they lived within the community of the saints. Many comparisons were helpful, but each of them illustrated the church's mission, governance or fellowship from a perspective that was different from the other. The work of teachers like Paul and Apollos was somewhat like the labors of a farmer. At one minute the farmer is fertilizing his fields; at another he is planting; later he hoes and waters. Finally, he harvests.

It is helpful to compare the church to a body or to a field but neither has a foundation or superstructure built on it. Viewed differently, the church is like a well-designed building. Considered differently, Paul, Apollos and other teachers were like builders. At one point they lay a foundation. Then, they select the kind of building material they will use. They calculate the weight-bearing supports and design the rooms. Each step in the process is essential, but unless the foundation is right, none of it will be. Paul makes the point that the foundation of the church is Christ. The church will never be right unless it is built on the foundation of Christ and the apostles, with the understanding that Christ is the cornerstone by which everything is measured (Ephesians 2:20).

Family (Ephesians 3:14-15)

Aspects of a well-framed building illustrate what the church is, but like every comparison, likenesses break down at some point. For example, a building is relatively static. Once erected it does not move. The church is a living organism made up of diverse people. Each Christian has his or her personal needs and peculiarities. Each is to be appreciated for his or her personal worth. When considerations for individual members are factored into the mix, the church is more like a family. It is not like a family in every respect, but in some ways it is. No Christian needs to be perfect in order to find acceptance. Fathers, mothers, daughters and sons muddle along, doing some semblance of their best but living up to no ideal. The church, like a family, is a place of love, mutual appreciation and support.

Kingdom (Colossians 1:13-14)

During the heyday of Greek culture, in the fifth century before Christ, a few city states were democracies, but even among the Greeks democracy was more an ideal than a realized accomplishment. Cities and empires were ruled more often by rulers or emperors. The welfare of farmers and craftsmen depended on the wisdom and the goodwill of kings. When the king was a good man, balanced in his enforcement of just ways, people flourished. By common consent, an ideal king produces the most efficient and just government. The problem is that no earthly king lives up to the ideal.

The kingdom of heaven, meaning the church of the Lord, has an ideal king and an ideal government. The church is not like a kingdom in every respect, just as it is not like a body or a building or a family in every respect. At the same time, the ideal of a kingdom applied to the church illustrates important aspects of what Christ wants His people to be. Jesus is like a king in His regal bearing, in the glory and honor due Him, and in the obedience He commands. The task of the church is to read His Word and to decide what He wants Christians to be and to do. The church does not gather as a democracy, take a vote and overrule the Lord. It leans on Christ for its law.

House of God (1 Timothy 3:14-15)

When Paul called the church "the house of God" (1 Timothy 3:15), it was not quite the same as comparing the church to a family or to a building. The church is also a "household" (NASB). It is a people who are united by values and a common commitment to a way of life. When the church assembles for worship or when it goes to work on Monday morning, its conduct is to be guided by the common confession each member of the household has made. Behavior in the household of God is not limited to a Bible class or an assembly on the Lord's Day. It comprises the way one treats fellow workers on the job, giving an honest day's work for a day's pay, treating a wife or a husband with consideration and respect, helping a neighbor in need, scrupulously keeping one's word, and being a support to the community in which one lives.

Conclusion

Christians sometimes emphasize one metaphor that draws attention to a particular aspect of church life and neglect others. If they do, it may result in a skewed view of the church built by Christ. The community of Christian people was a new thing in the world of the first century. It was not quite like any association or fellowship of people the world had seen. The church is more complex and more unique than a body or a building or even a family. Still, in structures and institutions of the ancient world, Jesus and Paul found elements where they could make fruitful comparisons with the church. A metaphor by its nature is limited in the degree to which it can teach. Each metaphor in the New Testament emphasizes one aspect of what Christ wanted His people to be; no one metaphor is adequate to express all the church's complexity. A body illustrates the church's unity, a building its foundation, and a kingdom its rule. All the metaphors together guide Christians in their life as believers.

Questions

1. What is the difference between a metaphor and simile? Give an example of each.
2. Using the analogy of a body, how does Christ relate to the parts of the body?
3. What important truth about the church does comparing it to a body illustrate?
4. What other teacher at Corinth did Paul mention who was instrumental in building up the church in the city?
5. What important truth about the church does comparing it to a building illustrate?
6. To what did Paul liken the church in addition to comparing it to a building in 1 Corinthians 3:5-11?
7. From what has God delivered Christians in order that they might partake of His kingdom?
8. What do Christians have in His kingdom that has been purchased with His blood?
9. What was the house or household of God where Paul wanted Timothy to conduct himself properly?
10. Why do some translations have "the household of God" instead of "the house of God"? What is the difference?

Discussion Starters

1. Why do biblical authors use figures of speech? What may a figure of speech do that literal language may do poorly?
2. Churches often speak of themselves as a family. Is it an apt figure of speech? In what ways is the church like a family?
3. Drawing on your own experiences, which of the five metaphors discussed in this lesson best illustrates the nature of the church? Why?
4. What difficulties may the use of metaphors present for modern readers when they interpret the Bible?

The Church in Prophecy and Reality

Isaiah 2:2-4

2 Now it shall come to pass in the latter days That the mountain of the LORD's house Shall be established on the top of the mountains, And shall be exalted above the hills; And all nations shall flow to it.

3 Many people shall come and say, "Come, and let us go up to the mountain of the LORD, To the house of the God of Jacob; He will teach us His ways, And we shall walk in His paths." For out of Zion shall go forth the law, And the word of the LORD from Jerusalem.

4 He shall judge between the nations, And rebuke many people; They shall beat their swords into plowshares, And their spears into pruning hooks; Nation shall not lift up sword against nation, Neither shall they learn war anymore.

Isaiah 9:6-7

6 For unto us a Child is born, Unto us a Son is given; And the government will be upon His shoulder. And His name will be called Wonderful, Counselor, Mighty God, Everlasting Father, Prince of Peace.

7 Of the increase of His government and peace There will be no end, Upon the throne of David and over His kingdom, To order it and establish it with judgment and justice From that time forward, even forever. The zeal of the LORD of hosts will perform this.

Daniel 2:40-45

40 "And the fourth kingdom shall be as strong as iron, inasmuch as iron breaks in pieces and shatters everything; and like iron that crushes, that kingdom will break in pieces and crush all the others.

41 "Whereas you saw the feet and toes, partly of potter's clay and partly of iron, the kingdom shall be divided; yet the strength of the iron shall be in it, just as you saw the iron mixed with ceramic clay.

42 "And as the toes of the feet were partly of iron and partly of clay, so the kingdom shall be partly strong and partly fragile.

43 "As you saw iron mixed with ceramic clay, they will mingle with the seed of men; but they will not adhere to one another, just as iron does not mix with clay.

44 "And in the days of these kings the God of heaven will set up a kingdom which shall never be destroyed; and the kingdom shall not be left to other people; it shall break in pieces and consume all these kingdoms, and it shall stand forever.

45 "Inasmuch as you saw that the stone was cut out of the mountain without hands, and that it broke in pieces the iron, the bronze, the clay, the silver, and the gold – the great God has made known to the king what will come to pass after this. The dream is certain, and its interpretation is sure."

Acts 2:47

47 ... praising God and having favor with all the people. And the Lord added to the church daily those who were being saved.

Acts 11:26

26 And when he had found him, he brought him to Antioch. So it was that for a whole year they assembled with the church and taught a great many people. And the disciples were first called Christians in Antioch.

Introduction

The Old Testament holds forth the promise of a coming kingdom of God. The revelation of Christ and the apostles in the New Testament clarifies the nature of the kingdom. The reign of Christ was to be over a spiritual kingdom; His kingdom would have no material borders. Prophecies about the coming kingdom in the Old Testament are prophecies about the church. When Jesus was born, Jews at that time anticipated a kingdom altogether different from the church that emerged after Peter's sermon on Pentecost. A brief look at what had happened to the Jewish people during the centuries leading up to Christ explains why the kingdom anticipated by great numbers of Jews did not turn out to be the same as the reality.

For some 200 years after Malachi (ca. 400 B.C.), the Jewish people themselves know little of what was taking place in their homeland. The Persians ruled them until the coming of Alexander the Great, ca. 335 B.C. After that, Greek rulers reigned in Judea. Alexander's successors fought over the land while the Jews trudged along, squabbling internally and forced into poverty by external forces. In the three decades following 200 B.C. the Jews emerged from their dark age. They fought off Greek overlords and from about 170 to 63 B.C. were more or less independent. When the rebellion began the leader of Jewish armies was Judas; "the Maccabee" they called him. The name meant "the hammer." For a time following Judas, the Maccabean kingdom was a significant force in the Near East. It came to an end in 63 B.C. when the Romans enveloped Judea. The coming of Rome set the stage for the rule of Herod the Great and the beginning of the New Testament period.

When Jesus was born, Judea had been under Roman rule for a little more than a generation. Rule by foreigners was fresh and chafing. Expectations for the coming of a king like David grew to a fevered pitch. They called the promised king "Messiah," a Hebrew word that means "anointed." "Christ" is the Greek word that means the same. Among the Jews, anticipation of the coming of the anointed of God was in the air. When the Messiah actually appeared, i.e., when Jesus began preaching and healing in Galilee, He had no task more difficult than to convince the Jews that God's anointed was to conquer by submitting. Suffering was to be the path to victory. Victory would be over sin. No kingdom like David's or even the Maccabees' was in the offing. A careful reading of the Old Testament reveals a kingdom different from what the Jews expected.

Peaceful (Isaiah 2:2-4)

In the gardens of the United Nations building in New York City is a monument erected by the old Soviet Union in 1959. On it are inscribed the words of Isaiah 2:4: "They shall beat their swords into plowshares, And their spears into pruning hooks; Nation shall not lift up sword against nation, Neither shall they learn war anymore." The eloquent words of Isaiah have been inscribed on scores of monuments scattered over the planet. They constitute one of the noblest expressions of the longing for peace found in any language. The New Testament reveals that the prophecy of the kingdom promised and anticipated by Isaiah was fulfilled when saved men and women were added to the church built by Christ.

Isaiah and Micah were contemporaries who prophesied in the 8th century B.C. Isaiah lived in Jerusalem and advised kings. Micah's home was Moresheth, a village some 20 miles southwest of Jerusalem. Micah's words in 4:1-4 are almost identical to those of Isaiah 2:2-5. When the prophets lived, King Sennacherib of Assyria and his armies moved through Judah and other Western Mediterranean lands; resistance was futile. Under the best of circumstances, families were butchered or left to die of starvation. Sennacherib laid siege to Jerusalem and mocked the hope Judah's King Hezekiah placed in deliverance from God (Isaiah 36-37). The longing for peace expressed by Isaiah and Micah are all the more pungent given the dire circumstances under which they lived.

Isaiah looked for a time in the indefinite future when peace would reign. That age would be introduced by the exaltation of Jerusalem, Zion and the house of God. The fulfillment of Isaiah's prophecy was realized in the kingdom ruled by Jesus of Nazareth from the right hand of God (Colossians 1:13). Paul did not hesitate to contrast the "Jerusalem which now is" with the "Jerusalem above" (Galatians 4:25-26). The author of Hebrews identified "Mount Zion" with the "heavenly Jerusalem" (Hebrews 12:22). The revelation of Christ and apostolic teachers is that the material Jerusalem, Zion and the house of God foreshadowed the spiritual reality of the church. To the degree that men and women embrace the ideals of Jesus Christ, the church is a kingdom where people exchange instruments of war for peace. Swords become plowshares and spears pruning hooks. The ways of violence and warfare have flown away.

Powerful (Daniel 2:40-45)

Jesus and the apostles embraced a concept that the world has never accepted. Even among Christians, it is in faint supply. The concept is this: The way of power and the way of peace work hand in hand. Victory and weakness are not mutually exclusive. Daniel described the kind of power the world has come to take for granted, a kingdom "strong as iron" that breaks in pieces and crushes all the others (Daniel 2:40). In the centuries before and after Daniel, iron kingdoms have had to deal with the infiltration of intrigue, lust and treachery. Sooner or later, earthen clay weakens the iron and the kingdom falls. Daniel wrote of goodness that undermines kingdoms of violent conquest. It was that way for Rome and for those who preceded and followed her. In the midst of power defined by swords and spears, by hydrogen bombs and stealth warplanes, God has "set up a kingdom which shall never be destroyed" (v. 44).

The New Testament defines the stone that God carved from the mountain as the kingdom which began with a crucifixion. It is the church built by Christ. The Lord of this kingdom said to the weary, "I am gentle and lowly in heart, and you will find rest for your souls" (Matthew 11:29). He appealed to words of Isaiah and applied them to Himself, "A bruised reed He will not break, And smoking flax He will not quench" (Matthew 12:20; Isaiah 42:3). Paul understood the implications of the cross, but he steadfastly maintained that weakness was a forerunner of victory. The Christ crucified in weakness was raised by the power of God (2 Corinthians 13:4). As for himself, Paul said, "I will boast in the things which concern my infirmity" (11:30), and "For when I am weak, then I am strong" (12:10). As for all those who share faith in Christ, the apostle wrote, "For we also are weak in Him, but we shall live with Him by the power of God toward you" (13:4). Kingdoms of iron rise and fall; the stone carved from the mountain by God is eternal.

Personified
(Isaiah 9:6-7; Acts 2:47; 11:26)

Tip O'Neill, an American politician, famously quipped, "All politics is local." He might just as well have said, "All politics is personal." Kings and presidents rule by appearance of a personal following. Mortal kings fail because they are subject to personal faults and to rival powers. Even when they reign for a lifetime, kingdoms over which they rule crumble in dust. To say that politics is personal is a recognition that rulers come and go; kingdoms rise and fall.

No distinction between earthly nations and the rule of God is more important than this: The kingdom of God draws life from its King. He is eternal in the heavens; He does not fail. His kingdom abides forever. Isaiah wrote of God's kingdom realized in terms of a person, a child. The government of Christ's church rests on a Savior crucified in weakness. He is Everlasting Father, Prince of Peace. It is to no abstract system of rule to which Christians pledge themselves; it is to a personal Lord. Paul wrote, "I know whom I have believed" (2 Timothy 1:12). The faith of the apostle was in the Lord who rules from God's right hand. By His death, Jesus has saved from sin. He adds the saved to His church. Those who partake of His kingdom call themselves after His name. The name Christian first used at Antioch (Acts 11:26) has become the universal designation for the people who own Him as Lord.

Conclusion

The inclination to identify the rule of God with an earthly kingdom did not end when Christ died in weakness. Speculation about a rapture or a battle of

Armageddon or millennial reign of Christ all spring from convictions that an earthly rule of Christ will, after all, prevail. So many strains of premillennialism have been adopted by various denominations that it is difficult to make generalizations. They are alike in their affirmation that the return of the Lord will be marked by a 1,000-year earthly reign of Jesus. The realization that the church of the Lord is the kingdom of God and that the kingdom of God is a spiritual reality remains illusive. Those who believe that God still has a favored place for the people of Israel or that the coming of the last day depends on events in the Near East or that the temple of Solomon and the sacrifices of Leviticus will be reinstated on the temple mount in the literal city of Jerusalem have seriously misunderstood the prophecies of the Old Testament and the revelation of the New.

Questions

1. What empire ruled the Jews between Malachi and the conquest of Alexander the Great?
2. How is the Jewish kingdom usually designated that ruled from about 170 B.C. until the Roman conquest?
3. What does the Hebrew word "Messiah" mean in English?
4. What prophet contemporary with Isaiah wrote a similar statement to Isaiah 2:2-5?
5. What world empire threatened the Jewish kingdom during the time of Isaiah?
6. With what metal did Daniel compare the strength of the kingdom which would be crushed by the stone carved out by God?
7. How long did God reveal to Daniel that the kingdom symbolized by the stone would last?
8. What names did Isaiah give to the Child God promised to give?
9. Upon whose throne did Isaiah say that God's Son would reign?
10. In what New Testament city were the disciples first called Christians?

Discussion Starters

1. How would you convince a non-believer that Isaiah's prophecy about a coming time of peace has been fulfilled in the church? What objections might be raised?
2. In what ways do strength and power coexist with weakness and suffering among the people of God? Give illustrations.
3. Why is the personal element in the rule of Christ of overriding importance? How does His personal rule compare to the rule of earthly kings?
4. What is premillennialism? Why have some Christians clung to the belief that Jesus will reign over a material kingdom on earth?

This We Teach
Winter Quarter

Building on the foundational truths studied last quarter, these studies now turn to some basic doctrines held and taught in the church for all Christians. These include the oneness of the church, the Holy Spirit, authority, grace, faith, obedience, repentance, confession and baptism. These we teach.

Lesson 1 • Week of Dec. 7, 2014
Is the Church a Denomination?

Matthew 16:18

18 And I also say to you that you are Peter, and on this rock I will build My church, and the gates of Hades shall not prevail against it.

John 17:20-23

20 I do not pray for these alone, but also for those who will believe in Me through their word;

21 that they all may be one, as You, Father, are in Me, and I in You; that they also may be one in Us, that the world may believe that You sent Me.

22 And the glory which You gave Me I have given them, that they may be one just as We are one:

23 I in them, and You in Me; that they may be made perfect in one, and that the world may know that You have sent Me, and have loved them as You have loved Me.

Acts 4:12

12 Nor is there salvation in any other, for there is no other name under heaven given among men by which we must be saved.

Acts 11:26

26 And when he had found him, he brought him to Antioch. So it was that for a whole year they assembled with the church and taught a great many people. And the disciples were first called Christians in Antioch.

Romans 16:16

16 Greet one another with a holy kiss. The churches of Christ greet you.

1 Corinthians 1:10-13

10 Now I plead with you, brethren, by the name of our Lord Jesus Christ, that you all speak the same thing, and that there be no divisions among you, but that you be perfectly joined together in the same mind and in the same judgment.

11 For it has been declared to me concerning you, my brethren, by those of Chloe's household, that there are contentions among you.

12 Now I say this, that each of you says, "I am of Paul," or "I am of Apollos," or "I am of Cephas," or "I am of Christ."

13 Is Christ divided? Was Paul crucified for you? Or were you baptized in the name of Paul?

Introduction

Is the church a denomination? Perhaps the question should be asked differently: Is the church Jesus built a denomination, or is the New Testament church a denomination? A knee-jerk response is "No. End of discussion." The questions call for a more thoughtful response however. Christians do well to consider a number of other matters that logically precede questions about denominationalism. For example, does a norm exist from which the doctrines and practices of denominations have evolved? That brings the questioner quickly to Scripture. Those who look to Jesus of Nazareth for life have believed and continue to believe that the Lord sent a second Comforter, the Holy Spirit, who inspired the apostles and others to set forth definitively and authoritatively God's design for His church (John 14:26; 1 Corinthians 2:13). The 27 books of the New Testament constitute the norm, the departure point. The 39 books of the Old Testament were also inspired; they point the way toward the "fullness of time" (Galatians 4:4) when the Son of God would manifest Himself. When Christians are careless with the norm, when they allow their personal preferences or doctrinal bias to override the authority of Scripture, divisions are inevitable. Divisions are inherently denominations.

Other questions are not far behind: Can conscientious believers hope to interpret the Bible with a measure of consistency? Can Christians be confident that they have followed the biblical norm? Can they be sure that Christ has added them to the fellowship of believers that follows the model for the church provided by Scripture? Jesus answered those questions when He prayed for the disciples shortly before He was crucified. Jesus asked that His followers might "be one, ... that the world may believe that you sent Me" (John 17:21). Jesus believed His followers could understand the revelation of the Spirit and be one. The Christian ideal is that all those who confess Jesus as Lord might be one. Christians cling to this ideal in the confidence that what the Lord prayed for is possible.

Unity among followers of Christ does not demand that all agree on every point of Bible interpretation, but it does require that they agree on the essentials. The definition of what those essentials are has occupied and continues to occupy the best minds and the noblest hearts who confess Christ as Lord.

Of this, we may be confident: Believers do well when they look to Scripture for guidance as they wrestle with questions concerning essentials of the faith, Christian fellowship and the oneness of the body of Christ.

The Church Is One
(Matthew 16:18; John 17:20-23)

The confession of Peter made this much clear: The oneness of the church of Christ is not a task to be accomplished; it is a fact to be confessed. When Jesus told Peter that He would build His church on the confession that He was the Christ (Matthew 16:16, 18), the Lord had no plethora of denominations in mind, each with its own governing body, creed and ideals. The church Jesus built inherently was to be one. At the same time, the Lord recognized that teachers would distort the gospel. Division would occur, but Christians ought never to accept division casually. The revelation God gave in Scripture is not to be faulted for making division inevitable. Shortly before He died, Jesus made it clear that division would drag down the kingdom of heaven. Division would impede reaching the lost, and it would detract from the glory due to God.

The night before the crucifixion, Jesus gathered with His disciples. The first three Gospels describe the institution of the Lord's Supper during His final meal with them. In John's gospel, Jesus engaged in a long discourse, reassuring and comforting them (John 13–17). He promised them another Comforter, the Holy Spirit, who would cause them to remember all that He had said (14:26) and who would guide them into all truth (16:13). Jesus spoke of Himself figuratively as a vine, and He said His disciples would be like branches drawing life from the stalk of the vine (15:5). Before He went out to Gethsemane, where He would be arrested and led to trial, the Lord paused to pray with His followers. In large part, His prayer was for their well-being. He knew that great challenges and hard times were in front of them. Jesus prayed for the multitudes, the untold millions stretching across the centuries, who would confess Him and seek the forgiveness of sins. He prayed for the church, the earthly body of believers, who would look to Him as Lord. He pleaded with God to help them to be one, to be united in their faith, goals and way of life (17:6-26). Despite Jesus' prayer, unity under the banner of Christ has proven to be elusive. Denominational divisions and loyalties testify to failure and to sin. Unity remains an ideal to which all those who own Jesus as Lord do well to give their best efforts.

The Church Identified With Jesus
(Acts 4:12; 11:26; Romans 16:16)

Important as unity is for disciples of Christ, unity cannot be purchased at the cost of truth. Neither the essential Christian confession of faith nor the holy lives of Christ's people are open for negotiation. Still, Christians are sometimes inclined to go beyond the teachings of the New Testament and define Christian doctrine and practice more narrowly than Scripture has defined them. The Pharisees of the New Testament fell into that trap. They went beyond the Law in defining work, Sabbath observance and dietary laws; then they charged Jesus with being liberal when He took issue with their traditions (e.g., Matthew 9:14; 12:2). The ideal for Christians is to speak with the Bible, which means neither compromising its commands nor going beyond them.

Christians are a people who adhere to a common confession of faith. It follows that the beginning point in the quest for unity is the acknowledgment of the lordship of Jesus Christ. Jesus of Nazareth, the son of Mary, was the Son of God. His lordship continues today as He reigns at God's right hand (Colossians 3:1). When He died on the cross, He bore the sins of all those who confess and obey Him (1 Peter 2:24). Peter laid down the gauntlet to Jewish opponents who were determined to silence him. "Nor is there salvation in any other," Peter said, "for there is no other name under heaven given among men by which we must be saved" (Acts 4:12). The church of Christ is a people whose essential identity is with Jesus, His divinity and His death for sins. Followers of Christ wear the name of the Savior. They are called Christians because He is Lord (11:26). No room for division or denominational loyalty attaches to churches of Christ (Romans 16:16).

The Church's Struggle Against Division (1 Corinthians 1:10-13)

Division in the ranks of the church is always a terrible thing, but some divisions are the lesser of two evils. Some divisions, Paul said, are necessary (1 Corinthians 11:19). If unity must be purchased at the expense of truth, the price is too dear. New Testament authors warned Christians that they must be eternally vigilant against those who wished to compromise essential biblical teachings (Acts 20:28-30; 1 Timothy 4:1-3; 2 Peter 2:1; 1 John 4:1). Paul encountered divisions in the church at Corinth, but some of them, at least, were not about essential doctrinal truths. Some divisions were the result of personal rivalry, preacher preferences and petty selfishness. No stand for the truth was at issue; no noble loyalty to Christ justified Corinthian behavior. When division is rooted in personal cantankerousness, no benefit accrues to the body of Christ.

Rivalries among individuals vying for dominance in the church at Corinth likely ran deep. They manifested themselves in expressed loyalties to certain teachers. It is not certain that Peter had ever been to Corinth; Christ certainly had not been there, at least not in person. Yet some were maintaining that they attached more authority and prestige to Paul than to Apollos or Peter. Others believed Apollos ought to have the final word in matters of dispute. Others likely grew tired of the bickering about Paul and Apollos and said that Peter or his representatives trumped them both. Doing them all one better, some said that Christ was their only authority. If there were substantive doctrinal or moral issues involved, Paul said nothing of them. Disputes were petty and personal, but the division that plagued the church was real.

Conclusion

When Christians confess the truths recorded in the New Testament and when they believe and practice the apostolic message, they do not contribute to divisions. The church that Jesus built is not a denomination. It is the point from which departures have come. Deviations from the confession and the practice of the New Testament church have resulted in denominations.

Although many observers of the larger Christian scene will judge churches of Christ to be one denomination among others, those who are members strive to follow the New Testament. Their stated goal is to go back past denominational division to restore the church Jesus built and, in the process, to be only Christians. Whether they have succeeded in that goal must be determined by a close examination of what the New Testament teaches. When Christians look to the New Testament and find commands and apostolically approved examples for the message they teach, the way of salvation they pronounce, the manner of worship they practice, and the kind of governance that guides them, they proclaim their refusal to be part of the denominationalism that has long plagued the larger Christian scene.

Questions

1. Whom did Jesus tell His disciples He would send to them after He was gone?
2. What did Jesus declare would not prevail against the church He would build?
3. In addition to His immediate disciples, for whom did Jesus pray in John 17?
4. What did Jesus expect the world to know because of the unity it would see among His disciples?
5. What did Peter say was the sole source by which men and women lost in sin could be saved?
6. Where and under what circumstances were disciples of Christ first given the name "Christians"?
7. When Paul wrote to the Roman church, what did he call the churches from which he sent greetings?
8. What were the likely sources of divisions and disputes in the Corinthian church? What were their quarrels about?
9. From whom had Paul learned about divisions in the Corinthian church?
10. Around whom did parties or sects form in the church at Corinth?

Discussion Starters

1. What question should logically precede all other questions about denominationalism? Why?
2. Because unity and truth are mutual aims of Christians, what temptations arise for them to compromise truth for the sake of unity? Give examples, and explain.
3. In what ways are Christians tempted to go beyond the commands and examples of the New Testament, and how are they tempted to fall short of them?
4. Insofar as divisions are the result of personal preferences, what should Christians do in order to promote unity and peace within their numbers?

The Holy Spirit and Today's Christian

Romans 8:9-11

9 But you are not in the flesh but in the Spirit, if indeed the Spirit of God dwells in you. Now if anyone does not have the Spirit of Christ, he is not His.

10 And if Christ is in you, the body is dead because of sin, but the Spirit is life because of righteousness.

11 But if the Spirit of Him who raised Jesus from the dead dwells in you, He who raised Christ from the dead will also give life to your mortal bodies through His Spirit who dwells in you.

Romans 8:14-17

14 For as many as are led by the Spirit of God, these are sons of God.

15 For you did not receive the spirit of bondage again to fear, but you received the Spirit of adoption by whom we cry out, "Abba, Father."

16 The Spirit Himself bears witness with our spirit that we are children of God,

17 and if children, then heirs – heirs of God and joint heirs with Christ, if indeed we suffer with Him, that we may also be glorified together.

Romans 8:26-27

26 Likewise the Spirit also helps in our weaknesses. For we do not know what we should pray for as we ought, but the Spirit Himself makes intercession for us with groanings which cannot be uttered. **27** Now He who searches the hearts knows what the mind of the Spirit is, because He makes intercession for the saints according to the will of God.

Galatians 5:22-23

22 But the fruit of the Spirit is love, joy, peace, longsuffering, kindness, goodness, faithfulness,

23 gentleness, self-control. Against such there is no law.

Ephesians 3:14-19

14 For this reason I bow my knees to the Father of our Lord Jesus Christ,

15 from whom the whole family in heaven and earth is named,

16 that He would grant you, according to the riches of His glory, to be strengthened with might through His Spirit in the inner man,

17 that Christ may dwell in your hearts through faith; that you, being rooted and grounded in love,

18 may be able to comprehend with all the saints what is the width and length and depth and height –

19 to know the love of Christ which passes knowledge; that you may be filled with all the fullness of God.

2 Timothy 1:6-7

6 Therefore I remind you to stir up the gift of God which is in you through the laying on of my hands.

7 For God has not given us a spirit of fear, but of power and of love and of a sound mind.

Introduction

An aura of mystery surrounds the Holy Spirit. The name itself contributes to the perception, especially when the reading is "Holy Ghost" as in the King James Version. The mystery is on a different order than that which surrounds the Father and the Son. Jesus was one of us, a flesh and blood man. Although "God is Spirit" (John 4:24), He is also heavenly Father. The Holy Spirit is the Godhead among us, within us. Although Scripture closely associates the Holy Spirit with the Word (Ephesians 6:17), it is difficult to understand the Bible to teach anything other than the personal indwelling of the Spirit in the believer (Romans 8:11; Galatians 4:6). Yet what did Paul mean by the Holy Spirit "in you" (Romans 8:11)? Does the Holy Spirit invade our brains, direct our thoughts, or lead us in mysterious ways?

Whatever one may think about the Holy Spirit, no one can deny His central place in the New Testament. A quick concordance count in the New King James Version yields some 328 occurrences of "spirit" or "Spirit." In a substantial percentage of cases, it is "Spirit," written with an uppercase "S," because translators have understood the word to refer to Deity. Christians have tended to deal with the role of the Spirit in one of two ways. (1) Push the Holy Spirit aside. Those who want faith to proceed from evidence and logical reasoning would rather concentrate on the plan of salvation, moral rectitude, God-ordained worship and concrete behavior. (2) Become infatuated by the Holy Spirit. These Christians urge churches to sponsor workshops and special classes on the Holy Spirit. Too much emphasis can never be given to the subject. Yet reading and reflection suggest a moderate approach. The Holy Spirit is not the all-in-all of the Christian's relationship with God; neither ought His role be relegated to the sidelines.

Led by the Spirit
(Romans 8:9-11, 14-17, 26-27)

Paul appealed to the indwelling Spirit as a truth of the Christian faith and experience (Galatians 3:2). It required no proof. But lest we attach too much significance to the apostle's language of indwelling, we might observe that he used the terminology broadly. Sincere faith, Paul wrote, indwells the saved (2 Timothy 1:5).

God indwells the faithful (2 Corinthians 6:16). The word of Christ dwelt in Colossian Christians (Colossians 3:16). Christ indwells the redeemed and is their "hope of glory" (1:27). Identifying himself with Christians everywhere, Paul went so far as to confess that sin had a grip; it "dwells in me," he said (Romans 7:17). The passages taken together raise a question. Does the Holy Spirit dwell in the faithful in some way that is different from the indwelling of God, of Christ, of faith or even of sin? Stated differently, is the indwelling Spirit a figurative expression for the manifestation of the will of the Spirit taken into a Christian heart?

No one who believes the Bible doubts that the Holy Spirit dwells in Christians; the questions focus on the manner of His indwelling. Shortly before He died, Jesus promised the apostles that He would send them a Helper who would teach them and miraculously bring to their minds what He had said (John 14:26). The "Spirit of truth," He said, would guide them "into all truth" (16:13). For the apostles, the Spirit worked in miraculous ways that would not characterize His work in all whom He indwelt, but we may at least conclude that Jesus promised a personal indwelling of the Spirit. Does the promise of Jesus that the Holy Spirit would personally indwell the apostles provide a context for the promise of Peter on Pentecost (Acts 2:38)? The apostle said that those who repented and were baptized would be saved. Further, he said they would receive "the gift of the Holy Spirit." If the promise of Jesus to the apostles is any indication, Peter promised that the Spirit would personally indwell the obedient. Paul's vivid assertions about the indwelling Spirit add support to the conclusion that the indwelling of the Spirit goes beyond the influence of the Spirit-inspired Word (Galatians 4:6; Romans 8:9). The Spirit works in and through the Word He inspired. In the process, He gives life to mortal bodies by quickening in believers the will to obey God (v. 11). He helps with the prayers of Christians (v. 26), searches their hearts, and intercedes on their behalf (v. 27).

Gifted by the Spirit
(Galatians 5:22-23; 2 Timothy 1:6-7)

The Holy Spirit gave the apostles miraculous powers, but He manifests Himself in ways that are not always miraculous. Those who are "sons of God," Paul said, are "led by the Spirit of God" (Romans 8:14). One way the Spirit leads is by giving Christians the power to do what God wants them to do (v. 11). The Spirit-inspired Word in the hearts of believers is their guiding light. When Christians see the fruit of the Spirit (Galatians 5:22-23) in their lives, the fruit bears witness with the Holy Spirit that they are among those who share in the promise of life. The Spirit, Jack Cottrell writes, "*marks* us as God's children indirectly through what He enables us to do. By objectively observing His mark upon our lives, we ... can have assurance that we belong to God's family." [1] The Spirit provides Christians with the power to produce His fruit in their lives, thereby bearing witness with the spirits of believers that they are God's children (Romans 8:16).

A Christian goes beyond biblical promises if he thinks that the indwelling Spirit is a guarantee he will make only godly choices. The Spirit wrenches freewill choices from no one, and sin continues to dwell in mortal bodies even after one has been baptized into Christ (Romans 7:17). Overpowering emotions sometimes spring from yearnings that ought never to be attributed to the Spirit. Christians embark on a perilous path when they adopt an I-can-do-no-wrong stance and justify sin by appealing to the indwelling of the Holy Spirit. When Paul urged Timothy to "stir up" (NKJV) or to "kindle afresh" (NASB) the gift of God within him (2 Timothy 1:6), his admonition was a reminder that self-confident boldness is the result of a Christian fashioning his personal desires in conformity with the revelation of the Holy Spirit.

Strengthened by the Spirit (Ephesians 3:14-19)

Paul began Ephesians 3 with "For this reason" (v. 1), but he digressed from his initial intent in order to describe the nature of his work among the Ephesians (vv. 2-3). Beginning with verse 14, he repeated the phrase "For this reason" and offered up a prayer on their behalf. He prayed that his readers would find the power to be the people of faith and godliness that embracing Christ required. The Holy Spirit was to be the source of that power. The Spirit would enable believers to find might in their inward persons to bring to fruition the transformed lives God expected of His people. The apostle blended the enabling power of the Spirit with obedience. Being "strengthened with might through His Spirit in the inner man" (v. 16) brought no emotional breakdown; it excited no ecstasy resulting in meaningless babble. The might given by the Spirit was a quiet, unobtrusive thing that the apostle associated with Christ's dwelling in the hearts of believers through faith.

To be rooted and grounded in love as defined by Paul (1 Corinthians 13) was essential to finding the power to live faithful and godly lives. Love and faith were the reasons for and the results of the indwelling Holy Spirit. It seems never to have occurred to Paul that anyone would have associated the work of the Spirit with occasional experiences. The Christian journey begins with a knowledge of God. From there, it proceeds to the steadiness of faith and love empowered by the Spirit (Ephesians 3:19).

Conclusion

The ease with which New Testament authors interchange phrases such as "the Spirit of God" or "the Spirit of Christ" with "Holy Spirit" (e.g., Romans 8:9) causes some to conclude that the Holy Spirit is a manifestation of God, not a separate person of the Godhead. Despite the vehemence with which many defend the word, "trinity" occurs nowhere in the Bible. Through most of the 1800s, influential gospel preachers rejected the term. To this day, "trinity" is not a common word among churches of Christ.

Still, when Jesus promised the coming of a Helper who would guide the disciples "into all truth" (John 16:13), He seems to have spoken neither of Himself nor of the Father. In a single verse, Paul coupled "The grace of the Lord Jesus Christ, and the love of God, and the communion of the Holy Spirit" (2 Corinthians 13:14). He seems to have envisioned the work of the Spirit as distinct from that of the Father and that of the Son (Romans 8:26-27). Because "trinity" is not a biblical word, perhaps it is best to avoid it, but the Bible does confront Christians with a Godhead that is at once three and one. The one God has revealed Himself as Father, Son and Holy Spirit. The Spirit has His own role to play within believers; He comforts and empowers to the end that they be obedient and holy. Whatever one may think of the word "trinity," the concept of God who is three and who is one is biblical.

Questions

1. How can we know whether translators mean for us to understand "spirit" as a divine being?
2. With what is the work of the Spirit closely associated in the New Testament?
3. What did Paul say about one who does not have "the Spirit of Christ" (Romans 8:9)?
4. What does the Spirit testify that we are when it bears witness with our spirit (Romans 8:16)?
5. What does the Spirit do when He helps with our weaknesses?
6. Into what component parts did Paul break down the fruit of the Spirit (Galatians 5:22-23)?
7. How did Paul say that the gift of God had been imparted to Timothy (2 Timothy 1:5-7)?
8. How did Paul describe the spirit God has given to His people (2 Timothy 1:7)?
9. What did Paul pray God would grant to the Ephesian Christians?
10. How did Paul say that Christ would dwell in the hearts of believers?

Discussion Starters

1. Why do you think some believers avoid talking about the Holy Spirit while others seem to want to talk of nothing else?
2. How is the Spirit similar to other things that Paul said dwell in believers? How is the Spirit different from those things?
3. Do you believe the Holy Spirit personally dwells in you as a Christian and that He gives you power for Christian living? Explain.
4. Do you believe Christians ought to avoid the word "trinity"? Justify your answer.

Authority in the Godhead

Exodus 3:4-14

4 So when the LORD saw that he turned aside to look, God called to him from the midst of the bush and said, "Moses, Moses!" And he said, "Here I am."

5 Then He said, "Do not draw near this place. Take your sandals off your feet, for the place where you stand is holy ground."

6 Moreover He said, "I am the God of your father – the God of Abraham, the God of Isaac, and the God of Jacob." And Moses hid his face, for he was afraid to look upon God.

7 And the LORD said: "I have surely seen the oppression of My people who are in Egypt, and have heard their cry because of their taskmasters, for I know their sorrows.

8 "So I have come down to deliver them out of the hand of the Egyptians, and to bring them up from that land to a good and large land, to a land flowing with milk and honey, to the place of the Canaanites and the Hittites and the Amorites and the Perizzites and the Hivites and the Jebusites.

9 "Now therefore, behold, the cry of the children of Israel has come to Me, and I have also seen the oppression with which the Egyptians oppress them.

10 "Come now, therefore, and I will send you to Pharaoh that you may bring My people, the children of Israel, out of Egypt."

11 But Moses said to God, "Who am I that I should go to Pharaoh, and that I should bring the children of Israel out of Egypt?"

12 So He said, "I will certainly be with you. And this shall be a sign to you that I have sent you: When you have brought the people out of Egypt, you shall serve God on this mountain."

13 Then Moses said to God, "Indeed, when I come to the children of Israel and say to them, 'The God of your fathers has sent me to you,' and they say to me, 'What is His name?' what shall I say to them?"

14 And God said to Moses, "I AM WHO I AM." And He said, "Thus you shall say to the children of Israel, 'I AM has sent me to you.' "

Exodus 20:1-7

1 And God spoke all these words, saying:

2 "I am the LORD your God, who brought you out of the land of Egypt, out of the house of bondage.

3 "You shall have no other gods before Me.

4 "You shall not make for yourself a carved image – any likeness of anything that is in heaven above, or that is in the earth beneath, or that is in the water under the earth;

5 "you shall not bow down to them nor serve them. For I, the LORD your God, am a jealous God, visiting the iniquity of the fathers upon the children to the third and fourth generations of those who hate Me,

6 "but showing mercy to thousands, to those who love Me and keep My commandments.

7 "You shall not take the name of the LORD your God in vain, for the LORD will not hold him guiltless who takes His name in vain."

Daniel 7:13-14

13 I was watching in the night visions, And behold, One like the Son of Man, Coming with the clouds of heaven! He came to the Ancient of Days, And they brought Him near before Him.

14 Then to Him was given dominion and glory and a kingdom, That all peoples, nations, and languages should serve Him. His dominion is an everlasting dominion, Which shall not pass away, And His kingdom the one Which shall not be destroyed.

Matthew 28:18-20

18 And Jesus came and spoke to them, saying, "All authority has been given to Me in heaven and on earth.

19 "Go therefore and make disciples of all the nations, baptizing them in the name of the Father and of the Son and of the Holy Spirit,

20 "teaching them to observe all things that I have commanded you; and lo, I am with you always, even to the end of the age." Amen.

Titus 3:4-7

4 But when the kindness and the love of God our Savior toward man appeared,

5 not by works of righteousness which we have done, but according to His mercy He saved us, through the washing of regeneration and renewing of the Holy Spirit,

6 whom He poured out on us abundantly through Jesus Christ our Savior,

7 that having been justified by His grace we should become heirs according to the hope of eternal life.

Introduction

When a Roman centurion wanted to explain his faith to Jesus, he said, "For I also am a man under authority" (Matthew 8:9). Passing centuries had honed in the Romans a near worshipful respect for authority. Their military, statecraft, even religion worked within the bounds of those who gave and those who received orders. The empire was strong when authority was father to duty, when soldier and citizen stepped into whatever breach threatened. Like Israel, the empire floundered when "everyone did what was right in his own eyes" (Judges 21:25).

For an army or an empire, authority, responsibility and discipleship are essentials. When values and morality are the subjects, the worth of authoritative lines of accountability are often less obvious. For the Christian, God is the source from whom authority flows. Goodness is built into the brick and mortar of the universe because God is good. Any meaningful use of the word "good" implies the Being of God. He alone has the right to step back from creation and pronounce it "very good" (Genesis 1:31). Without God, all is randomness and chaos, atoms and stars lurching along, going nowhere. An atheist or an agnostic has difficulty justifying whatever arbitrary authority he chooses for a moral compass. For him, rules are impossible; right and wrong can never be anything more than personal preference – a preference he has no right to impose on anyone. The most heinous behavior becomes acceptable once one dismisses God from the equation.

The theory of authority finds legs in God's self-revelation. Evidences of God in the material universe allow one to entertain the possibility that He has spoken (Psalm 19:1-3; Acts 14:17). Examination of the Bible leads from the possibility of authority to the fact. The universe had a beginning; it is moving to a conclusion. Sin raises its head when men and women shake their fists in God's face and say: "Your authority amounts to nothing. I am going to do it my way. I will be my own god." Suffering and shame are not arbitrary; they are byproducts of rebellion. God's lovingkindness has been such that He found a residue of goodness within people. Appealing to goodness, He sent a Savior. Take away the authority that flows from God, and the basis for reason, hope and promise will disappear.

I AM WHO I AM (Exodus 3:4-14; 20:1-7)

After the death of the Patriarchs, faithfulness to God slipped away from the descendants of Jacob as they settled into Egyptian life (Exodus 1:6-7; Joshua 24:14). The golden calf Aaron fashioned at Sinai testified to idolatry that had become ingrained in the people (Exodus 32:3-4). Losing sight of spiritual authority, Israel sank into a "Slough of Despond" in Egypt.[1] Although the Israelites were in the depths of despair, God remembered them. To Amram and Jochebed, a couple descended from Levi, God gave a child who was named Moses (2:1, 10; 6:20). By God's providence, for the first 40 years of his life, Moses was reared by Egypt's royal family, where his fame as a man of learning grew (Acts 7:22-23). After he killed an Egyptian, he lived the next 40 years as a refugee east of Egypt in Midian, where he married and had children (Exodus 2:11-15, 21-22; 4:20). At age 80, God appeared to him in a burning bush on Mount Sinai and commissioned him to deliver Israel from Egyptian bondage (3:2, 9-10). The task was to absorb the rest of his life.

God's appearance to Moses on the mountain signaled the return of authority to the descendants of Israel. The lawgiver's turning aside to see a bush perpetually burning but never consumed was an important event for the calling of Israel and eventually for the new covenant between God and spiritual Israel. God identified Himself to Moses through association with Abraham, Isaac and Jacob. He told the shepherd trained in the ways of the Egyptians that He had heard the cry of His people. He had determined to save them and to give them the land He had promised to their fathers. Moses was to be His representative. He was to lead the nation from Egypt. Moses demurred. He asked the voice in the burning bush what name the God of Abraham wore? God answered, "I AM WHO I AM." Hebrew scholars argue over the best way to translate the phrase. The ancient Greek translation rendered it, "I AM THE ONE WHO IS." Because God gave the phrase to Moses as if it were a proper name, several translations render it with uppercase letters. Clearly, God wanted Moses to understand that His authority was eternal. He was able to bring the great empire of Egypt to its knees.

When God brought Moses back to Sinai, he was at the head of a people great in number but weak in organization and power. At Sinai, God began to fashion Israel; He established His authority over the nation. He made a covenant with Israel. A covenant is an agreement, but the covenant between God and Israel was not between equals. God set the terms for the agreement, and Israel ratified it by submission. The religious and moral foundation for the covenant was in the Ten Commandments (Exodus 20:1-17; Deuteronomy 5:7-21). Religion and morality flowed from God's authority to the Law.

The Ancient of Days (Daniel 7:13-14)

From the limited perspective of human eyes, God's authority waxes and wanes. Under David and Solomon, Israel became a great nation only to wither in the course of time. Some 500 years after Solomon, the proud kingdom was a helpless captive in the rice fields of Babylon. Daniel and his friends might have had misgivings about God's authority over the nations when they were traded off as hostages when Jehoiakim was king (Daniel 1:1). The Babylonians likely made eunuchs of them and assigned them to the palace of Nebuchadnezzar, where they were to learn the ways and the gods of a strange people. Daniel might have been tempted to wonder why the God whose temple was behind the walls of Jerusalem allowed such suffering. Was the God of Israel sovereign over the nations as they had supposed Him to be?

God's providential care for Daniel stretched over decades. The prophet learned that the means by which God asserted His authority was not limited to the rise and fall of nations. Daniel saw God act in dreams and visions, in miracles and mysteries. God humbled King Belshazzar with a message inscribed in the walls of his palace (Daniel 5:24-28). During the reign of the same king, Daniel received a vision in the night where the Lord unveiled His plan for a kingdom that would be unlike anything the world had seen. The scene began with a "Son of Man" who presented Himself before "the Ancient of Days" (7:13-14). The eternal God who revealed Himself to Daniel ruled while the generations of men rolled from one into the next. He worked in ways that were spectacular and in ways that went unnoticed. God determined to assert His authority by the giving of a kingdom to a "Son of Man." It would be an everlasting dominion;

it would never pass away. Earthly kingdoms and human power were pawns in His hand when God wanted to establish His authority on the earth.

Father, Son and Holy Spirit (Matthew 28:18-20; Titus 3:4-7)

God's threefold nature appears only dimly in the Old Testament. God's creation of the world begins, "And the Spirit of God was hovering over the face of the waters" (Genesis 1:2), but it would have been difficult to know much of the Holy Spirit before the revelation of Christ. The promise of a coming Anointed One, a Messiah, runs deep in the Old Testament, but that He was to be divine is somewhat veiled. Jesus revealed God to the human family to a degree that men never knew Him before. God's fatherhood was not unknown in the Old Testament, but neither was it front and center. God's grace and lovingkindness were there from the beginning, but their fullness was manifested only through the Son.

The authority of the Father over the world and over human history, along with His grace and His desire to save, came to fruition on the cross. After Jesus' crucifixion and resurrection, He met with the disciples on a mountain in Galilee and asserted, "All authority has been given to Me" (Matthew 28:18). Jesus was no second-tier God. The "Word became flesh" (John 1:14), and "the Word was God" (v. 1). In the words of Paul, "For in him dwells all the fullness of the Godhead bodily" (Colossians 2:9). The authority of God, the authority of Christ, and the authority of the Spirit are one. The grace by which the lost have sins washed away and are born again is the hope of sinners for eternal life.

Conclusion

For a Christian, the very possibility of authority is predicated on the existence of God and His revelation. As the source of life and its sustainer, God told man and woman to tend the Garden of Eden. He forbade their eating of the tree of the knowledge of good and evil (Genesis 2:17). Later, God told Noah to build an ark; then He told Abraham to leave Haran and to travel southward to Canaan. God gave the Ten Commandments to the Israelites and led them from Egypt back to Canaan. In the end, all His designs were fulfilled by the sending of a Son to redeem for Himself a people. Because God gave Him authority, men and women know how they are to live. Values are meaningful; purpose and direction are possibilities.

Questions

1. What must any meaningful discussion of good and evil presuppose?
2. What did Moses do to acknowledge that the ground around the burning bush where God spoke to him was holy?
3. With which of the Patriarchs did God identify Himself when He spoke to Moses?
4. What did God tell Moses He was going to do for the people of Israel?
5. When Moses asked God what His name was, how did God answer him?

6. Where were the people of Israel when God gave them the Ten Commandments through Moses?

7. To what king and kingdom was Daniel subject when he saw the night vision of which Daniel 7:13-14 is a part?

8. What did the Ancient of Days present to the Son of Man, who appeared before Him?

9. How much authority did Jesus tell His disciples that God had given Him?

10. Using the authority God had given Him, where did Jesus send His disciples to preach the gospel?

Discussion Starters

1. Why does an atheist or an agnostic find it impossible to apply terms such as "right" or "wrong" to any human behavior?

2. What evidence does the Bible offer that idolatry became firmly entrenched in Israel during the 400-plus years between Joseph and Moses?

3. How many passages in the New Testament can you find that either cite or echo the words of Daniel 7:13-14? Read some of them aloud before the class.

4. According to what Paul told Titus, how has God saved sinners? Where does God's grace fit into the plan of salvation?

Authority in the Word

Ephesians 3:1-5

[1] For this reason I, Paul, the prisoner of Christ Jesus for you Gentiles –

[2] if indeed you have heard of the dispensation of the grace of God which was given to me for you,

[3] how that by revelation He made known to me the mystery (as I have briefly written already,

[4] by which, when you read, you may understand my knowledge in the mystery of Christ),

[5] which in other ages was not made known to the sons of men, as it has now been revealed by the Spirit to His holy apostles and prophets.

Ephesians 5:15-17

[15] See then that you walk circumspectly, not as fools but as wise,

[16] redeeming the time, because the days are evil.

[17] Therefore do not be unwise, but understand what the will of the Lord is.

2 Timothy 3:14-17

[14] But you must continue in the things which you have learned and been assured of, knowing from whom you have learned them,

[15] and that from childhood you have known the Holy Scriptures, which are able to make you wise for salvation through faith which is in Christ Jesus.

[16] All Scripture is given by inspiration of God, and is profitable for doctrine, for reproof, for correction, for instruction in righteousness,

[17] that the man of God may be complete, thoroughly equipped for every good work.

2 John 9-11

[9] Whoever transgresses and does not abide in the doctrine of Christ does not have God. He who abides in the doctrine of Christ has both the Father and the Son.

[10] If anyone comes to you and does not bring this doctrine, do not receive him into your house nor greet him;

[11] for he who greets him shares in his evil deeds.

Revelation 22:18-19

[18] For I testify to everyone who hears the words of the prophecy of this book: If anyone adds to these things, God will add to him the plagues that are written in this book;

¹⁹ and if anyone takes away from the words of the book of this prophecy, God shall take away his part from the Book of Life, from the holy city, and from the things which are written in this book.

Introduction

Magic and superstition are hardly absent from the modern world, but they were pervasive in the worlds of the Old and New Testaments. When a shaman reinforced what he said with mysterious rituals, devotees believed the words took on a life of their own, moving through time and space to bring about what he directed. Little wonder that Israel was forbidden to have any part in such magic (Deuteronomy 18:10-12); it was a form of idolatry. Modern people sometimes betray a residue of the ancient superstition about the power in words. A phrase such as "If my house were to catch fire" is likely to be followed by "Knock on wood." Fear of words lingers even among the scientifically sophisticated. Superstitions die hard.

A word spoken was no light matter among the ancients. Archaeologists have uncovered texts in Egypt, some dating to 2 millenniums before Christ, that are often collectively called "Execration Texts." They are curses that were sometimes written on a bowl, on an image of an enemy's god, or even on the skull of a beheaded enemy. Ancient people released the power of the words by smashing the vessel with a club or by hurling it against a wall. Jeremiah might have done something similar when he took an earthen vessel, described Israel's sins, smashed the vessel, and declared that God would similarly smash the city of Jerusalem (Jeremiah 19:1-15). Nothing is said of words being on the vessel, but the symbolism is not to be overlooked. God's words in the mouth of Jeremiah had power. Once released, God's will would be accomplished through them (vv. 2-3, 15).

John was drawing on the ingrained sense of power in words when he began his gospel: "In the beginning was the Word, and the Word was with God, and the Word was God" (John 1:1). For ancient people, a word or a name was more than a convenient tag. A spoken word was a living symbol of a person, thing, concept or act. John declared that the person of Jesus Christ was seamlessly attached to the Being of God as a name is attached to the person it represents. Jesus was the source of creation, the essence of eternal power. The name spoken is synonymous with His authority. In the person of Jesus, the Word of God became manifest in human form; the Word is the grace, the love and the promise of God.

The Mystery of Christ
(Ephesians 3:1-5; 5:15-17)

In Ephesians 3, Paul began with a description of the task God had assigned to him. "For this reason," he wrote (Ephesians 1:1), and then he digressed to discuss the unfolding of God's plan of redemption through the mystery of Christ (3:2-13). The digression ended in verse 14 with the repeat of "For this reason" and continued his thought. The digression, if we should call it that, sets forth the authority that supported the apostle in his preaching. The mystery that had been imperfectly understood by Israel was now in plain view. Paul's authority came from Jesus, who had been proclaimed Christ by His life, death, resurrection and ascension. God had poured new wine into new wineskins. Sin was no longer to be a barrier in the relationship between God and man. The same way to life opened for the Jew was also available for the Gentile. God's orderly management of His plan of salvation had been unveiled in Christ and committed to Paul and others like him.

Paul said that God had given him a "dispensation" (Ephesians 3:2 NKJV), a "stewardship" (NASB), or an "administration" (NIV84). With the words "the dispensation of the grace of God," the New King James Version suggests that God carefully worked His will through Christ so that sinners might be saved by grace. The Greek word lying behind the translations suggests the management of a household. God managed human affairs so that salvation from sin could result. To Paul, God gave the mission to proclaim that His work in Christ was no afterthought. Salvation by grace through faith had been in the mind of God through the call of Abraham, the giving of the Law, the reigning of kings, and the preaching of prophets. The mystery at long last was in full view.

What God revealed to Paul, He had written in words. The revelation given to the apostle by the Spirit was available to the Ephesians when they read his words. As Paul continued the letter, he came more explicitly to the authority that supported what he proclaimed. They would be wise to lay aside past sins and choose the way of obedience. The authority of God was at the root of the doctrines and morality the apostle preached.

The Holy Scriptures (2 Timothy 3:14-17)

Scripture is an indispensable link between God's right to rule authoritatively and the realization of God's will in the lives of people. In His Word, God speaks, commands and teaches. Although some claim that God speaks to them personally, it is difficult to take them seriously. Some say one thing, and others say things that are entirely different. By contrast, Scripture has been tested across centuries. It has demonstrated itself to be true, a God-given source for guidance in faith and morality. In the Bible, Christians have a book, concrete and tangible. Believers can hold Scripture in their hands and know that they have the counsel of God.

Do Christians sometimes stress knowledge of the Bible to the point that they detract from worship that is to be reserved for God alone? The word "bibliolatry" has been used contemptuously of those who emphasize the Bible to the neglect of prayer and other aspects of a living faith. In a public prayer, a brother may refer to worship of the Bible. Can the Bible become an idol? In the process of holding to the Bible as a tangible gift from God, do Christians sometimes forget the living God, who is seated above it and who has given it as an instrument for teaching and guidance? Questions like these need to be asked, but Christians should notice that Paul considered the Bible to be the authoritative source for the church's teaching and practice. The problem of too little emphasis on the Bible appears to be more widespread than that of too much.

Paul did not hesitate to remind Timothy that guidance from Scripture had begun early in his life by a godly mother and grandmother (2 Timothy 1:5; 3:15). He told his student that Scripture would make him "wise for salvation through faith which is in Christ Jesus" (v. 15). The apostle declared that Scripture had been breathed into holy men, who had transferred words from God into written form. The written words of the Bible were trustworthy sources for doctrine, teaching and instruction in righteousness. By the use of Scripture, a godly man or woman could be equipped for every good work (vv. 16-17). The subject of the apostle was authority. For Paul, the Word stood as the authority for Christian living.

The Doctrine of Christ
(2 John 9-11; Revelation 22:18-19)

Churches of Christ are communities that share a common confession of faith and way of life. The confession comes first. Doctrine matters. The apostle John lived when the New Testament in its entirety was not widely available. Religious authority was in the spoken word of the apostles and those who taught the apostolic message. Churches not yet grounded in the faith and without the New Testament in its final form tended to be easy prey for false prophets, who did not hesitate to bend the teachings of Christ and the apostles to serve their own purposes. Preachers masquerading as prophets appeared on the doorsteps of Christians, teaching strange things and demanding that churches support them. In his first letter, John said these preachers had gone out from them, but they had never really been of them (1 John 2:19). He urged churches to test those who claimed to be prophets (4:1).

In his second letter, John went further. He called the false prophets anti-christs and said they were deceivers (2 John 7). They did not have the authority of Christ behind them. What they taught compromised and perverted the message revealed to the apostles by the Spirit. The doctrine of Christ cannot be infinitely stretched into whatever shape a man might find satisfying. John urged his readers to give no support and to offer no greeting to false prophets. To give them encouragement or money was to participate in their deeds. John likely wrote Revelation shortly after his letters. He continued to urge Christians to measure all they heard by words that had the authority of Christ and His apostles behind them.

Conclusion

Authority for Christian people resides first in God Himself and in Jesus, the manifestation of the Godhead in human flesh (Colossians 2:9). He is the authoritative Word; but after He died on the cross, things remained that needed to be revealed. After the church came into being, the Holy Spirit spoke through the apostles and guided them in the writing of the New Testament (1 Corinthians 2:13; Ephesians 3:4). The New Testament continued the God-given truths declared by the Son. In the Bible, Christians have the Word of God to guide them. Any teaching that reaches beyond the authority of Christ and the apostles has gone too far; any that falls short is not enough.

Questions

1. How did ancient people suppose that words written on pottery might be released to bring about evil?
2. What prophet hurled an earthen jug against a wall and declared that Israel would be broken like the jug?
3. What does the word "dispensation" mean in Ephesians 3:2? What other ways might the word be translated?
4. How did Paul say the mystery of salvation had been made known to him?
5. How did Paul expect his readers to know the mystery of the gospel?
6. What did Paul tell the Ephesians they should do to be wise?
7. At what point in his life had Timothy become acquainted with the Holy Scriptures?
8. For what did Paul say Scripture was profitable?
9. Whom did John tell his readers they ought not to greet or fellowship with?
10. What did John declare God would add to the one who added to the words of His prophecy?

Discussion Starters

1. What did Paul mean when he said the dispensation of God's grace had been given to him? How are Christians heirs to God's dispensation?
2. How are the authority of Jesus and the authority of Scripture similar? How are they different?
3. Do Christians sometimes divert worship from God in order to worship the Bible? Is the charge of "bibliolatry" ever justified? Explain.
4. What is the danger when Christians encourage and extend fellowship to those who have seriously compromised the biblical message?

Authority for God's People

Deuteronomy 4:4-6

4 But you who held fast to the LORD your God are alive today, every one of you.

5 Surely I have taught you statutes and judgments, just as the LORD my God commanded me, that you should act according to them in the land which you go to possess.

6 Therefore be careful to observe them; for this is your wisdom and your understanding in the sight of the peoples who will hear all these statutes, and say, "Surely this great nation is a wise and understanding people."

1 Chronicles 15:11-15

11 And David called for Zadok and Abiathar the priests, and for the Levites: for Uriel, Asaiah, Joel, Shemaiah, Eliel, and Amminadab.

12 He said to them, "You are the heads of the fathers' houses of the Levites; sanctify yourselves, you and your brethren, that you may bring up the ark of the LORD God of Israel to the place I have prepared for it.

13 "For because you did not do it the first time, the LORD our God broke out against us, because we did not consult Him about the proper order."

14 So the priests and the Levites sanctified themselves to bring up the ark of the LORD God of Israel.

15 And the children of the Levites bore the ark of God on their shoulders, by its poles, as Moses had commanded according to the word of the LORD.

Acts 4:32-34

32 Now the multitude of those who believed were of one heart and one soul; neither did anyone say that any of the things he possessed was his own, but they had all things in common.

33 And with great power the apostles gave witness to the resurrection of the Lord Jesus. And great grace was upon them all.

34 Nor was there anyone among them who lacked; for all who were possessors of lands or houses sold them, and brought the proceeds of the things that were sold.

Hebrews 13:17

17 Obey those who rule over you, and be submissive, for they watch out for your souls, as those who must give account. Let them do so with joy and not with grief, for that would be unprofitable for you.

Introduction

Authority, obedience and discipline often go unappreciated in a world obsessed with individual rights and freedom of expression. Authority and kindred words are community-oriented. Whether the subject is a CEO at the helm of a corporation or a governor administering affairs of state, authority to some degree is prerequisite to getting the job done. When people must cooperate, authority has to be vested in the hands of someone. With the vesting of authority comes the potential, and often the fact, of abuse. Whether the subject is a business enterprise, a government, a church or a home, it is both risky and essential to grant authority. Authority presupposes obedience or else discipline, when obedience is lacking. Authority is abused when the person wielding it uses it in a self-serving or arbitrary manner.

The downside of authority is in the imperfections of those wielding it. If it were possible to have perfectly wise and benevolent people in charge, autocratic control would be best everywhere. Because no such people exist, nations choose democratic governments to spread authority around. They judge their leaders by the degree to which they approach wise and benevolent rule. In human affairs, those in charge are tainted with imperfections; it is otherwise in the kingdom of God. God gives no arbitrary laws to His people. The Ruler of heaven and earth has no master plan to keep people from having fun. He knows the behaviors that hurt people, and He forbids them. The law God has given, Moses told Israel, is "for our good always" (Deuteronomy 6:24). Coming from God, "thou shalt not" means "do yourself no harm."

However, people may feel deprived in the short term; in the long-term, obedience to God results in blessed and noble lives. Christians do not wait for heaven to enter the joys of godly living; they experience them now. In heaven, they expect the joy of godliness to be enhanced. Death and sin will have flown away. In this world, sin has a seasonal appeal (Hebrews 11:25); fools latch onto it and are crushed under its weight. Rebellion against God has no nobility. If God wielded authority in an impulsive and arbitrary way, as human rulers often do, rebellion might have a certain nobility. Given the nature of the God we serve, the wise and the blessed obey Him.

Statutes and Judgments (Deuteronomy 4:4-6)

Although the Old Testament was written almost entirely in Hebrew, the word "Deuteronomy" is Greek. Loosely translated, it means "the second giving of the Law" or, more loosely, "the Law summarized." Some things in the book had not been recorded earlier, but much of it had. When Moses led the Israelites to the banks of the Jordan as they were preparing to enter Canaan, the lawgiver gathered the people together. In three speeches (Deuteronomy 1:6–4:40; 5:1–26:19; 27:1–30:20), Moses rehearsed for the Israelites their heritage and history. He reminded them of the nobility of their Law and urged them to respect and obey God. No more wonderful statement of what it means to be the people of God can be found than that which is in the speeches of Deuteronomy.

In his first discourse, Moses traced the steps of the Israelites during the 40 years they had wandered in the wilderness. The history was prelude to exhortation. He urged Israel not to add to nor to detract from the Law God had given them (Deuteronomy 4:2). When they settled in the land, Moses said blessings would follow if they obeyed God, who had preserved their lives and led them from Egyptian bondage. Neighboring people would observe their decent and honest lives guided by the statutes and ordinances of the Lord and would step back in amazement. In the sight of those who served idols, the people of Israel would show themselves to be holy and wise. Families would be strong. Larders would be full. Enemies would falter before them. The Israelites' neighbors would fail to see that the Law God had given was the source of their strength; they could only observe, "Surely this great nation is a wise and understanding people" (v. 6).

Moses guaranteed no life free from calamity, but he did promise that obedience to God would bear them through good times and bad. In subsequent centuries, the Israelites failed to be faithful to God, but had they been true to Him, droughts, floods, windstorms and locust plagues likely would have still happened. Accidents of nature aside, the Law would have lifted the quality of their lives to a level other nations would never have known. Looking to God for authority and being faithful to Him would have been a blessing. Near the end of his third speech, Moses pleaded with the people: "Choose life," he said, "that both you and your descendants may live" (Deuteronomy 30:19).

According to the Word of the Lord (1 Chronicles 15:11-15)

God wanted obedience to be a settled disposition of mind, not an emergency measure to deal with a crisis. The authority of God was to be baked into the lives of the Israelites. God's authority was at issue when David decided to move the ark of God from the house of Abinadab in Kirjath Jearim to Jerusalem. David and his people were careless about the move. Without any consultation of the Law, they built an ox cart to transport the ark and lined the route to Jerusalem with celebration and dancing. When the oxen stumbled and the holy ark nearly fell from the cart, a man named Uzzah put out his hand to steady it. God was less than impressed with the levity and disrespect that attended the moving of the ark. His anger flared, and Uzzah died (1 Chronicles 13:6-11).

The death of Uzzah sobered the king. He stored the ark in the house of Obed-Edom and returned to Jerusalem. During the three months that followed, David built a proper place for the housing of the ark. More important, he resolved to attend to the direction of the Law when he moved it again. The Law specified that the ark was to be carried by its poles on the shoulders of Levites (Exodus 25:14; 1 Chronicles 15:15). When David followed the directions God had given for moving the ark, all went well. God's people trifle with the holiness and authority of God to their own peril.

Of One Heart and Soul (Acts 4:32-34)

Nearly a millennium passed between David's moving of the ark to Jerusalem and the founding of the Lord's church in Jerusalem. During the intervening years, Scripture records many examples of blessings that God's people accrued by respecting His authority; few examples are more inspiring than that of the early Christians in Jerusalem. The brotherly love that bound them together was noticeable. Rich and poor alike shared in a common store of material blessings. The apostles proclaimed the resurrection of the Lord; grace abounded.

The common sharing of property seems to have been a matter unique to the situation in Jerusalem. Neither Acts nor the letters offer any hint that churches generally followed the practice. Still, Jerusalem Christians teach us that respect for God's authority extends to the support believers offer to one another. Blessings abound for believers who place God's authority higher than love for material things.

Obey Those Who Rule Over You (Hebrews 13:17)

Submission to the authority of God as expressed in His Word is of primary importance. His directions are often specific. It is wrong to lie or steal. A sinner who wants to have his sins washed away by the blood of the Lamb must act on his faith. He must repent and be baptized (Acts 2:38). But in the day-to-day life of the church, countless situations arise in which human judgments have to be made. How can the church best encourage those who are weak in faith? What methods of evangelism are most effective? Where will the church meet? The questions are endless; the church needs leadership. In addition, pressures from within and without arise to compromise New Testament doctrine. Vigilance for teaching the truth never ceases. Teaching new generations of Christians is a necessity.

In His wisdom, God ordered that churches appoint elders from their numbers who will guide churches in matters of expedience and who will learn of God's authority in order that He may be honored. In that spirit, the author of Hebrews urged his readers to submit to godly leaders and to obey them. Few blessings are of more importance to a church than respected and godly elders.

Conclusion

God has given the church a daunting task in its exercise of leadership. Government officials have the power of law to enforce their directives. Employers have the power of the purse. The one who signs the paychecks may not always be right, but he is always boss. In the church, leadership is more pure. Its authority is the product of Christians who respect their shepherds. If any elder loses the respect of the church, turmoil usually follows. Those he is to shepherd pay him no mind. If godly elders are to lead well, those who are being led must respect their judgments and submit willingly to their authority. Authority is a blessing for God's people. Authority blesses them in the living of good lives, in the adherence to the teachings of the New Testament, and in the building of strong and loving homes. The absence of authority is chaos; it results in everyone doing what is right in his own eyes. It is the way of turmoil and death.

Questions

1. What does the Greek word "Deuteronomy" mean? Why did the fifth book of the Bible receive that name?
2. Who did the speaking for most of Deuteronomy? How many speeches are there?
3. When the Israelites were careful to observe God's laws and statutes, what did their neighbors testify about them according to Deuteronomy 4:6?
4. Drawing on your knowledge of earlier events, under what circumstances had the ark come to be stored in a private home?
5. How did David plan to move the ark of God from its storage place in a private home to Jerusalem?
6. According to the Law, who was to carry the ark of God? How were they to carry it?
7. Why was Uzzah stricken by God so that he died?
8. How did the early church at Jerusalem make provision so that no one was poor among them?
9. What was the testimony of the apostles to the people of Jerusalem?
10. What reason did the author of Hebrews give his readers for being obedient to their rulers?

Discussion Starters

1. Why is it necessary for a group of people who work together to vest authority in some of its members? Why is authority an important word for a community?
2. Was the punishment of Uzzah too severe? Did he deserve to die for trying to steady the ark? Explain and justify your answer.
3. How is leadership in the church similar to, yet different from leadership in government or business?
4. Is a life obedient to God likely to be more fulfilling and happier as a result, even in this world? Do God's commands take joy away from life? Explain.

The Gift of Grace

Romans 6:17-23

17 But God be thanked that though you were slaves of sin, yet you obeyed from the heart that form of doctrine to which you were delivered.

18 And having been set free from sin, you became slaves of righteousness.

19 I speak in human terms because of the weakness of your flesh. For just as you presented your members as slaves of uncleanness, and of lawlessness leading to more lawlessness, so now present your members as slaves of righteousness for holiness.

20 For when you were slaves of sin, you were free in regard to righteousness.

21 What fruit did you have then in the things of which you are now ashamed? For the end of those things is death.

22 But now having been set free from sin, and having become slaves of God, you have your fruit to holiness, and the end, everlasting life.

23 For the wages of sin is death, but the gift of God is eternal life in Christ Jesus our Lord.

Ephesians 2:4-10

4 But God, who is rich in mercy, because of His great love with which He loved us,

5 even when we were dead in trespasses, made us alive together with Christ (by grace you have been saved),

6 and raised us up together, and made us sit together in the heavenly places in Christ Jesus,

7 that in the ages to come He might show the exceeding riches of His grace in His kindness toward us in Christ Jesus.

8 For by grace you have been saved through faith, and that not of yourselves; it is the gift of God,

9 not of works, lest anyone should boast.

10 For we are His workmanship, created in Christ Jesus for good works, which God prepared beforehand that we should walk in them.

Titus 2:11-14

11 For the grace of God that brings salvation has appeared to all men,

12 teaching us that, denying ungodliness and worldly lusts, we should live soberly, righteously, and godly in the present age,

13 looking for the blessed hope and glorious appearing of our great God and Savior Jesus Christ,

14 who gave Himself for us, that He might redeem us from every lawless deed and purify for Himself His own special people, zealous for good works.

Introduction

Grace is a complicated word. A Bible school definition is "unmerited favor." No doubt, God's unmerited favor conferred on sinners is grace, but the phrase "God's unmerited favor" raises questions. If merit has nothing to do with God's favor, what inspires it? All are sinners, but not all are saved. Does God bestow grace arbitrarily? Does He choose some for salvation and others for damnation by a sovereign decree that originated in Himself before the world began? Does human response to God's invitation to life have anything to do with His grace? If human response does matter, the word "unmerited" needs examination. One might argue that humble faith in Christ and submission to His will are good things, but if God saves a sinner because of something good he does, what has become of "unmerited favor"?

Closer examination of God's grace demonstrates that He confers "unmerited favor" in general terms. The human family is blessed by the grace of God. At His own initiative, He reached out to mankind through His Son, Jesus Christ. No merit is inherent in the bestowal of His love and His grace. Because of His grace, God saves individuals who choose faith and, through faith, obey Him. "Unmerited favor" does not extend to the choice of select individuals. God has not predestined some to be saved and others to be lost. To remove from people the need to choose life in Christ is to misunderstand "unmerited favor." Men and women are not less responsible because God in His grace has reached out to save.

Still, churches of Christ have often been accused of treating the New Testament doctrine of grace as if it were a stepchild. The criticism has been especially strong among those with Calvinistic leanings, but in recent decades, it has also come from within the ranks of the church. Perhaps gospel preachers have spoken of grace with reservation because they have recognized the Calvinistic baggage often attached to the word. Regardless, the New Testament teaches that God sent His Son to open the door of life to sinners at His own initiative, i.e., by His grace. God reached out His hand to sinners, not the other way around. The doctrine of grace is not peripheral to the gospel proclamation; it lies near the heart.

Set Free From Sin (Romans 6:17-23)

For Paul, conversion to Christ required the sinner to be obedient (Romans 6:17). At the same time, eternal life was the free "gift of God" (v. 23). Those who hear the gospel must make a decision for Christ in order to be saved. That salvation is God's free gift does not preclude the possibility that God placed a choice before the sinner. Moses set before the Israelites the way of life and the way of death (Deuteronomy 30:15); then he pleaded with the people to "choose life, that both you and your descendants may live" (v. 19). Joshua called the Israelites together to say, "Choose for yourselves this day whom you will serve" (Joshua 24:15). Similarly, Roman Christians were presented with a choice when they heard the gospel. Paul said they had believed and "obeyed from the heart" (Romans 6:17). Any of them might have refused God's grace, though they did not.

By His grace, God predestined a plan of salvation. The carrying out of His plan entailed the incarnation of His Son in "the fullness of time" (Galatians 4:4). Jesus gave His sinless life in order to purchase for Himself a people, a glorious church without spot or wrinkle (Ephesians 5:27). God brought all of this about because He is a gracious God. He took the initiative to save while people were enslaved to sin. The demand that sinners respond in faith to the gospel and obey Him is no compromise of the doctrine of grace. No one who obeys the gospel or bends his will to righteousness has thereby merited the eternal life God gives by grace.

Sin has a grip on humankind. "All have sinned" (Romans 3:23), but the doctrine of total hereditary depravity is a human invention. It has been woven into a tight tapestry for the sake of philosophical consistency, but it has no standing in the New Testament. Men and women are capable of faith, i.e., they are capable of presenting their "members as slaves of righteousness for holiness" (6:19). Obedience to God is no occasion for self-righteous boasting. Sin separated men from God. Only God's initiative, only His grace, has made the movement from death to life possible. But God's grace does not imply that men and women have no choice to make, no obedience to render. When a sinner obeys the gospel, God takes away his sin. He stands before God justified and saved because God graciously executed a plan of salvation.

The Gift of God (Ephesians 2:4-10)

When John wrote "For God so loved the world that He gave His only begotten Son" (John 3:16), he was affirming nothing different than what Paul affirmed in Ephesians: God is "rich in mercy, because of His great love" (2:4). John did not write of grace in terms of God choosing individuals to be saved or lost by divine orders determined before time began. He wrote in general terms of God's love for the world. When Paul wrote "by grace you have been saved" (vv. 5, 8), the word "you" in Greek was plural. He was not telling individual believers how and why they were saved. The individual is saved by virtue of his sharing in the church, the family of God. God's grace is universal, freestanding. Any sinner who reaches back to the extended hand of God is saved by grace. A sinner is blessed by God's unmerited favor when he chooses faith and responds to faith's call through obedience.

Faith's response, whether in having sins washed away in baptism or godly living in any of its dimensions, gives the sinner no claim on life because he is meritorious. Neither baptism nor generosity nor any other aspect of Christian living is of value devoid of faith and love. All that God has done so that people can be saved from sin is summed up under the word "grace." All that men and women are to do is summed up under the word "faith." Salvation is by grace through faith. Paul was clear on the matter: "For we are his workmanship, created in Christ Jesus for good works" (Ephesians 2:10). Paul would have lacked faith if he had responded to the call "Arise and be baptized, and wash away your sins, calling on the name of the Lord" (Acts 22:16) with a refusal or a delay. Throughout Scripture, faith and obedience are two sides to the same coin. Faith and obedience result in salvation not because the sinner deserves it but because God's grace foreordained it.

That Brings Salvation (Titus 2:11-14)

Paul was insistent that God confers salvation on those who otherwise would be lost in sin because He is a gracious Lord. Nothing else accounts for the coming of Christ and His bearing of human sins on the cross. At the same time, the apostle was acutely aware that the doctrine of salvation by grace through faith left him open to criticism. His opponents said: "If salvation is by grace, the more a person sins, the more grace God extends. If grace is a good thing, let us sin, and let grace abound. The more sin, the more grace." Paul's response could be paraphrased, "God forbid that anyone accuse us of such nonsense" (Romans 3:8; 6:2). The apostle considered grace to be an impetus for holy living, not an excuse for sin.

Paul's opponents began their reasoning with the assumption that when a person sins, he gets away with something. Like a child who ignores the consequences of what he does in favor of not getting caught, people sometimes view sin as acceptable if they can get away with it. For Paul, there is no getting away with it. Sin is inherently destructive, whereas righteousness, by the nature of what it is, brings joy and goodness. The one who enjoys God's grace by means of his faith in Christ adopts a package deal. God's grace extends to the holy life God expects of His people. God's grace teaches us that "denying ungodliness and worldly lust, we should live soberly, righteously, and godly in the present age" (Titus 2:12). Disobedience is not a call for more grace; it is a rejection of grace. No one ever gets away with sin. Ungodliness is its own punishment.

Conclusion

Left to their own devices, people have perceived their gods as capricious, arbitrary and vengeful. God reveals Himself in the Bible as loving, gracious and holy. It is God's nature that He gives. His creation of the material universe and His giving men and women a small corner of it to rule speaks to His grace. God desired fellowship with creatures made in His image (Genesis 1:27), and man came into being. The possibility of fellowship with God entailed the possibility of sin, and men have chosen to sin. The doctrine of grace makes sense only when sin has entered the picture. Because He is a gracious God, He determined to open to men and women a path to a renewal of life, a new birth. The cost of human redemption testifies to the consequences of sin, and it testifies to the grace that paid the price. That can be said without inventing any doctrine of total hereditary depravity or erasing from human consciousness the ability to choose good and reject evil. His grace colors all that God's people believe and do.

Questions

1. What did God do to extend His grace to mankind?
2. Where does human merit fit into the picture of God's grace?
3. To what did Paul say the Roman Christians had become obedient?
4. To what had the Roman Christians become slaves after their slavery to sin no longer bound them?
5. What did Paul say are the wages of sin? What is the free gift of God?
6. Who is "the prince of the power of the air" who Paul said works in "the sons of disobedience" (Ephesians 2:2)?
7. What has Christ made of those who were formerly dead in trespasses and sin?
8. Why did God save men and women by His grace? What should be the way of life of His workmanship?
9. What did Paul say the grace of God has taught believers?
10. To what percentage of mankind has the grace of God that brings salvation appeared?

Discussion Starters

1. Is "unmerited favor" an adequate definition for grace? Does salvation by grace mean that no obedience is required? Explain.
2. How did Paul respond to critics who claimed that the logical outcome of his doctrine was "Let us sin so that grace may abound"?
3. If "grace" is the word for God's part in salvation from sin, what is the word for the response of people? What does God's grace tell us about Him?
4. If salvation is by grace, why did Paul go to great lengths to describe the nature of the obedience God requires? Are Christians saved by obedience? Explain.

The Power of Faith

Acts 16:30-34

30 And he brought them out and said, "Sirs, what must I do to be saved?"

31 So they said, "Believe on the Lord Jesus Christ, and you will be saved, you and your household."

32 Then they spoke the word of the Lord to him and to all who were in his house.

33 And he took them the same hour of the night and washed their stripes. And immediately he and all his family were baptized.

34 Now when he had brought them into his house, he set food before them; and he rejoiced, having believed in God with all his household.

Romans 10:14-18

14 How then shall they call on Him in whom they have not believed? And how shall they believe in Him of whom they have not heard? And how shall they hear without a preacher?

15 And how shall they preach unless they are sent? As it is written: "How beautiful are the feet of those who preach the gospel of peace, Who bring glad tidings of good things!"

16 But they have not all obeyed the gospel. For Isaiah says, "LORD, who has believed our report?"

17 So then faith comes by hearing, and hearing by the word of God.

18 But I say, have they not heard? Yes indeed: "Their sound has gone out to all the earth, And their words to the ends of the world."

James 2:14-26

14 What does it profit, my brethren, if someone says he has faith but does not have works? Can faith save him?

15 If a brother or sister is naked and destitute of daily food,

16 and one of you says to them, "Depart in peace, be warmed and filled," but you do not give them the things which are needed for the body, what does it profit?

17 Thus also faith by itself, if it does not have works, is dead.

18 But someone will say, "You have faith, and I have works." Show me your faith without your works, and I will show you my faith by my works.

19 You believe that there is one God. You do well. Even the demons believe – and tremble!

20 But do you want to know, O foolish man, that faith without works is dead?

21 Was not Abraham our father justified by works when he offered Isaac his son on the altar?

22 Do you see that faith was working together with his works, and by works faith was made perfect?

23 And the Scripture was fulfilled which says, "Abraham believed God, and it was accounted to him for righteousness." And he was called the friend of God.

24 You see then that a man is justified by works, and not by faith only.

25 Likewise, was not Rahab the harlot also justified by works when she received the messengers and sent them out another way?

26 For as the body without the spirit is dead, so faith without works is dead also.

Introduction

Paul made it clear that the blessings of God come by grace through faith (Ephesians 2:8). The reason we have hope and life is rooted in God's grace. Our part is to give ourselves in faith to God through Christ. After experiencing the grace of God, He calls for the response of faith. Faith begins with understanding, which, in turn, is predicated on revelation. Spiritual, mental and even physical limitations mean that men and women cannot come to know God from intuitive senses within. We know Him as a God of grace because that is what He has shown Himself to be. God's long history with humankind, a history that culminates in the coming of the Son, is His self-revelation. It is His grace in action.

Faith is born in the concrete events of time. Salvation from sin begins with embracing the apostolic witness (Acts 4:13). The testimony of the apostles, of the women who went to the tomb after the crucifixion, of some 500 in Galilee, and of others reveals that Jesus died and was raised from the dead. The resurrection was among the things of first importance (1 Corinthians 15:3-4); by that singular act, God declared Jesus to be His Son (Romans 1:4). From the testimony of the apostles, hearers have learned the teaching, the miracles and the example of the Lord. The New Testament rests on the bedrock of apostolic testimony. Belief is born from the encounter between the sinner and the witness of the apostles. For the saved, it results in the confession of faith.

Faith is belief, but it is more than belief. It is also trust and obedience. A scientist believes his data, but ideally, he stands detached from the data. He has no vested interest and no emotional attachment to his confidence that the earth revolves around the sun or that water is two parts hydrogen and one part oxygen. He will adjust his belief as new data appears. Faith for a Christian is on a different order. The believer is not tentative about the confession that Jesus is the Son of God. A Christian gives not only his mind but also his heart to God. He is committed. The belief of demons in facts about Jesus is not unlike the belief of scientists in their data. By contrast, faith in Christ requires the heart and will. Obedient response is dyed into the fabric of faith. When obedience fails, faith has not measured up to the faith that saves. Belief by itself is like water without a vessel to shape and transport it. The response of faith is more than emotional turmoil or a moment in time when the sinner allows Jesus to enter his heart. It is the embracing of a way of life. It is repentance; it is change. The Bible in its entirety is about the way to live by faith.

Believe on Jesus (Acts 16:30-34)

The jailer at Philippi has the distinction of being the only voice in the Bible who put the question "Sirs, what must I do to be saved?" in those exact words (Acts 16:30). The crowd on Pentecost was asking the same thing when they responded, "Men and brethren, what shall we do?" (2:37), but those who put the question to Peter already knew the God of Israel. Imperfect as it might have been, they knew something too of Jesus Christ. The jailer at Philippi was a Gentile. He may have had some inkling of Jewish notions about God, but he knew nothing of Jesus of Nazareth, of His resurrection, or of God's promises fulfilled by His Son. The jailer had a longer way to go than most of those on Pentecost who wanted to know what to do. Paul and Silas began by teaching the facts of the gospel. To be saved, the jailer had to believe on the Lord Jesus Christ. The fleshing out of what they were to believe about Jesus was the subject as the missionaries "spoke the word of the Lord to him and to all who were in his house" (16:32).

Paul and Silas' purpose as they spoke to the jailer was not to satisfy his curiosity about an interesting teacher who had lived in Palestine. Nor was it to explain why they had run into trouble with Roman law. The missionaries spoke to convince and to convict. When they finished, the jailer and his household believed, but their faith entailed more than prayers and tears. They acted. They washed the wounds of those who told them of Christ. At some point, Paul and Silas told them that to be saved from their sins they needed to confess their faith, to turn in repentance from the old gods they had served, and to be buried with Jesus in baptism (Colossians 2:12). "And immediately he and all his family were baptized" (Acts 16:33). Repentance and baptism were not works of merit; they earned no salvation for the jailer. The obedience of the jailer and his family was faith doing what faith inherently does. They put their trust in Jesus and did what He commanded. The faith that saves necessarily includes the response of faith. Repentance and baptism are not acts separate from faith; they are a part of what faith is.

Faith Comes by Hearing (Romans 10:14-18)

Christ gave His church the mission of preaching the gospel (Matthew 28:19-20). From the standpoint of its facts, the good news is spread like any other news. A speaker or author uses words to tell the story of Jesus the Christ as another spreads news of a wildfire or the birth of a child. Nothing is mysterious about it. The response of people when they hear the good news is more complicated. Some respond to the message with faith; others turn their backs. Paul told the Romans that sinners have no choice to make until they hear the gospel preached. In order for people to be saved, preachers must proclaim the truth, and their fellow believers must send them. Those who send participate in the Great Commission alongside those who go (3 John 5-8).

The denominational world has come up with many reasons to explain why some respond favorably to the message of Christ and Him crucified while others are content to go their way lost in sin. Some maintain that because men and women are totally depraved, they cannot choose faith. According to this viewpoint, the sinner can only wait until the Holy Spirit miraculously infuses faith in the heart and mind. Confronted with the gospel, the sinner can only "pray through" until faith is given to him or her. Some maintain that the reception of faith is accompanied by ecstatic feeling, weeping and mysterious babbling. The sinner cannot choose to believe, so it is said, because he is utterly vile. The only prospect for faith is some version of the so-called sinner's prayer. Those lost in sin are urged to pray something such as, "I am a sinner. God grant me faith. Make me know and believe that Jesus Christ died for my sins." The New Testament knows of no such response. Paul said that "faith comes by hearing, and hearing by the word of God" (Romans 10:17). At the point of hearing, a lost soul must make a choice. The engagement of will, mind and heart resulting in confession and obedience is the essence of faith.

Faith Without Works Is Dead (James 2:14-26)

From the earliest days of the church, nonbelievers have charged that salvation by grace through faith requires the sinner to do nothing. God makes all the choices. He predestines the saved and grants faith to those He has chosen. However, Paul told his critics that if they understood him to say the sinner was a mere passive receptacle with no choices to make, they were mistaken. God forbid that I should teach such a thing, he said (Romans 3:8; 6:2). To come to Christ in faith requires an active turning from sin (v. 6). James dealt with the same kind of distortion of the gospel in his letter: "Thus also faith by itself, if it does not have works, is dead" (James 2:17). A work, by definition, is a positive response and a decision for obedience. James illustrated this by referring to the example of Abraham, the same example Paul used to teach that no one is saved by his own merit (Romans 4:3-5). For both James and Paul, the response of Abraham to God was as much the Patriarch's faith as his trust in God's promises. Obedience to God is "faith working through love" (Galatians 5:6).

Conclusion

Those who ask "Is a sinner saved by faith or by works?" are asking the wrong question. The New Testament teaches that all people are sinners (Romans 3:23) and that no one can save himself because of his own merit (4:2-4). Confusion is the result when people fail to distinguish between works of merit that do not save and works that flow from faith. Faith saves, but faith without works is a contradiction of terms. Paul carefully distinguished between meritorious works and works of faith. Many in the modern religious world want to dismiss the controversy as much ado about nothing. Decidedly, it is not. Works of merit result in a prideful stance before God because one demands justification on the basis of what he has done. Such arrogance is offensive to God. A humble response to the offer of God's grace in Christ through obedience of His commands is no claim to salvation by merit. Obedience to God and faith in Him are inseparable. When people separate faith from obedience, they move toward an emotion-driven faith that slips into and out of sin without consideration of the consequences.

Questions

1. What is the proper response when sinners hear of God's grace in Christ?
2. By what singular act did God declare Jesus to be His Son?
3. What question did the Philippian jailer ask Paul and Silas?
4. What answer did Paul and Silas give to the jailer?
5. What did the jailer and all his house do immediately after Paul and Silas spoke the word of the Lord to them?
6. By what means did Paul tell the Roman Christians they had come to believe the gospel?
7. What passage did Paul cite from the prophet Nahum to underscore the importance of preaching?
8. What did James have to say about faith unaccompanied by works?
9. Which of the Patriarchs did James use to demonstrate that faith and works are both necessary?
10. What woman from Jericho did James mention, who was justified by her works?

Discussion Starters

1. How is the Christian's faith in Christ different from and similar to a scientist's belief in his data?
2. How would you respond to someone who claims that when Paul told the jailer to believe on Jesus, he needed to do nothing more to be saved?
3. What is the difference between works of merit and works that follow from faith? Which of the two are necessary to be saved? Explain.
4. What is the difference between Paul's comparison of faith and works in Romans 4 and James' in James 2? How are the two alike?

The Necessity of Obedience

Matthew 7:21-23

21 Not everyone who says to Me, "Lord, Lord," shall enter the kingdom of heaven, but he who does the will of My Father in heaven.

22 Many will say to Me in that day, "Lord, Lord, have we not prophesied in Your name, cast out demons in Your name, and done many wonders in Your name?"

23 And then I will declare to them, "I never knew you; depart from Me, you who practice lawlessness!"

Acts 5:27-32

27 And when they had brought them, they set them before the council. And the high priest asked them,

28 saying, "Did we not strictly command you not to teach in this name? And look, you have filled Jerusalem with your doctrine, and intend to bring this Man's blood on us!"

29 But Peter and the other apostles answered and said: "We ought to obey God rather than men.

30 "The God of our fathers raised up Jesus whom you murdered by hanging on a tree.

31 "Him God has exalted to His right hand to be Prince and Savior, to give repentance to Israel and forgiveness of sins.

32 "And we are His witnesses to these things, and so also is the Holy Spirit whom God has given to those who obey Him."

Romans 13:1-5

1 Let every soul be subject to the governing authorities. For there is no authority except from God, and the authorities that exist are appointed by God.

2 Therefore whoever resists the authority resists the ordinance of God, and those who resist will bring judgment on themselves.

3 For rulers are not a terror to good works, but to evil. Do you want to be unafraid of the authority? Do what is good, and you will have praise from the same.

4 For he is God's minister to you for good. But if you do evil, be afraid; for he does not bear the sword in vain; for he is God's minister, an avenger to execute wrath on him who practices evil.

5 Therefore you must be subject, not only because of wrath but also for conscience' sake.

1 Thessalonians 1:7-9

7 ... so that you became examples to all in Macedonia and Achaia who believe.

8 For from you the word of the Lord has sounded forth, not only in Macedonia and Achaia, but also in every place. Your faith toward God has gone out, so that we do not need to say anything.

9 For they themselves declare concerning us what manner of entry we had to you, and how you turned to God from idols to serve the living and true God.

Introduction

Obedience to God is necessary for salvation because faith in God is necessary. To speak of faith is to speak of obedience. Conceivably, a person might submit to baptism, assemble with the church, and adopt moral principles laid down in the Bible – all without believing that God exists. In such a case, his behavior gives no praise to God (cf. Hebrews 11:6). Mere obedience without faith does not result in laying hold of eternal life. Alternately, one might believe as demons believe (James 2:19). Without obedience, the believer offers no glory to God. The faith that saves is obedient; the obedience that saves flows from faith. Each might be considered without the other in the abstract, but when the subject is redemption, neither faith nor obedience saves when considered alone. The New Testament, at times, focuses attention on faith in God. At other times, it focuses on obedience to God. But always the one presupposes the other.

Grace is cheapened by those who tell a sinner that if he opens his heart to Jesus, an emotional catharsis will sweep him into the arms of the Savior. By contrast, lost souls in the New Testament are commanded to repent and be baptized (Acts 2:38). Grace is no less grace when one must open his hand to receive the gift. Salvation by faith is no less by faith when the sinner obeys God's commands. In countless ways, the New Testament repeats what James said succinctly: "Thus also faith by itself, if it does not have works, is dead" (James 2:17).

Doing the Will of God (Matthew 7:21-23)

The Sermon on the Mount (Matthew 5–7) is programmatic for the manner in which Jesus wants His people to live. In the sermon, Jesus set forth the principles that were to undergird the kingdom of heaven. God would turn away no one. "Ask, and it will be given to you," Jesus said, "seek, and you will find" (7:7). But entailed in asking and seeking is more than a momentary emotional response born of guilt and desperation. Guilt and desperation are hardly anathema, but they are pathways to reconciliation with God only when accompanied by repentance and change. If a tree bears worthless fruit, Jesus said it is worthless (v. 17). If an emotional response to God results in no obedience, it is not faith-driven. Faith that saves is obedience to the will of God. "The criterion for entry to *the kingdom of heaven* (cf. 'entering into life' in vv. 13-14) is, as vv. 16ff. have shown, practical obedience, not an appeal to Jesus as *Lord*, however urgent (cf. 25:11 for equally urgent and equally fruitless repetition)." [1]

To underscore His metaphor about the necessity of fruit for those who want to enter life, Jesus was more explicit. Entry into the kingdom of heaven will not result from a tearful "Lord, Lord," He said, unless it is followed by doing the will of God. The use of "holy language" is not enough. Legion are those who can talk religion with a circle of friends. Pious talk is not faith. In another place, Jesus asked, "But why do you call Me 'Lord, Lord' and not do the things which I say?" (Luke 6:46). Those whose behavior belies their pious words sometimes deceive themselves en route to deceiving others. The Teacher from Nazareth said that false prophets will be genuinely surprised, in some cases at least, when they hear God turning them away from eternal life on judgment day. They will point to their prophecy in the name of the Lord, to the demons they cast out, and to the miracles they performed. Jesus responded by saying, in effect, "Whatever you did, I had nothing to do with it." Adoring crowds surrounding a teacher is no sign that he has taken up the mantle of faithful obedience.

Obeying God, Not Men (Acts 5:27-32)

After the church came into being on the first Pentecost after the resurrection, tension between the kingdom of heaven and official Judaism did not end. Early in the story of the church, Peter and John healed a lame man in the temple precincts (Acts 3:6-7). On the following day, temple authorities arrested them and hauled them before the Jewish high court. When the Sanhedrin questioned them, Peter proclaimed Christ. The fear of repercussions from the crowds prevented authorities from silencing the fishermen from Galilee with the kind of force they had used against Jesus. They threatened them, strictly forbade them to speak further of the Nazarene, and released them. Peter and John went back to their preaching.

The high priest and his supporters arrested the apostles a second time. The people of the church feared for their lives. The two apostles were thrown into prison, where they might have languished indefinitely, except that God did not allow it. He sent His angel, who led them from the common jail back to the company of the church. They next day found them preaching in the temple again.

Still fearing the crowds, Jewish authorities were cautious when they seized the apostles and stood them before the Sanhedrin. They reminded the apostles that they had been forbidden to preach. Peter's response cut to the heart of the matter: "We ought to obey God rather than men," he said (Acts 5:29). When the choice is clear, when a Christian must decide whether to obey God or men, the choice must be for God. It is no light thing to refuse obedience to secular law, but in dire circumstances, it must be done. Even then, Peter and the early church did not take up arms in rebellion. They quietly and peaceably did what God told them to do. Their defense was in His hands.

No Authority Except From God (Romans 13:1-5)

When those who profess Christianity are in the majority or have popular support, they are inclined to press secular government into their service. The secular power of the papacy during the Middle Ages illustrates the point. For a century and longer, the pope ruled over a temporal kingdom, commanded an army, and executed offenders. By contrast, Jesus told Pilate, "My kingdom is not of this world" (John 18:36). The church has no interest in wielding the power of the sword, but neither is secular government a matter of indifference for the believer. Stable and just governments frame a world where preachers can herald the message of Christ and souls can respond without fear and find salvation from sin. Christians have a profound stake in orderly government.

For the mass following Jesus had, He refused any hint of secular power. When some wanted to make Him king, He refused to meet with them (John 6:15). When confronted with taxation, He offered no objection (Matthew 17:27; 22:21). Jesus was neither a devoted political activist nor a disinterested observer of government. The apostles followed in the same vein. Obedience to God included submission to secular government, even when the government was less than ideal. For Paul, the Roman government, for all its injustice, was "God's minister to you for good" (Romans 13:4). At the point where governments demand believers to choose between obedience to God and obedience to them, Christians are to obey God. Paul did not expect that to be the normal state of affairs.

Turning to God (1 Thessalonians 1:7-9)

The Romans divided the Grecian peninsula into two major parts. Macedonia was the northern province with major cities such as Philippi and Thessalonica; Achaia was the southern part with cities such as Athens and Corinth. Word of Paul's reception at Thessalonica had spread to all parts of Greece. Paul commended the Thessalonian Christians because their obedience of the gospel had included both a turning from the world in repentance and a turning to Christ with faith. Turning from the world may entail making a new circle of friends and changing habits. Many find it more difficult to turn from the world than to turn to Christ. Paul commended the Thessalonians for forsaking idols and turning their backs on the excesses of sin. At the same time, he knew old habits would be difficult to break. He devoted a portion of the letter to the encouragement of continued obedience (1 Thessalonians 4:1-8).

Conclusion

Conflict between Jesus and the Pharisees illustrates the different ways they defined obedience. The Pharisees wanted to codify acceptable religious behavior to a degree that went beyond the Law of Moses. They faulted the disciples for removing grain from the husk on the Sabbath because it was work, at least as they had defined it. Jesus insisted that satisfying hunger was more important than the regulations of the Pharisees. According to Jesus, obedience to God requires the godly to order priorities and make judgments. God intended the Sabbath to be a blessing, not a strait jacket to make people chafe and groan (Mark 2:27). Jesus modified the Pharisees' definition of obedience, but He steadfastly insisted that disciples obey God. Paul, like Jesus, demanded that believers obey God, but he went on to make a distinction between obedience motivated by a desire to gain merit and obedience motivated by the response of faith and love. Good works do not earn forgiveness for anyone; instead, they are dyed into the fabric of faith.

Questions

1. Why is saying "Lord, Lord" by itself no pathway to heaven?
2. What three things did Jesus say some would claim as evidence that they were subjects of the kingdom of heaven?
3. How will Jesus respond to those who do not follow profession with obedience?
4. What did Peter and John do in the temple that resulted in their arrest?
5. Who questioned Peter and John when they stood before the council of the Jews?
6. How did Peter justify his preaching when the council had forbidden him to speak?
7. What advantages do stable, just governments provide when believers want to tell the world of Christ?
8. What kind of response did Paul say Christians would receive from secular powers when they lived good lives?
9. Which two Roman provinces did Paul mention had received word of his favorable reception at Thessalonica?
10. What did Paul say the Thessalonians had turned from and turned to?

Discussion Starters

1. Why must obedience to God be incorporated into the definition of the faith that saves? Why are faith and obedience inseparable?
2. To what extent are Christians to obey secular powers? Why do Christians have a stake in stable and orderly governments?
3. Why is it sometimes more difficult to turn from the world than it is to turn to Christ? Why is a willingness to obey God important for each?
4. How did the teachings of Jesus about obedience differ from those of the Pharisees?

The Gospel Message

Mark 16:15-16

15 And He said to them, "Go into all the world and preach the gospel to every creature.

16 "He who believes and is baptized will be saved; but he who does not believe will be condemned."

1 Corinthians 15:1-4

1 Moreover, brethren, I declare to you the gospel which I preached to you, which also you received and in which you stand,

2 by which also you are saved, if you hold fast that word which I preached to you – unless you believed in vain.

3 For I delivered to you first of all that which I also received: that Christ died for our sins according to the Scriptures,

4 and that He was buried, and that He rose again the third day according to the Scriptures.

Galatians 1:6-10

6 I marvel that you are turning away so soon from Him who called you in the grace of Christ, to a different gospel,

7 which is not another; but there are some who trouble you and want to pervert the gospel of Christ.

8 But even if we, or an angel from heaven, preach any other gospel to you than what we have preached to you, let him be accursed.

9 As we have said before, so now I say again, if anyone preaches any other gospel to you than what you have received, let him be accursed.

10 For do I now persuade men, or God? Or do I seek to please men? For if I still pleased men, I would not be a bondservant of Christ.

Ephesians 1:13-14

13 In Him you also trusted, after you heard the word of truth, the gospel of your salvation; in whom also, having believed, you were sealed with the Holy Spirit of promise,

14 who is the guarantee of our inheritance until the redemption of the purchased possession, to the praise of His glory.

Introduction

The Greek word translated "gospel" literally means "good news." As a verb, it means "to announce good news." Both the noun and the verb may be used in a generic sense. For example, Gabriel spoke "glad tidings" to Zechariah when he told the latter that he and his wife would have a son (Luke 1:19). Paul had been pleased to hear "good news" about the Thessalonian church from Timothy (1 Thessalonians 3:6). "Glad tidings" and "good news" in these passages are translated from the same word that means "to preach the gospel" in other contexts.

In most cases, where "gospel" or "to preach the gospel" appears, it has a technical meaning. It refers specifically to the proclamation that, in the person of Jesus of Nazareth, God appeared in human form. He showed Himself to be the Son of God "by miracles, wonders and signs" (Acts 2:22). He taught the way of God and "went about doing good" (10:38). In the end, He died on the cross as a payment for sin (1 John 2:2). God removed all doubt about His being the Son of God by raising Him from the dead (Romans 1:4). The gospel is the message that men and women can be saved by coming to God through His Son, Jesus Christ. Being declared innocent because Christ died for them, the redeemed hope for eternal life in the age to come.

The implications of the gospel message are profound. If Jesus is the Christ, the universe is His creation. Men and women are responsible moral creatures. Right and wrong are built into the structure of existence. How a person treats his fellow human beings matters on an eternal scale. Every person will stand before God at judgment and give an account for how he or she has lived. Although the human body may have similarities to that of an orangutan, or even a housefly for that matter, people are different in kind from all other living things. The Latin phrase culled from Genesis 1:26 is *imago Dei*, meaning "in the image of God." The gospel is about the relationship between God and man and about the working out of God's plan to redeem a people to wear His name.

Preach the Gospel (Mark 16:15-16)

Although the wording is different, all four of the Gospels describe the death and resurrection of Christ. Afterward, all four record the universal commission Jesus gave His disciples. In Matthew, He met with the 11 disciples on a mountain in Galilee. He told them that God had given all authority to Him. Drawing on His authority, He sent them to make disciples of all nations. They were to baptize the lost in the name of "the Father and of the Son and of the Holy Spirit" (28:16-20). Mark recorded a time shortly after the resurrection where Jesus appeared to the 11 "as they sat at the table." The mission was the same. "Go into all the world and preach the gospel to every creature. He who believes and is baptized will be saved" (16:14-16).

In Luke, Jesus appeared to the 11 behind closed doors in Jerusalem. He told them that "repentance and the remission of sins" was to be preached to all nations. Of the apostles, Jesus said, "You are witnesses of these things" (24:46-47). Like Luke, John recorded a meeting between Jesus and His disciples where He said, "As the Father has sent Me, I also send you" (20:21). The good news sent by God was proclaimed orally at first by those who had witnessed the resurrection. After that, the Holy Spirit inspired the recording of the message in the New Testament. From there, it has been passed down to faithful men (2 Timothy 2:2), who, more than 2,000 years later, continue to proclaim Christ.

In both Matthew and Mark, the Great Commission includes the command to baptize believers. Baptism is a living, bodily confession of faith. It is a spiritual reenactment of the death, burial and resurrection of the Lord (Romans 6:4). When a person is baptized, God lifts the burden of sin from him and transfers the guilt and punishment to Jesus (1 Peter 2:24; 3:21). This is an active confession of the believer's faith. One goes down into the waters of baptism estranged from God; he is raised a new creature, reborn into the family of God. Baptism is no mechanical act; neither is it optional. It is an act of faith that participates with repentance and confession, and its efficacy is in the sacrifice of Christ. Until a lost soul has expressed faith in baptism, he is lost in sin. The Greek word translated "faith" can just as well be translated "belief." Jesus said it plainly in Mark: The one who believes and is baptized shall be saved; the one who does not have belief – or faith – remains lost in sin.

Death, Burial, Resurrection (1 Corinthians 15:1-4)

The gospel is about the death, burial and resurrection of Jesus Christ. In the church at Corinth, questions had arisen about the resurrection. Some seemed to think that it was "spiritual," that is, a non-bodily resurrection. Paul corrected the notion by rehearsing the testimony of the apostles. He made it clear that their being saved required them to believe and hold fast to the confession of faith they had professed when they became Christians.

Scholars argue over whether the word "first" in 1 Corinthians 15:3 refers to the sequence of Paul's preaching or to the relative importance of what he preached. Where the New King James Version has "For I delivered to you first of all," the New American Standard Bible declares that the death, burial and resurrection of Jesus were "of first importance." In either case, salvation began with the message that God had become incarnate in Jesus of Nazareth. He had been delivered to the hands of sinners and crucified. In His suffering and death, He had paid the price for human redemption. After His burial, God brought Him forth from the dead. The gospel is good news for humanity. Sin has no dominion over those who come to God through Jesus Christ.

No Other Gospel (Galatians 1:6-10)

Galatians is the only letter in the New Testament written to several churches in one specific Roman province. Paul and Barnabas had preached the gospel in cities scattered through what today is south-central Turkey. Within a short time, maybe a few months, believers from Judea who were "zealous for the law" (Acts 15:5; 21:20) followed them through the cities and persuaded Gentiles that they had to obey the Law of Moses in order for Christ to save them. As soon as Paul heard of the matter, he wrote the Galatian letter. Paul often began his letters with compliments and encouragement. Not so with Galatians. The letter is filled with disbelief and indignation.

The teachers who had followed Paul and Barnabas into Galatian churches wanted Gentiles to observe circumcision as well as Jewish dietary rules and feast days (Galatians 4:10-11). Paul told Gentile believers that if they bent to the demands of the false teachers, they would be compromising the gospel to an intolerable degree (5:4). The Judaizing Christians declared themselves to be followers of Christ, but the "gospel" they proclaimed was no gospel at all. To embrace it was to fall from grace. Galatians 1:6-10 stands as an eternal reminder to Christians that they must examine the message of those who claim to preach Christ. No one is to be believed, supported or followed unless he proclaims the gospel set forth by the apostles and recorded in the New Testament.

The Gospel of Salvation (Ephesians 1:13-14)

Paul encouraged the Christians at Ephesus by rehearsing with them the path they had traveled spiritually. The beginning of life had come when they had "heard the word of truth" (Ephesians 1:13). The word of truth was the gospel, the good news. They had heard and believed the word of truth, and their faith had resulted in their being "sealed with the Holy Spirit of promise" (v. 13). What did their being sealed with the Holy Spirit entail? Was the sealing a misty feeling that had crept over them? Was the sealing of the Spirit identical to allowing Jesus to enter into their hearts?

Sealing for Christians was more substantial and observable than misty feelings. On Pentecost, Peter told those who confessed faith to be baptized. In baptism, God would forgive their sins and convey the gift of the Spirit (Acts 2:38). The Spirit was the seal, the guarantee of their inheritance (cf. 2 Corinthians 1:22; 5:5). The sealing of the Spirit reminded Ephesian Christians of the time when they had heard the truth, believed the truth, and obeyed the truth. They simultaneously had been baptized for the remission of sins and sealed by the Spirit of promise. Having heard the gospel, they responded in faith. As a result, they shared in the Lord's blessings.

Conclusion

The path along which sinners travel from death to life is neither a mechanical process nor solely a subjective, emotional experience. If receiving Christ is not a starched-shirt event, devoid of melted hearts and tears, neither is it a come-as-you-are affair, where each is left to his or her own preferences. Faith and love are the wellsprings from which repentance and obedience bubble up. Without the forsaking of sins such as sexual immorality (1 Thessalonians 4:3), lying and thievery (Ephesians 4:25, 28), faith is in vain. Without submission to the Lord in baptism, the sinner continues to bear the burden of sin (Acts 22:16).

Questions

1. What is the literal meaning of the Greek word translated "gospel"?
2. What things did Paul say are of first importance for the gospel?
3. How many of the Gospels record some version of the Great Commission?

4. What did Jesus tell the disciples would be the result for those who believed and were baptized?
5. What were the disciples doing when Jesus appeared to them in Mark's gospel and told them to take the gospel to every creature?
6. What had Corinthian Christians received, taken their stand on, and been saved by?
7. What had the death, burial and resurrection of Christ been in accord with?
8. In what modern country was the Roman province of Galatia?
9. What kinds of teachers had moved in behind Paul and Barnabas?
10. What did Paul call the "word of truth," which had been received by the Ephesian Christians?

Discussion Starters

1. What was the "other gospel" proclaimed to Galatian Christians? Why was the "other gospel" an intolerable compromise of the gospel of Christ?
2. What biblical evidence supports the conclusion that the Ephesians were sealed by the Holy Spirit when they were baptized into Christ?
3. When Jesus said "He who does not believe will be condemned" (Mark 16:16), was He implying that baptism is not essential for salvation? Defend your answer.
4. Why do Christians need to compare vigilantly what they hear about the gospel to what they read in the New Testament? Are "other gospels" still being proclaimed?

Repentance and Confession

Acts 2:36-38

36 "Therefore let all the house of Israel know assuredly that God has made this Jesus, whom you crucified, both Lord and Christ."

37 Now when they heard this, they were cut to the heart, and said to Peter and the rest of the apostles, "Men and brethren, what shall we do?"

38 Then Peter said to them, "Repent, and let every one of you be baptized in the name of Jesus Christ for the remission of sins; and you shall receive the gift of the Holy Spirit."

Acts 3:18-20

18 But those things which God foretold by the mouth of all His prophets, that the Christ would suffer, He has thus fulfilled.

19 Repent therefore and be converted, that your sins may be blotted out, so that times of refreshing may come from the presence of the Lord,

20 and that He may send Jesus Christ, who was preached to you before.

2 Corinthians 7:8-11

8 For even if I made you sorry with my letter, I do not regret it; though I did regret it. For I perceive that the same epistle made you sorry, though only for a while.

9 Now I rejoice, not that you were made sorry, but that your sorrow led to repentance. For you were made sorry in a godly manner, that you might suffer loss from us in nothing.

10 For godly sorrow produces repentance leading to salvation, not to be regretted; but the sorrow of the world produces death.

11 For observe this very thing, that you sorrowed in a godly manner: What diligence it produced in you, what clearing of yourselves, what indignation, what fear, what vehement desire, what zeal, what vindication! In all things you proved yourselves to be clear in this matter.

Matthew 10:32-33

32 Therefore whoever confesses Me before men, him I will also confess before My Father who is in heaven.

33 But whoever denies Me before men, him I will also deny before My Father who is in heaven.

Romans 10:9-10

9 ... that if you confess with your mouth the Lord Jesus and believe in your heart that God has raised Him from the dead, you will be saved.

10 For with the heart one believes unto righteousness, and with the mouth confession is made unto salvation.

1 Timothy 6:11-14

11 But you, O man of God, flee these things and pursue righteousness, godliness, faith, love, patience, gentleness.

12 Fight the good fight of faith, lay hold on eternal life, to which you were also called and have confessed the good confession in the presence of many witnesses.

13 I urge you in the sight of God who gives life to all things, and before Christ Jesus who witnessed the good confession before Pontius Pilate,

14 that you keep this commandment without spot, blameless until our Lord Jesus Christ's appearing.

Introduction

The process by which a person becomes saved by the blood of Christ appears to be fairly straightforward. Over the centuries, the series of events by which an individual is transferred from the kingdom of darkness to the kingdom of light has been repeated countless times. At its simplest, the gospel confronts a sinner who knows nothing of the Creator God. Christians send a messenger, and the sinner learns that Christ took on flesh, died on the cross as a payment for sin, and was raised from the dead. A person believes the message to be true. He trusts in Christ and asks what the Lord wants him to do to be saved. The messenger tells the person to turn from sin, to confess his faith publicly, and to be baptized for the remission of sins. When he obeys, God lifts the burden of sin and adds the person to His church. The new Christian then lives a godly life until the Lord's return, when the Lord claims him as His own.

The ramifications of Christian living are many; difficult questions must be worked out through careful study of the Bible in interaction with fellow believers. Still, the basic steps by which one who is lost in sin progresses into the Christian pilgrimage is fairly simple. No theological degree or philosophical sophistication is required to understand the way people, such as the jailer of Philippi, become Christians (Acts 16:31-33). Despite the simplicity of the process, people have fussed and argued about every step. Some maintain that the number of the saved has been set from eternity by God. It is said that repentance comes first, then faith. After that, God miraculously gives faith. Many maintain that the sinner cannot believe because people are born depraved. One totally depraved cannot muster the will to believe. Repentance and baptism are works, so it is said. If salvation is by grace, some argue that nothing the sinner does has anything to do with redemption from sin.

The arguments are endless. A process that appears simple in its setting forth in the Bible has become exceedingly complex in human hands. Christians will be well-served when they move past speculation and complexities. Becoming a Christian is as simple as the New Testament sets it forth to be.

Repentance, Baptism and Conversion
(Acts 2:36-38; 3:18-20)

On the first Pentecost after the resurrection of Jesus, as the Lord had promised (Mark 9:1), God poured out the Holy Spirit on the apostles (Acts 2:4). Jews from all parts of the Roman Empire and beyond had gathered in Jerusalem for the great feast day. In the commotion that surrounded the coming of the Spirit, the apostles spoke miraculously in the languages of the multitudes. Peter's sermon was recorded. It, no doubt, was representative of what they all proclaimed.

Some 50 days had passed since Jesus had been crucified, but the apostles were not about to let the event lie dormant in the city's streets. Peter told the crowds about Jesus. He rehearsed what God had done through Him and proclaimed the resurrection of the dead. In the end, thousands believed. They wanted to know what the resurrected Lord wanted them to do (Acts 2:37). Peter told them to repent, to turn from their sins, and to be baptized in order to be saved (v. 38). Those who obeyed the Lord were added to the church (v. 47). Becoming a Christian hardly seemed complex. People believed and confessed. They asked what to do and were told to act on their faith by repenting and being baptized.

A few days later, Peter and John healed a lame man in the temple courts (Acts 3:6). A crowd gathered, and Peter proclaimed the message of Pentecost again. What the prophets had said, Peter affirmed had come to pass. Christ had to suffer. By repenting and turning to Christ, those who were lost in sin would have their sins forgiven. They would be saved. Thousands obeyed the gospel. They repented and were baptized in the same way others had done on Pentecost. Throughout the ages, until the Lord returns, people will come to Christ in the same way.

Godly Sorrow and Repentance
(2 Corinthians 7:8-11)

Repentance is no small undertaking. It is a turning away from sensuality, greed, idols – anything that causes people to dishonor God or to harm one another. At the same time, it is a turning to Christ, a trusting in His grace. An initial repentance follows faith, but repentance is a never-ending process. Some sins stop immediately, but others continue to raise their heads throughout life. Lust, greed, anger and bitterness are often crucified an inch at a time.

Paul wrote the Corinthian church a letter where he took them to task. He was uncertain how they would receive his admonition. Titus brought him word from Corinth that the church had examined itself and repented of its wrongs. The source of the repentance had been sorrow for behavior that had dishonored God and grieved the apostle. The simplicity of the church's response is worth underscoring. The Corinthian Christians recognized the wrong they were doing, and they changed. Repentance is about the way people change their thinking and their behavior once they know the will of God.

Confessing Jesus
(Matthew 10:32-33; Romans 10:9-10)

Confessing, like repenting, encompasses a one-time demand and a long-term commitment. There can be no secret discipleship. Secrecy will either overcome discipleship, or discipleship will overcome secrecy. The conversion stories in Acts imply public confession. The exact wording of the Christian confession of faith is not as important as the message the candidate for baptism conveys. When Paul wrote "With the mouth confession is made unto salvation" (Romans 10:10), he made at least this much clear: The one who wants salvation must be convinced and confess aloud that Jesus of Nazareth was the Son of God, that God raised Him from the dead, and that He reigns at God's right hand.

Confession is woven into the fabric of discipleship. Godly parents would have difficulty denying a child regardless of how much they might disapprove of choices the child had made. Similarly, a disciple should never entertain the possibility of denying Christ even though trials may be severe and the ways of God beyond finding out. Jesus underscored the importance of confession when He told disciples that His confessing of them before God required that they confess Him before men. For emphasis, He stated the same thing negatively. Those who deny Jesus in the presence of men will find that He denies them in the presence of God. Jesus lives among the people of the world through the confession His disciples make of Him, a confession that extends to both words and deeds.

The Good Confession (1 Timothy 6:11-14)

In a public setting, before witnesses, both Timothy and Jesus gave voice to their faith in the fact that God reigns in the affairs of men. The confession of Jesus was a model. His devotion to the Father and the holiness of His life were not at issue. For Timothy, on the other hand, weaknesses of the flesh, weariness with struggle, and uncertainty about the future tended to wear down Christian resolve. Timothy needed to recall the commitment he had made to the Lord.

Paul bracketed his appeal to Timothy's confession with admonitions (1 Timothy 6:11, 14). The Christian life is a struggle; it requires one to fight "the good fight of faith" (v. 12). Neither Timothy nor any believer reaches such holiness of will and mind that he needs no reminder to flee from the love of money and what it buys (v. 10). Paul urged his child in the faith to deny the material ambitions that drive many people and to pursue righteous and godly living instead. Timothy's good confession followed that of Jesus'. It would be the wellspring for a well-ordered life, but it would require courage and self-discipline. The apostle returned to exhortation. Both teacher and student were on the path to eternal life. By keeping the commandments of the One they confessed, each could hope to be counted "blameless until our Lord Jesus Christ's appearing" (v. 14).

Conclusion

Confession is the public declaration of faith. The good confession Jesus made before Pilate and the one Timothy made before many witnesses involved an oral declaration and a steadfast determination to obey God. For Timothy and others, though not for Jesus, confession calls for turning from sin and turning to God. It calls for repentance. Repentance and confession, like every other nook and cranny of Christian living, grow from faith and trust. Faith is at once simpler and more complex than people often suppose. To believe in Christ is to consider true the testimony of firsthand witnesses, but Christ requires belief firmly embedded in trust and obedience. Jesus told His hearers that they did a work pleasing to God when they believed in Him (John 6:29). Faith begins and ends with people who decide Jesus is the Christ and follow-up that decision by loving, trusting and obeying His will. Those who deny that repentance, confession, baptism and godly living are integral to faith use the word differently than Jesus and the apostles.

Questions

1. What message does a sinner learn when he hears the gospel?
2. How did Peter conclude his sermon on the Day of Pentecost?
3. What question did those who heard Peter on Pentecost put to him?
4. What did Peter tell believers on Pentecost to do to be saved?
5. Where were Peter and John when they healed the lame man?
6. What did Peter tell the crowd that gathered after the healing of the lame man they needed to do to have their sins blotted out?
7. How did the Corinthians respond to the letter Paul wrote to them?
8. What did Paul say godly sorrow would bring about?
9. What did Jesus say He would do for those who confessed Him?
10. Before whom did Timothy make the good confession?

Discussion Starters

1. Why did Paul say confession leads to salvation? Why is public confession of great importance for one who owns Jesus as Lord?
2. How have people made the simple process of coming to Christ for salvation a complex matter?
3. Is repentance a work required for salvation? What kind of work is it? Why are works of any kind required if salvation is by God's grace?
4. Why would anyone argue that repentance has to come before faith? Is a sinner able to believe the gospel by his own free will?

Immersion in Precept

Matthew 28:18-20

18 And Jesus came and spoke to them, saying, "All authority has been given to Me in heaven and on earth.

19 "Go therefore and make disciples of all the nations, baptizing them in the name of the Father and of the Son and of the Holy Spirit,

20 "teaching them to observe all things that I have commanded you; and lo, I am with you always, even to the end of the age." Amen.

Mark 16:15-16

15 And He said to them, "Go into all the world and preach the gospel to every creature.

16 "He who believes and is baptized will be saved; but he who does not believe will be condemned."

John 3:3-7

3 Jesus answered and said to him, "Most assuredly, I say to you, unless one is born again, he cannot see the kingdom of God."

4 Nicodemus said to Him, "How can a man be born when he is old? Can he enter a second time into his mother's womb and be born?"

5 Jesus answered, "Most assuredly, I say to you, unless one is born of water and the Spirit, he cannot enter the kingdom of God.

6 "That which is born of the flesh is flesh, and that which is born of the Spirit is spirit.

7 "Do not marvel that I said to you, 'You must be born again.' "

Romans 6:3-6

3 Or do you not know that as many of us as were baptized into Christ Jesus were baptized into His death?

4 Therefore we were buried with Him through baptism into death, that just as Christ was raised from the dead by the glory of the Father, even so we also should walk in newness of life.

5 For if we have been united together in the likeness of His death, certainly we also shall be in the likeness of His resurrection,

6 knowing this, that our old man was crucified with Him, that the body of sin might be done away with, that we should no longer be slaves of sin.

Introduction

When King James assigned translators to the King James Version (1611), their task, he told them, was to use language current in the Church of England insofar as possible. Their adherence to the instructions resulted in words such as "bishop" and "deacon" in the translation. Both represented officials in the Church of England in the early 17th century, even if their responsibilities were considerably different from those of bishops and deacons in the New Testament church. "Bishop" is a rough English transliteration of the Greek word *episkopos*, meaning "overseer"; "deacon" transliterates *diakonos*, meaning "servant."

Among the words transliterated rather than translated in the King James Version was "baptize" in its noun and verb forms.[1] The words are kin to the Greek word *bapto*, meaning "to dip." The latter word is used, for example, in John 13:26, where Jesus said, "It is he to whom I shall give a piece of bread when I have dipped [*bapto*] it." Words rooted in *bapto* indicate dipping, plunging or immersion. The Church of England sprinkled infants and called it baptism. The translators of the King James Version had an incentive to transliterate the Greek words as "baptize" and "baptism" rather than translate them as "immerse" and "immersion." Later translations continued to follow the practice that predated the King James Version.

Among strict Jews who were contemporaries with Jesus, ceremonial washing was common. Archaeologists have uncovered large vats scattered widely over Palestine. The *mikvoth*, as they were called, were used for ritualistic bathing. The ceremonial bathing of Pharisees was not the same as the immersion practiced by John the Baptist and the disciples of Jesus. The Jews washed themselves repeatedly to take away defilements that others might have transferred to them. John, by contrast, called on candidates to repent before he baptized them. His baptism was a singular event. It was for the "remission of sins" (Mark 1:4), not ceremonial defilement. Both the baptism of John and the baptism commanded in the Great Commission were different in concept from the ritualistic washing of the Jews. Those who refer to Jewish "baptisms" that preceded John the Baptist fail to consider significant differences between the two.

The Command
(Matthew 28:18-20; Mark 16:15-16)

After Jesus died on the cross, Joseph of Arimathea asked Pilate if he could take down the body of Jesus and bury it. Permission was granted, and the corpse of Jesus was laid in a new tomb (Matthew 27:57-60) near the crucifixion site (John 19:41). Matthew recorded only one appearance of the resurrected Jesus in Jerusalem (Matthew 28:9). Jesus told the women to whom He appeared that they were to convey news of His resurrection to the disciples and that they were to meet Him in Galilee (26:32; 28:7, 10). Significant events in the life of Jesus took place in Galilee (cf. 4:14-16).

By general consent, Matthew addressed himself to Jewish disciples. He seems to have made a conscious effort to draw parallels between the lawgiver Moses and Jesus. Jesus honored the Law Moses had given (Matthew 5:17; 7:12), but as the Son of God, He had more authority than Moses. As Moses went up on a mountain to receive the Law, Jesus set His programmatic sermon before the disciples on a mountainside (Matthew 5–7). He honored the

Law, but also went beyond the Law. After God raised Him from the dead, it was fitting that He appeared on a mountain in Galilee and set before His disciples the mission to bring the gospel to all nations. The disciples were to teach and baptize in the name of the Father, Son and Holy Spirit (28:18-19). The two went together: teaching and baptizing. The two were bookends. Sandwiched between them were faith, repentance and confession. Following baptism, His disciples were to continue to teach. The Lord intended that the gospel change the way people live. Jesus said that the baptized ones were "to observe all things that I have commanded" (v. 20).

After the resurrected Jesus appeared to the disciples in Galilee, He returned to Jerusalem and appeared to the disciples while they were having a meal. That He "rebuked their unbelief" suggests they had not taken the mission He had given them in Galilee seriously (Mark 16:14). Jesus repeated the commission. He told them they were to preach the gospel to every creature. Those who believed and were baptized would be saved. Those who refused to believe would continue to be lost in sin (vv. 15-16).

No one can read the commission in either Matthew or Mark and doubt that Jesus commanded the disciples to baptize believers. All the commands given by the Lord had urgency attached to them. Obedience was to be immediate. No one suggests that believers wait a few days or months before they repent or confess Christ. Yet many understand baptism to be an appendage to obedience, an option that one may choose to carry out at his convenience. When Acts records the carrying out of the Great Commission, believers immediately responded and were baptized (2:41; 16:32-33). Why? Because baptism was "for the remission of sins" (2:38; 22:16) and the one who believed and was baptized would be saved (Mark 16:16). Until the sinner acted on his faith with repentance and baptism, he continued to bear the burden of sin.

New Birth and New Creation
(John 3:3-7; Romans 6:3-6)

The most unavoidable and radical changes anyone experiences are birth and death. In order to convey the magnitude of the change in store for believers, both Jesus and the apostles resorted to metaphors of being born and of dying. When lost souls come to Jesus in "obedience to the faith" (Romans 1:5; 16:26), they are born, and they die. A spiritual birth and a spiritual death take place when a penitent believer obeys the Lord by being baptized for the remission of sin.

"Regeneration," "the new birth," and "being born again" are different ways to designate the same spiritual reality. The first occurrence of the figure of speech took place when a Jewish ruler named Nicodemus came to Jesus (John 3:1-2). The ruler wanted to talk about the miracles Jesus had done, but the Lord had more lofty things in mind. The Jewish ruler was convinced that God had sent Jesus, but Jesus wanted to move on to what His coming meant. To enter the kingdom of God, Jesus told him, a person must be born again (v. 3).

Nicodemus failed to grasp the meaning of Jesus. "How can a man be born when he is old? Can he enter a second time into his mother's womb and be born?" he asked. Jesus clarified, "Unless one is born of water and the Spirit, he cannot enter the kingdom of God" (John 3:4-5). The translation in the New King James Version is misleading. The Greek has no word for the article ("the") before "Spirit." Without "the," being born of water and Spirit can more easily be read as one and the same process. With the addition of "the," one might think that being born of water is different from being born of the Spirit. Those who want to read baptism out of the words of Jesus teach that being born of water is natural birth and being born of the Spirit is an emotional union between the sinner and Jesus. Being born of "water and the Spirit," so it is said, are two different things.

The assertion that being "born of water" refers to natural birth is forced. Neither in the Bible nor in the secular world where Jesus lived did people speak of natural birth as being born of water.[2] John the Baptist began his ministry by baptizing, calling on people to repent and change their lives (John 1:26-28). Obeying God from the heart was like being reborn. After the baptism of Jesus, John continued with his mission (3:23). The disciples of Jesus also began to baptize. They proclaimed the same repentance John had preached (v. 26; 4:1). Entering the kingdom of God required a new way of life. It brought a new relationship with God because, in Christ, sins were removed. Like Jesus, Peter understood rebirth to culminate in baptism (1 Peter 1:3, 23; 3:21). Obedient believers were like newborn babes, needing nourishment from the Word of God (2:2).

Paul made the connection between the new birth and baptism explicit with the phrase "washing of regeneration" (Titus 3:5). Jesus, Peter and Paul tied the new birth securely to the time when the sinner obeyed the Lord in baptism, but Paul more commonly used the analogy of death and resurrection to illustrate the significance of baptism (Romans 6:3-4). The old man dies and is spiritually buried in baptism. He comes from the water a new person. The new birth and the raising up from baptism to "newness of life" (v. 4) turn out to be very near in concept (Colossians 2:12; Galatians 3:27). The obedient believer is reborn in baptism, resurrected to be a new creation. The newness consists of two factors. (1) Being reborn means that a Christian stands justified before God. Sins are no longer counted against him. (2) Rebirth means that the sinner adopts a new way of life based on righteousness. He lives a morally upright life; he embraces the kingdom of God. He gives and receives from the body of Christ.

Conclusion

Baptism – like repentance, confession and godly living – is an inescapable part of what it means to have faith in Jesus Christ. Good works will not result in anyone having a meritorious standing before God on the day of judgment. However, the faith that saves – as James (1:25; 2:22) and Paul (Romans 2:13) made clear – is a faith that acts. God demands from His people not the mere profession of faith, but the doing of faith. Baptism is more than a ritual; it is an act of faith.

Questions

1. What English word best translates the Greek word carried over into English as "baptism" or "baptize"?
2. According to Matthew, where was Jesus when He told His disciples to preach the gospel to the world?
3. In whose name did Jesus tell the disciples they were to baptize?
4. After the disciples had baptized believers, what else were they to do?
5. Why might the resurrected Jesus have appeared to the disciples a second time and repeated the substance of the Great Commission?
6. What two things did Jesus say would need to precede being saved?
7. To whom was Jesus speaking when He said, "Unless one is born again, he cannot see the kingdom of God" (John 3:3)?
8. What does a person need to do in order to be born of water and Spirit?
9. What passages in the New Testament explicitly speak of being saved in terms of a new birth?
10. After a sinner has been buried with Christ in baptism, in what did Paul say he would then walk?

Discussion Starters

1. What motivated translators of the King James Version to use terms associated with the Church of England at the time? What are some examples?
2. How was ceremonial washing by Jewish contemporaries of Jesus different from the baptism of John the Baptist and the disciples of Jesus?
3. Is being born of water and Spirit two different things, or is it a designation for one spiritual process? Justify your answer.
4. How is the analogy of death to the old man, burial in baptism, and being raised to walk in newness of life similar to being born again? Explain.

Immersion in Practice

Acts 2:40-42

40 And with many other words he testified and exhorted them, saying, "Be saved from this perverse generation."

41 Then those who gladly received his word were baptized; and that day about three thousand souls were added to them.

42 And they continued steadfastly in the apostles' doctrine and fellowship, in the breaking of bread, and in prayers.

Acts 8:34-39

34 So the eunuch answered Philip and said, "I ask you, of whom does the prophet say this, of himself or of some other man?"

35 Then Philip opened his mouth, and beginning at this Scripture, preached Jesus to him.

36 Now as they went down the road, they came to some water. And the eunuch said, "See, here is water. What hinders me from being baptized?"

37 Then Philip said, "If you believe with all your heart, you may." And he answered and said, "I believe that Jesus Christ is the Son of God."

38 So he commanded the chariot to stand still. And both Philip and the eunuch went down into the water, and he baptized him.

39 Now when they came up out of the water, the Spirit of the Lord caught Philip away, so that the eunuch saw him no more; and he went on his way rejoicing.

Acts 10:44-48

44 While Peter was still speaking these words, the Holy Spirit fell upon all those who heard the word.

45 And those of the circumcision who believed were astonished, as many as came with Peter, because the gift of the Holy Spirit had been poured out on the Gentiles also.

46 For they heard them speak with tongues and magnify God. Then Peter answered,

47 "Can anyone forbid water, that these should not be baptized who have received the Holy Spirit just as we have?"

48 And he commanded them to be baptized in the name of the Lord. Then they asked him to stay a few days.

Acts 19:1-5

1 And it happened, while Apollos was at Corinth, that Paul, having passed through the upper regions, came to Ephesus. And finding some disciples ² he said to them, "Did you receive the Holy Spirit when you believed?" So they said to him, "We have not so much as heard whether there is a Holy Spirit."

³ And he said to them, "Into what then were you baptized?" So they said, "Into John's baptism."

⁴ Then Paul said, "John indeed baptized with a baptism of repentance, saying to the people that they should believe on Him who would come after him, that is, on Christ Jesus."

⁵ When they heard this, they were baptized in the name of the Lord Jesus.

Acts 22:16

¹⁶ And now why are you waiting? Arise and be baptized, and wash away your sins, calling on the name of the Lord.

1 Peter 3:21-22

²¹ There is also an antitype which now saves us – baptism (not the removal of the filth of the flesh, but the answer of a good conscience toward God), through the resurrection of Jesus Christ,

²² who has gone into heaven and is at the right hand of God, angels and authorities and powers having been made subject to Him.

Introduction

Neither early 19th-century leaders in the effort to restore the church of the New Testament nor the 21st-century church maintains that baptism ought to be emphasized more than faith or repentance. If churches of Christ have given a disproportionate amount of energy to New Testament teachings on baptism, it has been in response to the shelving of the subject by the Christian denominational world. Faith, repentance and confession are fundamental responses to Christ, but in the New Testament, the sinner moves from being lost to being saved when he expresses faith by actively putting on Christ in baptism (Galatians 3:27).

Among Christian denominations, two overarching viewpoints on baptism prevail. (1) Large numbers practice infant baptism. They believe a child is born with inherited sin. A baby cannot believe or repent, but it can have a little water sprinkled or poured on it. This is supposed to be baptism, even if baptism by definition requires immersion. Those who baptize infants by sprinkling believe that God acts to take away inherited sin when a candidate is baptized by a duly ordained church official. (2) The other broad view maintains that faith, repentance and confession come first and that God has already acted to save before baptism. God gives faith, repentance and rebirth, so it is said, so that nothing more needs to happen at baptism. It is only the "outward sign of an inward grace" and, often, only an outward act necessary for admission to a particular denomination.

However, the New Testament teaches both by precept and practice that baptism by definition is an immersion in water; only believing, penitent persons are fit subjects for baptism; and God forgives sin when a believer obeys the Lord in baptism. Those who practice infant baptism are correct when they maintain that God takes away sins when baptism occurs. They are incorrect when they suppose that the faith and repentance are matters of no concern and when they substitute sprinkling or pouring for immersion. Those who baptize persons old enough to understand the gospel are correct when they practice immersion. They are incorrect when they suppose that sinners cannot muster the will to obey the gospel and when they maintain that rebirth occurs only for those whom God has predestined for life and that baptism has nothing to do with forgiveness of sins.

Who Should Be Baptized?
(Acts 8:34-39; 19:1-5)

Both Jesus and Paul set forth the doctrinal underpinning for baptism, but in the book of Acts, one encounters the way inspired men put the teaching into practice. An angel directed Philip the evangelist to the road that connected Jerusalem with the old Philistine city of Gaza (8:26). Philip encountered an Ethiopian official who had been to Jerusalem. On the way home, riding in a chariot, the Ethiopian was reading from Isaiah 53. Philip approached the man and, beginning where the Ethiopian was reading, taught him of Christ (Acts 8:35).

As the two traveled, they came to some water, and the Ethiopian wanted to be baptized. Both of them went down into the water (Acts 8:38); Philip baptized him; and they came up out of the water (v. 39). The narrative helps to answer at least two important questions about baptism. (1) Who are proper candidates for baptism? The Ethiopian was an adult. He asked questions, learned that he was lost in sin, and then asked to be baptized into Christ. (2) What is the proper procedure for baptism? The Ethiopian's baptism was a physical immersion in water.

A second incident that pictures the practice of baptism is when Paul came to the great city of Ephesus. He found about 12 men who knew something of Jesus, but not all they needed to know (Acts 19:7). They had been baptized according to the manner of John; that is, they had been baptized without proper knowledge of the death, burial and resurrection of the Lord. After Paul taught them better, their faith was complete, and they were baptized for the remission of sins. Their re-baptism illustrates that proper candidates for baptism need to understand and confess that Christ died for their sins and was raised from the dead.

Cornelius (Acts 10:44-48)

Jesus told His disciples to preach the gospel to every creature, but it took some time for the church to understand that Gentiles could obey the gospel as they were. They did not have to adopt the traditions of ethnic Judaism before they could be baptized into Christ. The church at Jerusalem came face to face with the matter when Peter preached the gospel to Cornelius and his household.

Too little had been required of the men at Ephesus before they had been baptized; they had been ignorant of Christ's death, burial and resurrection.

But more often, early Jewish believers required too much of candidates for baptism. They insisted that Gentiles needed to embrace circumcision and other ethnic components of Judaism before they could be saved (Acts 15:1). God settled the matter while Peter was preaching to Cornelius and his household. The Holy Spirit came on the Gentiles in the same manner that it had come on the apostles on Pentecost (11:15-17). Peter understood this to be a sign from God that Gentiles were to be baptized into Christ as they were; they did not need to become Jews first. Christ added them to His people just as He had added the Jews who were baptized on Pentecost. God showed no distinction between Jews and Gentiles (10:34).

Saving Power (Acts 22:16; 1 Peter 3:21-22)

A proper candidate for baptism makes a decision; he puts faith and trust in the work of Jesus Christ on the cross. Faith requires him to repent of past sins and to confess his faith publicly. Faith then compels him to ask for baptism so that his sins might be washed away by the blood of the Lamb (Acts 22:16). By His grace, God acts through baptism to take away the sins of the obedient believer. Peter compared the saving of a lost soul in baptism to the saving of the eight in the ark during the time of Noah. He said baptism is an antitype of the flood waters, by which the eight were saved. Baptism "now saves us" (1 Peter 3:21), he added.

Preachers sometimes speak of one going down into the waters of baptism as a dry sinner and coming up as a wet sinner. One needs to be careful with such language. Neither Cornelius nor the Ethiopian official could have known a great deal about Christ before they were baptized. Christians sometimes fret unnecessarily about the "validity" of their baptism. After the event, they may reflect on how little they knew about faith and repentance. Believers do well to remember that God by His grace acts to forgive sin. Forgiveness does not depend on passing a knowledge or sincerity test. One will grow in Christ (2 Peter 3:18); faith, repentance and confession, leading up to baptism, are at the level of one's ability to assimilate what he has learned. Forgiveness does not depend on the believer's merit or depth of understanding. God acts in baptism; He grants forgiveness based on the merits of the One who died on Calvary.

Life After Baptism (Acts 2:40-42)

Conversion to Christ is both putting off an old life of sin and putting on a new life. His new clothing is the righteousness of Christ. Baptism is the end of the process that transfers a sinner from the kingdom of darkness to the kingdom of light, but it is also the beginning of a life devoted to pleasing and praising God. On Pentecost, about 3,000 souls obeyed the gospel. Christ added them to the number of the saved. Multitudes more became Christians in the weeks and years that followed. Life after baptism has individual and corporate components. Individually, a Christian struggles to please the Lord through godly living. Corporately, he partakes of the body of Christ. In the church, he finds strength and gives strength. Christian living is more than an individual allowing Christ into the heart. It is also being a part of a family, a household and a kingdom.

Conclusion

In practice, baptism in the New Testament is "the answer of a good conscience toward God" (1 Peter 3:21). When a sinner becomes conscious of Jesus Christ – when he places faith in Him, repents of sin, and confesses Him to be Lord – his conscience leads the way. The sinner goes down into the waters of baptism, buries the old person in whom sin had reigned, has his sins washed away, and arises to newness of life. The taking away of sins is nothing a lost soul does for himself. God is the unseen Actor working through baptism. God grants the forgiveness of sin when the sinner acts on his faith and is baptized into Christ.

Questions

1. What has motivated modern churches of Christ to devote energy to the biblical teaching about baptism for the remission of sins?
2. Why did Philip go to the road to Gaza to preach the gospel?
3. What was the home country of the official to whom Philip preached?
4. Where in the Old Testament had the official been reading?
5. What question did Paul ask the disciples he found at Ephesus?
6. When the disciples learned more perfectly of Christ, what did they do?
7. What did Peter and others observe that convinced them Cornelius and his household should be baptized?
8. What did Ananias tell Paul to do to have his sins washed away?
9. What did Peter say happened at baptism when it was the answer of a good conscience toward God?
10. To what did the Lord add those who were baptized on Pentecost?

Discussion Starters

1. Have churches of Christ in the modern era emphasized baptism to the neglect of faith, repentance and grace? Defend your answer.
2. What two viewpoints about baptism tend to prevail among Christian denominations? What is wrong and right about each?
3. What is the human part in baptism, and what is God's part? What kind of knowledge and sincerity should a lost soul bring to baptism?
4. What part does the church have in the life of a Christian after he has been baptized into Christ?

This We Do
Spring Quarter

With this quarter's emphasis on worship and our participation in it, these in-depth studies enable us to re-examine concepts and practices we have studied before, but now we seek to renew our emphasis on each one. These we do.

Lesson 1 • Week of March 1, 2015
Worship, Part 1

Psalm 27:1-6

1 The LORD is my light and my salvation; Whom shall I fear? The LORD is the strength of my life; Of whom shall I be afraid?

2 When the wicked came against me To eat up my flesh, My enemies and foes, They stumbled and fell.

3 Though an army may encamp against me, My heart shall not fear; Though war may rise against me, In this I will be confident.

4 One thing I have desired of the LORD, That will I seek: That I may dwell in the house of the LORD All the days of my life, To behold the beauty of the LORD, And to inquire in His temple.

5 For in the time of trouble He shall hide me in His pavilion; In the secret place of His tabernacle He shall hide me; He shall set me high upon a rock.

6 And now my head shall be lifted up above my enemies all around me; Therefore I will offer sacrifices of joy in His tabernacle; I will sing, yes, I will sing praises to the LORD.

Psalm 148:1-4

1 Praise the LORD! Praise the LORD from the heavens; Praise Him in the heights!

2 Praise Him, all His angels; Praise Him, all His hosts!

3 Praise Him, sun and moon; Praise Him, all you stars of light!

4 Praise Him, you heavens of heavens, And you waters above the heavens!

Luke 4:16-19

16 So He came to Nazareth, where He had been brought up. And as His custom was, He went into the synagogue on the Sabbath day, and stood up to read.

17 And He was handed the book of the prophet Isaiah. And when He had opened the book, He found the place where it was written:

18 "The Spirit of the LORD is upon Me, Because He has anointed

Me To preach the gospel to the poor; He has sent Me to heal the brokenhearted, To proclaim liberty to the captives And recovery of sight to the blind, To set at liberty those who are oppressed;

19 "To proclaim the acceptable year of the LORD."

Revelation 4:8-11

8 The four living creatures, each having six wings, were full of eyes around and within. And they do not rest day or night, saying: "Holy, holy, holy, Lord God Almighty, Who was and is and is to come!"

9 Whenever the living creatures give glory and honor and thanks to Him who sits on the throne, who lives forever and ever,

10 the twenty-four elders fall down before Him who sits on the throne and worship Him who lives forever and ever, and cast their crowns before the throne, saying:

11 "You are worthy, O Lord, To receive glory and honor and power; For You created all things, And by Your will they exist and were created."

Introduction

The Hebrew and Greek words translated "worship" suggest a prostrating of self before God. In worship people express submission, acknowledge dependence, and offer praise to God. In the Greek language, the opposite of worshipful submission is hubris. Hubris is the arrogant pride that causes man to shake his fist in God's face. It is the frame of mind that asserts, "I am my own god. I will do whatever I please." Hubris is a self-defeating stance before the Almighty.

It is right when mortals worship God, but what they ought to do in order to give Him glory and praise is far from obvious. Left to their own devices, people engage in religious rites that range from the ridiculous to the grotesque. When Joshua led Israel into Canaan, the newcomers encountered gods and worship practices different from what they had learned in the wilderness. The Canaanites wove their gods into the processes of nature. Baal was the sky god who brought thunderstorms and rain; Asherah was the earth goddess who gave fertility and crops. To acknowledge the role of the gods in reproduction, men went to sacred prostitutes in shrines built on high places. They were hardly unique in building sensuality into the worship of idols. At their worst, the people of Israel embraced the practice with enthusiasm (Jeremiah 3:2).

Canaanites believed their gods to be powerful enough to demand what was most precious to them. In times of great danger, leading families brought their small children, their toddlers, to be slaughtered and offered as gifts to the gods. The practice was abhorrent to God (Leviticus 18:21), but two of Judah's kings, Ahaz (2 Kings 16:1-3) and Manasseh (21:1-6), made their sons "pass through the fire." These are extreme examples, but it is difficult to image any abominable practice that someone has not done and called it worship. Sin is so deeply entrenched in the human family that no one dares to define for himself what honors God. The righteous wait patiently for God to reveal how they should worship Him. It is hardly surprising that a great deal of the Bible directs people in appropriate ways to praise God. When men presume to decide for themselves what acceptable worship is, they go astray.

Old Testament Worship
(Psalm 27:1-6; 148:1-4)

Worship by the patriarchs and by the people of Israel under the Law of Moses appealed to the senses in ways that New Testament worship does not. While Israel was in the wilderness, God instructed Moses concerning the dimensions and the adornments of the tabernacle. God called a priesthood and instructed them about the way they were to offer sacrifices. After Israel settled in Canaan, the Lord chose a place where the priests were to serve and where the people were to bring their gifts. Rituals were elaborate, and rules were meticulously prescribed. The fear, the awesome presence of the Almighty, was the beginning place for faithfulness. Homage was to be offered to no deity other than Yahweh, and He defined the worship that pleased Him.

Important as the ceremony of worship was for Israel, Christians make a mistake if they suppose outward form to have been of singular importance under the Old Law. In the midst of ceremonial instructions, the Law emphasized that God wanted the heart of His people. Underlying sacrifice was love for the Lord (Deuteronomy 6:5). God was never pleased when people got the rituals right and neglected kindness for the poor or just dealing with neighbors (10:12-13; Micah 6:6-8). Worship in the Old Testament included prayers and psalms, repentance and praise. Tradition and history can be important instruments for the stirring of the heart. Such worship regularly finds expression in the Psalms.

The psalmists stood awestruck in the presence of God. The God who set Sinai to smoke struck fear. Life and death, misery and mirth, honor and shame hung in the balance. In the face of unknown and unknowable might, the psalmists sought familiar paths and scenery. The Jerusalem temple on its hill was only stone and mortar, yet it was the place where priests offered sacrifices and the place where God had put His name. Threatened by enemies, the pious sought council and refuge "in the secret place of His tabernacle" (Psalm 27:5). In public worship or in solitude with God, the psalmists found courage and strength to do what they could not do alone.

The Psalms teem with worship and praise. It is difficult to select a few and call them representative, but in Psalm 148 praise reaches the summit. The heavens, mountaintops, angels, moon and stars join in praise. The temple inspires its own kind of awe, but the cathedral of the heavens, the passageways of the seas – all nature contributes to the worship of the Almighty. From the sidelines, the psalmist partook of the praise.

Synagogue Worship (Luke 4:16-19)

Synagogues have no place in the worship of Israel as set forth in the Law. Community worship for Israel focused on the three great feast days, Passover (Feast of Unleavened Bread), Pentecost (Feast of Harvest) and Tabernacles

(Feast of Ingathering) (Exodus 23:14-17). The Sabbath was a day of rest, a family day, not a day of public assembly. The temple in Jerusalem, the priesthood of Aaron, and the kingship of David were the outward, visible signs that Israel belonged to the God who had called them from Egypt. All of that changed in 587 B.C. The temple, the city, the priesthood, the kingship were no more. Judah languished in captivity.

As captives in Babylon, the Jews turned their eyes to the Law of Moses with fervor. They began to assemble on the Sabbath to study and discuss the Law. In time they built places for assembly. The word "synagogue" means "assembly." With their homeland under occupation by foreigners, Jews scattered to other parts of the world. In time, synagogues became traditional. By the time of the New Testament, synagogues were a part of Jewish community life wherever they lived.

It is safe to conclude that God's providence directed Jews toward assembly in synagogues on the Sabbath. Jesus found them well entrenched. Luke describes an incident shortly after Jesus' baptism when He visited His hometown of Nazareth and assembled with friends and family in the local synagogue as was His custom (Luke 4:16-19). He read from the Scriptures and appealed to them as witnesses to the authority God had given Him. It was to the synagogues more than to the temple that the church was to look for a worship model. Churches, like synagogues, assemble weekly. They read from the Scriptures, offer praise in song and exhort one another to godly living.

Heavenly Worship (Revelation 4:8-11)

After the letters to the seven churches, the scene of John's vision in Revelation changes to the heavens. God transported the apostle in spirit to the great rainbow throne where the majesty of the Godhead appeared to his mortal eyes. Surrounding the throne were lesser thrones on which were seated 24 elders. Lightning and peals of thunder assaulted John's eyes and ears while four "living creatures" (Revelation 4:8) offered continual praise to the Almighty. Worship, it seems, is built into the structure of the universe. In this age and the age to come, created things search the limits of their being for praise appropriate for His majesty.

For centuries interpreters of the Bible have puzzled over the significance of John's vision for future events. God clearly wanted the vision to offer reassurance to persecuted Christians. The overall message is clear, even if the significance of its bits and pieces have been obscured by time. God would judge the powers who ruled over John and his readers as He had judged nations in the past. His sovereignty over the affairs of men is not to be doubted. It is not for the minutia of history that we look for in Revelation, much less the unfolding of a rapture and a millennial kingdom where Christ reigns from an earthly throne. Revelation offers a timeless message about the triumphal rule of God in human affairs and a message of praise and worship that are timeless in scope.

Conclusion

God demanded of Job that he account for his presumption in questioning God's rule. Where was Job when God laid the foundations of the earth,

"When the morning stars sang together, and all the sons of God shouted for joy" (Job 38:7)? The observations and measurements of men and women of science have not dampened the sense of awe and mystery that surround creation. That awe and mystery lie at the heart of worship. Whether the subject is Adam and Eve in the garden, modern engineering feats, or the coming and going of the generations, the posture of men in the presence of God is prostration. Worship is many pronged, but always it is obedience. Only God can prescribe what men do that honor Him. When people set about to worship God by dredging up what stirs their emotions, the result is catastrophic. Both the ancient people of Israel and the modern church risk God's ire when they presume to know more about worship than God does.

Questions

1. What do the most common words translated "worship" from the Hebrew and Greek mean literally?
2. What is the frame of mind that is the polar opposite of worship?
3. What are some of the elements of Old Testament worship that are prescribed in detail in the Law?
4. In addition to following the outward forms of worship as He prescribed, what else did God want His people to give Him?
5. When threatened by the wicked, what did the psalmist expect the God of Israel to do for him?
6. Where did the psalmist say that he wanted to dwell all the days of his life?
7. From what sources did the psalmist expect praise to come to glorify God?
8. At what point in the history of Israel did a tradition of synagogue worship begin?
9. Where was Jesus when He entered the synagogue and read from Isaiah?
10. What timeless message does John's vision of the throne room of God convey?

Discussion Starters

1. How do the religions of the Canaanites illustrate the problem when people decide for themselves what acceptable worship should be?
2. Does Christian worship find more parallels in Jewish synagogues or in temple services? How was synagogue worship similar and different from church worship?
3. Was God pleased when Israel focused solely on the outward form and ritual of worship? What else did God expect the people to offer Him?
4. What ought Christians to learn from the worship John saw in heaven? Do all elements of heavenly worship apply to the church? Explain.

Worship, Part 2

Exodus 3:1-6

1 Now Moses was tending the flock of Jethro his father-in-law, the priest of Midian. And he led the flock to the back of the desert, and came to Horeb, the mountain of God.

2 And the Angel of the LORD appeared to him in a flame of fire from the midst of a bush. So he looked, and behold, the bush was burning with fire, but the bush was not consumed.

3 Then Moses said, "I will now turn aside and see this great sight, why the bush does not burn."

4 So when the LORD saw that he turned aside to look, God called to him from the midst of the bush and said, "Moses, Moses!" And he said, "Here I am."

5 Then He said, "Do not draw near this place. Take your sandals off your feet, for the place where you stand is holy ground."

6 Moreover He said, "I am the God of your father – the God of Abraham, the God of Isaac, and the God of Jacob." And Moses hid his face, for he was afraid to look upon God.

Psalm 100:1-5

1 Make a joyful shout to the LORD, all you lands!

2 Serve the LORD with gladness; Come before His presence with singing.

3 Know that the LORD, He is God; It is He who has made us, and not we ourselves; We are His people and the sheep of His pasture.

4 Enter into His gates with thanksgiving, And into His courts with praise. Be thankful to Him, and bless His name.

5 For the LORD is good; His mercy is everlasting, And His truth endures to all generations.

Psalm 122:1

1 I was glad when they said to me, "Let us go into the house of the LORD."

John 4:19-26

19 The woman said to Him, "Sir, I perceive that You are a prophet.

20 "Our fathers worshiped on this mountain, and you Jews say that in Jerusalem is the place where one ought to worship."

21 Jesus said to her, "Woman, believe Me, the hour is coming when you will neither on this mountain, nor in Jerusalem, worship the Father.

22 "You worship what you do not know; we know what we worship, for salvation is of the Jews.

23 "But the hour is coming, and now is, when the true worshipers will worship the Father in spirit and truth; for the Father is seeking such to worship Him.

24 "God is Spirit, and those who worship Him must worship in spirit and truth."

25 The woman said to Him, "I know that Messiah is coming" (who is called Christ). "When He comes, He will tell us all things."

26 Jesus said to her, "I who speak to you am He."

Introduction

Worship includes both corporate and individual dimensions. For Israel the corporate dimension included the priesthood, the tabernacle or temple, sacrifices and feast days. For the church it includes assembly on the Lord's Day, the first day of the week. It includes singing, the Lord's Supper, giving, praying and learning from Scripture. The corporate dimension of worship is what God's people do as a family when assembled. In addition, worship has a personal dimension. The individual Christian hears "amazing grace, how sweet the sound" coming in song from the mouths of brothers and sisters. He or she joins his voice to theirs and feels the joy and hope that comes from sharing the promise of eternal life. The believer adds his heart to the prayer of the church. He melts in gratitude as he adds his "amen" to prayers offered. So it is with all the church does when it assembles. The individual blends his own heart, will and mind with those of fellow Christians. Worship is at once a community and an individual offering.

Because no two people are the same, the emphasis in worship may vary. One person may be concerned that the church follow the outward forms of worship as the Bible prescribes, and another may be concerned that individuals be stirred to heartfelt praise. Issues become confused when individual failures are transferred to the church. A distracted Christian, for example, may judge the worship of everyone to be sterile and devoid of emotional involvement because he personally felt no religious wonder during the assembly. Harmony is more likely to result when believers recognize individual differences and are concerned both with corporate worship and with individual hearts. Every believer should strive to worship with understanding and with spiritual energy (1 Corinthians 14:15).

Problems are likely to result when the individual goes to the church assembly in search of a feeling. He or she may be convinced that the church should experiment in order to find what invokes intense feelings of worship. Sometimes believers in essence say, "All right! Here I am. I came to church like I promised. Now it is your responsibility to make me feel religious." Such a disposition is likely to be displeased no matter what happens during the assembly. Believers have no need to choose between praise from sincere hearts and corporate worship that pleases God. They may strive for both.

Reverently (Exodus 3:1-6)

Reverence, like other aspects of worship, results when heart and mind are drawn into the eternal glory and lovingkindness of the Creator. For Moses, the encounter with the majesty of God came while he was tending the flocks of his father-in-law Jethro, "the priest of Midian," in the vicinity of Mount Horeb (Exodus 3:1). Horeb is an alternate name for Sinai. Moses would be back to the mountain within a few years at most. When he came back, he would be in company with the hordes of Israel. Descendants of Jacob will pause long enough with Moses at Horeb to receive the Law of God.

According to Stephen (Acts 7:23, 30), Moses was some 80 years old when he turned aside to see the bush that burned continually but was never consumed. He was a shepherd, used to oddities that appeared in the loneliness of desert places, but this phenomenon, if true, would surpass anything he had heard or seen before. Curiosity drove him on. Little did he know that beginning with the burning bush an adventure would stretch out before him and occupy the remainder of his days. The fire was curious enough, but the shepherd was unprepared for the voice that came from the fire, "Moses, Moses!" Moses heard the command to take his shoes off, and the explanation, "for the place where you stand is holy ground." The voice identified Himself: "I am the God of your father" (Exodus 3:4-6).

How much Moses knew about the Creator God when He spoke from the bush is uncertain. While growing to maturity as the Son of Pharaoh's daughter, he had been aware of where he had come from (Exodus 2:11). Stories of Abraham and Jacob likely captured his imagination more than the incantations and centuries-old ritual of Egyptian priests. At age 40, he left Egypt. Likely the priest of Midian taught him thoroughly in the ways of God. God took it for granted that names such as Abraham, Isaac and Jacob meant something to Moses. In the burning bush, Moses came face to face with the Almighty God whose Being stretches through time, who is the same "yesterday, today, and forever" (Hebrews 13:8). Little wonder that the shepherd hid his face, afraid to look at the bush from which the voice came (Exodus 3:6). Isaiah would sense the same fear centuries later (Isaiah 6:5). God is a father and friend, but Christians ought not to forget that He is the awesome Creator. To sing His praises, to address Him in prayer, to worship with the saints – all of it is to stand on holy ground.

Joyfully (Psalm 100:1-5; 122:1)

Worship is a somber undertaking filled with reverence and awe, but worship is also a time of joy and thanksgiving. One ought not to confuse joy in worship with fun in worship. Joy has within it a component of thoughtful reflection that fun lacks. Fun is for the purpose of instant gratification. Fun can easily take a selfish turn, a mocking turn, a sensual turn or even a cruel turn. Worshipers hardly fault a preacher who occasionally resorts to humor to make a point, but a diet of rollicking good times is like eating sugar cookies three meals a day. For the psalmist, worship allowed for one to "make a joyful shout to the LORD" (Psalm 100:1). There was room for gladness and singing, but for the author of Psalm 100, joy was intermingled with reflection. Praise is for the God "who has made us," for we have not made ourselves. "We are His people and the sheep of His pasture" (v. 3). Reflection issues forth in gratitude. He has blessed us. His mercy is everlasting. His truth endures to all generations. Joy pervades the psalm, but such joy was not the domain of belly laughs and giggles.

People cultivate the behavior that brings them gladness and joy. Going to church on Sunday, shaking hands with old friends, lifting voices in songs are times of gladness for those who have cultivated their hearts. Like an adult who enjoys the taste of broccoli or asparagus, the worshiper learns to enjoy the praise, the closeness, the fellowship of worship because he has cultivated the taste. Like the adult who eats sensibly, a worshiper finds that his soul is nourished by praise. For the author of Psalm 122, gladness swelled in him at the prospect of entering the "house of the LORD" (v. 1) with other worshipers, all of them united within the gates of Jerusalem.

Obediently (John 4:19-26)

While Jesus was alone at a well in Samaria, a woman from the nearby village came out to draw water. A conversation ensued in which Jesus spoke about Himself as living water. That Jesus spoke to her at all is surprising. Under normal conditions, a Jewish male would not strike up a conversation with an unknown woman, much less an unknown woman who was a Samaritan. Jews had only disdain for Samaritans. They were semi-Jews who claimed to follow the Law of Moses but rejected the rest of the Old Testament. Samaritans had their own temple on Mount Gerizim near the site of ancient Shechem. No love was lost between Jews and Samaritans.

The woman broached the subject of the temple. Was the place where God's people ought to worship on Mount Gerizim or was it on the temple mount in Jerusalem? She expected Him to claim that Jerusalem was the place for the temple. Jesus did not disappoint on that score, but He went further. Jesus foresaw a time when the physical place of worship would not be as important as the heart of the worshiper. The worship that pleases God, the Lord said, was to be in spirit, i.e., welling up from sincere hearts, and it was to be in truth. Worship offered in truth was praise offered as God prescribed (John 4:23-24). The words of Jesus are prophetic. After He died on the cross and the church came into being, acceptable worship would flow to God through the Savior Jesus Christ (14:6). Worship in truth is worship through Jesus of Nazareth.

Conclusion

The "how" of worship is widely debated. Roman Catholicism and other such traditions engage in rites that are centuries old but not mentioned in the New Testament. Many expect worship to stir strong emotions that become manifest in shouts, weeping or laughter. Assemblies that once were marked by pulpits and scriptural exhortations in the modern world have been turned over to rock 'n' roll. The music of worship has become the music of the nightclub; the Word slightly altered for the sake of the old folks. The modern church confronts the world in ways similar to the way Israel confronted Canaanite religion. The questions for them and for us are: Does the manner of worship matter? Is public worship a matter of popular taste?

The prophets understood that the way Israel worshiped had a great deal to do with what they thought about God. Obedience in worship was the beginning place for obedient living. Israel failed on both scores; as a result God sent judgment on the nation. For Israel and the church, acceptable worship is obedient worship.

Questions

1. How old was Moses when God appeared to him on Mount Horeb?
2. What is an alternate name Scripture assigns to Mount Horeb?
3. Who was the father-in-law of Moses?
4. How did Moses respond when God called to him from the burning bush?
5. How did God identify Himself to Moses?
6. Whom did the psalmist invite to join him in shouting joyfully to the Lord?
7. When the psalmist entered the gates of the Lord, what did he say resulted?
8. Where did Jesus talk to the woman at the well?
9. Where was the temple where those of the Samaritan religion worshiped?
10. Why is it surprising that the conversation between the woman at the well and Jesus took place?

Discussion Starters

1. Why do problems arise when a person worships with the church and insists that others make him or her feel religious? What is a better way of worship?
2. Why might one say that serving God is joyous? What is the difference between joy and fun?
3. What distinction was Jesus making when He spoke of worshiping in spirit and truth (John 4:23-24)? Can one worship in spirit or truth without the other? Explain.
4. Why is it essential for the church to look to Scripture for a pattern of worship? What are the dangers when people follow their personal inclinations in worship?

Using God's Word, Part 1

Nehemiah 8:1-8

1 Now all the people gathered together as one man in the open square that was in front of the Water Gate; and they told Ezra the scribe to bring the Book of the Law of Moses, which the LORD had commanded Israel.

2 So Ezra the priest brought the Law before the assembly of men and women and all who could hear with understanding on the first day of the seventh month.

3 Then he read from it in the open square that was in front of the Water Gate from morning until midday, before the men and women and those who could understand; and the ears of all the people were attentive to the Book of the Law.

4 So Ezra the scribe stood on a platform of wood which they had made for the purpose; and beside him, at his right hand, stood Mattithiah, Shema, Anaiah, Urijah, Hilkiah, and Maaseiah; and at his left hand Pedaiah, Mishael, Malchijah, Hashum, Hashbadana, Zechariah, and Meshullam.

5 And Ezra opened the book in the sight of all the people, for he was standing above all the people; and when he opened it, all the people stood up.

6 And Ezra blessed the LORD, the great God. Then all the people answered, "Amen, Amen!" while lifting up their hands. And they bowed their heads and worshiped the LORD with their faces to the ground.

7 Also Jeshua, Bani, Sherebiah, Jamin, Akkub, Shabbethai, Hodijah, Maaseiah, Kelita, Azariah, Jozabad, Hanan, Pelaiah, and the Levites, helped the people to understand the Law; and the people stood in their place.

8 So they read distinctly from the book, in the Law of God; and they gave the sense, and helped them to understand the reading.

Matthew 28:19-20

19 "Go therefore and make disciples of all the nations, baptizing them in the name of the Father and of the Son and of the Holy Spirit,

20 "teaching them to observe all things that I have commanded you; and lo, I am with you always, even to the end of the age." Amen.

1 Corinthians 9:16-18

16 For if I preach the gospel, I have nothing to boast of, for necessity is laid upon me; yes, woe is me if I do not preach the gospel!

17 For if I do this willingly, I have a reward; but if against my will,

I have been entrusted with a stewardship.

18 What is my reward then? That when I preach the gospel, I may present the gospel of Christ without charge, that I may not abuse my authority in the gospel.

2 Timothy 4:2

2 Preach the word! Be ready in season and out of season. Convince, rebuke, exhort, with all longsuffering and teaching.

James 1:21-25

21 Therefore lay aside all filthiness and overflow of wickedness, and receive with meekness the implanted word, which is able to save your souls.

22 But be doers of the word, and not hearers only, deceiving yourselves.

23 For if anyone is a hearer of the word and not a doer, he is like a man observing his natural face in a mirror;

24 for he observes himself, goes away, and immediately forgets what kind of man he was.

25 But he who looks into the perfect law of liberty and continues in it, and is not a forgetful hearer but a doer of the work, this one will be blessed in what he does.

Introduction

To a limited degree, God has chosen to reveal Himself through the phenomena of nature. We see His majesty, His authority and His consistency in the daily rising of the sun, in the rains that bring forth fruits, in the waves of the oceans and in the peaks of mountains. When revelation from nature has been lacking, God has resorted to words. In the early stages, God's Word came through living voices, through prophets, wise men and lawgivers, but living voices were limited in the numbers they could reach. In time God not only inspired His messengers to speak His Word, He instructed them to write it. A canon of scripture resulted, first the Old Testament and then the New (2 Peter 1:20-21). Wherever men could read, God's Word was with them to guide.

God's Word in written form had several advantages over the spoken word. First, it could be copied and made available wherever it was needed. Second, the written word was more stable than oral reports. Those who served God could go back to its words, reexamine its teachings, and draw from it a constant flow of blessings. Third, during times of national apostasy a scarcity of God's Word followed in the trail of faithlessness. Prophets were scarce; people had difficulty distinguishing the true prophets from the false. Immediately before the days of Samuel, the record says, "And the word of the LORD was rare in those days; there was no widespread revelation" (1 Samuel 3:1). The written word was a wellspring to which the faithful could return even under the darkest clouds of apostasy.

God's self-revelation in written form makes possible a people guided by an authoritative hand. Neither Scripture nor authority can be spoken of alone.

When Christians want to know what to believe or how to live, Scripture is there to direct their paths. Feelings are not authoritative in the realm of religion. A denominational conference is not authoritative. The feelings of equally sincere people direct them in opposite ways; degrees from denominational conferences define the faith of Christ differently. Unity among God's people begins with a common acceptance of Scripture as the place where Christian faith and practice are set forth definitively. The beginning place for God's glory to be realized among men is when people recognize and obey Scripture.

Hearing the Word (Nehemiah 8:1-8)

In order to have its desired effect on people, Scripture must move from the page into human hearts. During the long years of Babylonian captivity the people of Israel had lost Jerusalem. No descendant of David reigned, no descendants of Aaron presided at sacrifices, no temple stood on the holy mount, no feast days were observed, and no wise men sat in the city gates. The one point for spiritual stability toward which the faithful migrated was the Word. During the days of good King Josiah, about 50 years before Nebuchadnezzar destroyed Jerusalem, a copy of the Law of Moses was found in the temple. Drawing on the Law, the king inaugurated a great reform (2 Chronicles 34:1ff.).

When the Jews went into Babylonian captivity, faithful men took copies of the Law with them. In captivity Jews began to assemble on the Sabbath, to read the Word and discuss its precepts. They came to call their assemblies "synagogues" or "gathering places." The first Jews to come home from Babylonian captivity were under the leadership of Jeshua and Zerubbabel shortly after Cyrus conquered the great city in 539 B.C. (Ezra 1:1ff.). In the midst of struggle to survive, the returnees began offering sacrifices and rebuilt the temple (5:1). Some 80 years passed before Ezra (7:6-8) and Nehemiah (Nehemiah 2:1, 5) arrived with additional settlers. Ezra was "the priest, the scribe, expert in the words of the commands of the LORD" (Ezra 7:11); Nehemiah was governor and builder of the city walls.

Ezra arrived in Jerusalem shortly before the beginning of the seventh month during which the Feast of Tabernacles and the Day of Atonement fell. He decreed that Jews from all the towns and villages of Judah assemble in the holy city. They came with celebration. The scribe had brought a copy of the Law. He would teach them. In the public square before the Water Gate they built a wooden platform. With city officials at his side, Ezra read from the Law. Many had forgotten the old Hebrew tongue in which Moses had written. Ezra read the Hebrew and his assistants translated so all could know what God wanted from His people. When the law began to be read, out of respect all the people stood (Nehemiah 8:5). Afterward they raised their hands in praise, then bowed their knees, "faces to the ground" (v. 6). During the eight days of Tabernacles, Ezra read daily from the Law (v. 18). People listened with reverence.

Obedience to God involves more than reading or memorizing scripture. The mere reading of the Law by Ezra made for no great flowering of godliness. If Christians are to obey God, they must know what He has said. God spoke authoritatively to Israel, and He speaks authoritatively to the church through

Scripture. Knowledge of the Word ignites love for the Lord. Love and knowledge together issue forth in godly lives. Wherever people want to please God, Ezra's reading of the Law to the Jews in the seventh month offers inspiration and hope.

Preaching the Word (Matthew 28:19-20; 1 Corinthians 9:16-18; 2 Timothy 4:2)

God's self-revelation through His Son has allowed Christians to build upon and to modify concepts and commandments given in the Old Law, but use of the written Word is a constant. However, the commitment of the Word to written form has not diminished the importance of oral proclamation. Among the last teaching Jesus gave His apostles was that living voices were to proclaim the gospel. Preachers were to have an indispensable role in the bringing of salvation to humankind. The apostles were to preach and to make disciples. They were to baptize the lost into Christ and to teach the saved all that Jesus had commanded.

Paul could not conceive of doing anything other than proclaiming the gospel. He had not chosen to earn his living as a preacher as another might choose to be an electrician. Preaching was not "against my will" (1 Corinthians 9:17) in the sense that he proclaimed the gospel as a tiresome duty but in the sense that Christ had chosen him. The initiative to preach had come from the Lord; his own ambitions were not the driving forces behind his preaching. Preachers of previous generations were likely to take offense if someone mentioned their salary. They quickly let folks know that they received support so they could preach. Christ was their Master; the Word their directive. Preaching was in their blood. Among the last exhortations Paul made to Timothy was that he not hesitate to preach in all circumstances. "In season, out of season," he said; the Word was to be the medium for convincing and rebuking (2 Timothy 4:2). Longsuffering and persistence were to attend his ministry. "Be ready to preach at the drop of a hat," an older preacher advised, "and if necessary drop the hat."

Doing the Word (James 1:21-25)

The measure of the impact the Word has on the world is not in its consistency of thought or the rhetorical skills of those who proclaim it. The measure of the gospel is in the impact it has on people's lives. Jesus ended the Sermon on the Mount with a parable about a wise and a foolish builder. The wise builder was the one who heard "these sayings" of Jesus and did them. The foolish builder heard but failed to do them (Matthew 7:24-27).

No work that men and women do is sufficient to merit salvation. The lost are saved by grace through faith (Ephesians 2:8) by the merits of Christ's blood. But one fails to read and understand Scripture if he fails to see that faith requires positive obedience. No one had more to say about grace than Paul, but he saw no inconsistency between salvation by grace through faith and God's demand that believers obey His commandments. Paul declared, "For not the hearers of the law are just in the sight of God, but the doers of the law" (Romans 2:13). James proclaimed the same: "But be doers of the word," he wrote, "and not hearers only, deceiving yourselves" (James 1:22).

Conclusion

Scripture is not a thing to be displayed and admired on a shelf. The written Word first and then the Word proclaimed are the lifeblood of the family of God. Moses told fathers to teach the precepts of the Law to their children. When they sat in their houses or walked on the way, they were to talk about the Law. The Law was to be on the door-posts of their houses, bound to their hands, dangling before their eyes (Deuteronomy 6:6-9). But with all of that, Moses said that God wanted the Law to be held in the hearts of His people (v. 6). Christians are to use the Word. It is the practical guide for conduct and the spiritual inspiration for godly living. Scripture is a tangible link between the invisible God whom Christians serve and the day-to-day world of sin and strife. In His Word, God has left His people a powerful component to guide them. Through the Word, believers influence and mold the world.

Questions

1. What is the source of authority to which the church may go for guidance in doctrine and morality?
2. About how many years passed after the first returnees came to Jerusalem before Ezra and Nehemiah arrived?
3. How is Ezra described?
4. What was the name of the gate in the wall of Jerusalem before which the people gathered to hear Ezra read from the Law?
5. What did all the people do when Ezra began reading from the Law? Why?
6. Why did some of those with Ezra help the people understand the Law as Ezra read from it?
7. What did Jesus tell His disciples to do after they had made disciples of all nations?
8. Why did Paul say that he preached Christ? What motivated him?
9. What passages in Romans and in James complement one another in the insistence that those who do the Word are just before God?
10. How does a man observing himself in a mirror illustrate the need for obedience?

Discussion Starters

1. What advantage does a written Word have over oral statements by prophets? Why has God given a written Word to the church?
2. Because Christians have the Word in written form, why are preachers necessary? Why not give the lost a copy of the New Testament and skip the preacher?
3. How is financial support for a preacher similar to and yet different from the pay others might receive from their occupations?
4. Why is it true that God demands obedience from the one who wants salvation and also true that salvation is by God's grace and on the basis of faith?

Using God's Word, Part 2

Psalm 119:9-16

9 How can a young man cleanse his way? By taking heed according to Your word.

10 With my whole heart I have sought You; Oh, let me not wander from Your commandments!

11 Your word I have hidden in my heart, That I might not sin against You.

12 Blessed are You, O LORD! Teach me Your statutes.

13 With my lips I have declared All the judgments of Your mouth.

14 I have rejoiced in the way of Your testimonies, As much as in all riches.

15 I will meditate on Your precepts, And contemplate Your ways.

16 I will delight myself in Your statutes; I will not forget Your word.

Romans 10:14-17

14 How then shall they call on Him in whom they have not believed? And how shall they believe in Him of whom they have not heard? And how shall they hear without a preacher?

15 And how shall they preach unless they are sent? As it is written: "How beautiful are the feet of those who preach the gospel of peace, Who bring glad tidings of good things!"

16 But they have not all obeyed the gospel. For Isaiah says, "LORD, who has believed our report?"

17 So then faith comes by hearing, and hearing by the word of God.

2 Peter 3:14-18

14 Therefore, beloved, looking forward to these things, be diligent to be found by Him in peace, without spot and blameless;

15 and consider that the longsuffering of our Lord is salvation – as also our beloved brother Paul, according to the wisdom given to him, has written to you,

16 as also in all his epistles, speaking in them of these things, in which are some things hard to understand, which untaught and unstable people twist to their own destruction, as they do also the rest of the Scriptures.

17 You therefore, beloved, since you know this beforehand, beware lest you also fall from your own steadfastness, being led away with the error of the wicked;

18 but grow in the grace and knowledge of our Lord and Savior Jesus Christ. To Him be the glory both now and forever. Amen.

Introduction

The Bible is for the guidance of God's people – the Old Testament for Israel and the New for the church. The body of believers knows how to worship, and they know how to treat one another because God speaks in Scripture. In addition to guidance for the community, God has also given the Word for the comfort, encouragement and edification of individual believers. Hardships, pain, persecution and death are a part of earthly existence. To varying degrees, everyone is plagued by self-doubts; everyone lives with the uncertainty of disease and death. The joys of life are undeniable, but only a crazy man lives blissfully unaware that life too has its pains. In His Word, God has left an anchor for the soul. He has given His people an island of stability in a storm-tossed world.

A person is forgiven, saved and justified when he (or she) comes up from the waters of baptism. He is free from sin, but Christ does not remove baptized believers from the sinful world where they live or from the sinful flesh that calls to them. Jesus has given His disciples the twofold mission of guiding the world to godliness and of resisting the fleshly desires that live in themselves. The good news is that He has not left them to their own devices. His indwelling Spirit (Galatians 4:6) is an intercessor who helps with "groanings which cannot be uttered" (Romans 8:26). For Paul, the working of the Spirit and the working of the Word of God were so closely intertwined that the two could not be spoken of separately. "The sword of the Spirit," he said, "is the Word of God" (Ephesians 6:17; Hebrews 4:12). When the tempter is strong, when faith is weak, when living hope degenerates into routine religion, Christians need the strength that God supplies. They open the Bible and allow God to speak to them; then they bow their heads and speak to Him in prayer.

Protection Against Sin (Psalm 119:9-16)

In order for the precepts and laws of God to protect him, the believer must realize that sin is finely worked into human hearts. A theme throughout Scripture is that rebellion against God is the essence of self-destruction. Inexperienced youth are particularly susceptible to the deceptive ways of sin. Restless energy combined with unrelenting desire are a dangerous combination. Sexual allurements are particularly difficult for young people. The voice of wisdom in Proverbs parodies the response of a young man to easy sexual conquest. "Immediately he went after her, as an ox goes to the slaughter, or as a fool to the correction of the stocks" (Proverbs 7:22). Then he added, "He did not know it would cost his life" (v. 23). The psalmist asked, "How can a young man cleanse his way?" God's revelation, he said, is a shield against sin. Cleansing comes for those who take "heed according to Your word" (Psalm 119:9).

God's Word is protection against sin insofar as it is absorbed into the character of a person. One's character is formed by the decisions that are imbedded in the mind until response to sin is automatic. The English word "character" has evolved from a Greek word that refers to an impression stamped onto an object, like a die that impresses a trademark on a plate of steel. The godly digest God's

Word so that its stories, precepts and commands become engraved into the slate of one's character. The Word was no emergency shelter for the psalmist. It was the stuff of his life, his meditation, his delight. "Your word I have hidden in my heart," he said, "that I might not sin against You" (Psalm 119:11).

Experience teaches that sinners seldom find God in the immediate aftermath of rebellion. An adulterer's tears are real when he learns that his wife is suing for divorce. If he opens his Bible to miscellaneous places and reads, he may find little to satisfy him. Had he made the Word a companion from his youth, it could have been a shield against sin. As an emergency measure or a resort of desperation, it may offer little protection. Repentance and defense against future temptations are the result for those who seek God with wholeness of heart.

Source of Faith (Romans 10:14-17)

When Jesus and three of His disciples came down from the Mount of Transfiguration, they found a man whose son was demon possessed with symptoms similar to an epileptic (Mark 9:14-29). The father displayed only an anemic faith, but Jesus demanded more. The father's response to the Lord likely strikes a responsive chord in many believers: "Lord, I believe; help my unbelief" (v. 24). For most Christians, faith is not a strong current flowing unimpeded throughout their lives. Many baptized believers have times when their faith is weak and they struggle to trust that God cares or even exists. Prayer and Christian fellowship are important sources of faith, but the inspired Word is without peer as a stronghold for the believer. Paul held out a place for hope when he appealed to the "Holy Scriptures, which are able to make you wise for salvation" (2 Timothy 3:15).

Faith needs to be strengthened in some and kindled in others. The kindling of faith was Paul's concern in Romans 10. The Word is a source of faith in its written form, but it is also a source when spoken by faithful messengers. The first acquaintance most people have with Jesus comes about because someone spoke the Word to them. The telling of the story of Abraham, Israel and the prophets leads to the appearance of John the Baptist and finally to Jesus Himself. The gospel is the story of Jesus' death and resurrection by the power of God. It is a wonderful story to hear and read. The Word is the source for faith (v. 17).

Means of Growth (2 Peter 3:14-18)

Plants and animals alike grow, reproduce and die. When Peter admonished his readers to "grow in the grace and knowledge of our Lord and Savior" (2 Peter 3:18), he knew that if they did not grow, their faith would die. Christians can find nourishment for growth in Scripture. In particular, Peter recommended that his readers study and grow from things Paul had written (vv. 15-16).

Peter's insistence that Christians grow in Christ followed teachings on the Lord's return. A consistent New Testament theme is that the world and human life are proceeding toward an end. When the Lord comes again, all will stand before Him in judgment. He will mete out justice, eternal life or eternal death, according to the deeds of men (2 Corinthians 5:10). The end of the age is not a subject for the idly curious. The return of the Lord is important because it demands that people properly align their values. One lives differently if he believes the Lord will return in judgment. Because the world is passing away, Peter admonishes, "Be diligent to be found by Him in peace, without spot and blameless" (2 Peter 3:14). If the Lord delays His coming, no one should interpret that to mean He has changed His mind. He delays because He is "longsuffering toward us, not willing that any should perish" (v. 9). His delay is opportunity for Christian growth.

Conclusion

Progress in any undertaking will depend to some degree on the resources one has available. A child whose parents can provide educational and other benefits is more likely to succeed than one born into poverty. A businessman who begins with adequate capital is more likely to prosper than one who begins with nothing. What is true in other areas of life is also true for personal and spiritual growth. Three of the most important resources for God's people are the fellowship of Christians, communion with God in prayer and worship, and the teachings of Scripture. God left a record of Himself as Creator, Lord, Redeemer, Judge and Savior in His Word. Scripture educates believers by molding their characters, shaping their values, and giving meaning and direction to their lives. Confronted with a problem, the Christian does not open the Bible to a random passage and expect to find answers. Rather, the Bible is a resource for those who have made its message a part of their lives before the emergency arrives.

Questions

1. In Paul's thinking, what is inseparably associated with guidance by the Spirit?
2. According to Scripture, what inevitably accompanies rebellion against God?
3. What stage of life did the psalmist specifically ask about (Psalm 119:9)?
4. Where does the psalmist say that he had treasured up God's word?
5. What did the father of the demon-possessed boy ask Jesus to do?
6. What did Paul say had to precede hearing and believing?
7. What did Paul mean by saying the feet of God's messengers were beautiful?
8. What were the bounds to which Paul said the sound of the gospel had gone?
9. Who did Peter say had written some things that were hard to understand?
10. In what did Peter tell his readers that they needed to grow?

Discussion Starters

1. What does a person need to do to have God's Word be a permanent influence for good in his life? Why does religion by emergency seldom work?
2. Why is the faith of most people sometimes stronger and sometimes weaker? How does God's Word nourish faith so that it remains consistently stronger?
3. What happens to a Christian who does not grow in grace and knowledge? Why is growth essential for Christian living?
4. What are some of the resources God provides Christians so that their faith grows in strength? Which resource is most important to you?

Prayer, Part 1

Matthew 6:9-13

9 In this manner, therefore, pray: Our Father in heaven, Hallowed be Your name.

10 Your kingdom come. Your will be done On earth as it is in heaven.

11 Give us this day our daily bread.

12 And forgive us our debts, As we forgive our debtors.

13 And do not lead us into temptation, But deliver us from the evil one. For Yours is the kingdom and the power and the glory forever. Amen.

Matthew 7:7-12

7 Ask, and it will be given to you; seek, and you will find; knock, and it will be opened to you.

8 For everyone who asks receives, and he who seeks finds, and to him who knocks it will be opened.

9 Or what man is there among you who, if his son asks for bread, will give him a stone?

10 Or if he asks for a fish, will he give him a serpent?

11 If you then, being evil, know how to give good gifts to your children, how much more will your Father who is in heaven give good things to those who ask Him!

12 Therefore, whatever you want men to do to you, do also to them, for this is the Law and the Prophets.

1 Timothy 2:1-8

1 Therefore I exhort first of all that supplications, prayers, intercessions, and giving of thanks be made for all men,

2 for kings and all who are in authority, that we may lead a quiet and peaceable life in all godliness and reverence.

3 For this is good and acceptable in the sight of God our Savior,

4 who desires all men to be saved and to come to the knowledge of the truth.

5 For there is one God and one Mediator between God and men, the Man Christ Jesus,

6 who gave Himself a ransom for all, to be testified in due time,

7 for which I was appointed a preacher and an apostle – I am speaking the truth in Christ and not lying – a teacher of the Gentiles in faith and truth.

8 I desire therefore that the men pray everywhere, lifting up holy hands, without wrath and doubting

Introduction

Following faith, prayer is the next step for the person who wants to know God. Prayer is essential to faith because faith is personal. The one God who spoke and brought a universe into being, who sustains the movements of galaxies and atoms – the God of mountain peaks and wheat fields – is aware of and cares about the little frustrations and the big life-and-death issues of the smallest of His children. When godly souls pray, God hears. Because He hears, the course of events turns in new and unexpected ways. Prayer is more than a psychological phenomenon. It matters that Christians pray.

Prayer is not automatic and natural – like breathing or affection, for example. One may pray well or poorly. An unnamed disciple came to Jesus at one point and asked, "Lord, teach us to pray, as John also taught his disciples" (Luke 11:1). The Lord seemed pleased that a man wanted to learn about prayer. Rather than lecturing on abstract theories, Jesus prayed with His disciples. By doing this, He taught them how to pray. Prayer includes confession and petition, but mature, faith-filled prayer goes further. The worshiper expresses adoration, praise and thanksgiving when he prays. The worshiper asks for earth-moving events but bows before the sovereign wisdom and omniscience of the Creator. The worshiper asks God; he does not demand. The worshiper petitions and then understands that God, in His benevolent wisdom, brings about events.

Prayer is conversational, but it entails no lively exchange of words. The disciple may pray aloud, but God listens in silence. Prayer requires the under-girding of faith. The one who prays "must believe that He is, and that He is a rewarder of those who diligently seek him" (Hebrews 11:6). In events and in time, the disciple experiences the response of God to his words. For those who pray well, who ask in faith and trust in His providential care, the promise of Jesus holds true: "If you abide in Me, and My words abide in you, you will ask what you desire, and it shall be done for you" (John 15:7). Doubt has no place in prayer, at least not in well-done prayer. To pray while doubting is to be "like a wave of the sea driven and tossed by the wind" (James 1:6).

Learning to Pray (Matthew 6:9-13)

What is popularly called "the Lord's Prayer" is not so much a prayer by Jesus on His personal behalf as it is a model for prayer that He gave to the disciples. John 17 might be labeled more properly "the Lord's Prayer." In Matthew, the model prayer comes embedded in the Sermon on the Mount (Matthew 5–7). It is in a context where Jesus contrasted the public display of religion with sincere faith proceeding from the heart. He told His disciples that when they gave alms (6:2) or prayed (v. 5) or fasted (v. 16), they were not to seek their own praise by parading what they did. He showed them how to pray by praying with them. A slightly shorter version of the model prayer appears in Luke in response to the request "Lord, teach us to pray" (Luke 11:1).

Jesus taught His disciples to address God as "Father." Among Christians it has become commonplace, nothing unexpected at all, to say "Father" when God is the subject. "Father" is a metaphor for God; that is, the word focuses on particular aspects of God's relationship to people. Perhaps the title neglects elements in God's being that are of equal importance – His being Judge, for example, or Creator. What has a petitioner said about God when he begins a prayer "Our Father in heaven"? For one who has been blessed with a loving and sympathetic earthly father, the term may conjure up a considerably different image than it does for one who has never had a male presence at home who hugged or supported him. Children are legion whose mental image of a father is a scowling presence they dread and fear. Some fathers arrive at the house with several beers under their belts and notice children only to curse them. As adults, can these children relate to what Jesus meant when He taught His disciples to pray, "Our Father in heaven"?

Figures of speech are always imperfect; "Father" for God is no exception. The ministry of Jesus fleshed out the qualities of an ideal father, which help us understand who God is. The Father in heaven says, "Come to Me, all you who labor" (Matthew 11:28). He is not just any Father; He is the Friend and Guide for His Son, Jesus Christ. He longs to be our Father as He is the Father of Jesus. "My Father loves Me," Jesus said (John 10:17). "And he who loves Me will be loved by My Father" (14:21). On the cross, Jesus turned to God with "Abba, Father" (Mark 14:36), and Paul taught us all to imitate our Lord with the same words (Romans 8:15). Jesus taught His disciples to think of God as a Father in heaven. This metaphor entails a way of understanding self and one's standing in the eternal order of things in ways ancient people could hardly have fathomed. In the Old Testament, God is rarely "Father." Idolaters sometimes latched on to the unpredictability of their gods and found in those qualities "fatherhood." When a pagan spoke of Father Zeus, he hardly had anything in mind that resembled Jesus' "Abba, Father" from the cross.

Using Prayer (Matthew 7:7-12)

After Jesus offered the disciples a model prayer in the Sermon of the Mount, He came back to the subject. Petition is not the only element of prayer; perhaps it ought not be the predominant element. The model prayer offered praise: "Hallowed be Your name" (Matthew 6:9). It appealed to God to work His might in human affairs. The Christian prays especially for the church. "Help us," he prays, "to rise above our sins, our small, self-seeking ways. May Your kingdom enlarge its borders. May Your will be realized among the saved and may Your church be a model for peace and goodwill on earth." The model prayer teaches believers to praise God, to confess sin, and to plead for forgiveness. Prayer is much more than petition, though it is petition.

Petition itself is a form of praise. When one turns to God for favor, he confesses that natural disasters, the violence of men, and the randomness of disease place a question mark over every step of life. Christians petition God for intervention. "Give us this day our daily bread," Jesus taught His disciples to pray (Matthew 6:11). "Ask, and it will be given to you," He said later in the same sermon (7:7). Because God is almighty, He is able to give. When human efforts are to no avail, He stands above disease, accident and death. Nothing is impossible for Him (Luke 1:37).

When Jesus taught His followers to ask, seek and knock (Matthew 7:7-8), He implied that God gives more abundantly to those who know Him and who talk with Him. The petitioner must have faith and persistence to ask. Failing to ask means no blessing. Ideally, the petitioner will ask like a child whose life is in continual communication with his father. The petitioner asks because it is natural to ask; he asks with awareness that a loving father wants good things for him. The message in Matthew 6:9-13 and 7:7-12 is that the Creator, who rules in the affairs of nature and men, is a Father to His people. All the love, patience and care an ideal father shows his children are embodied in God.

Sharing Our Prayers (1 Timothy 2:1-8)

Prayer includes petition for self, but everything Jesus taught His people by word and example demands that Christians seek God's blessings for all men. Paul admonished Timothy to direct the church to lift up holy hands in prayer and petition for others. In particular, he urged his child in the faith to pray for those with positions high in government. Prayer that governments do their work well hardly implies approval of all they do.

Roman governors, proconsuls and emperors were not godly men, but the apostle knew that orderly government was an ally of God's people. Even a rule like that offered by Rome was preferable to anarchy. Christians pray that those who bear the load of secular power might come to know God or at least that they might grant Christians the clemency to follow God's ways without persecution. Peaceful, stable governments are often a precondition for the winning of lost souls to Christ. The prayer of Christians is that men and women everywhere will be able to earn a living and support their families. Peace and order are friends of the kingdom of God because Christians are a peaceful and orderly people, a blessing for this world.

Conclusion

In the Bible, prayer is a command (cf. 1 Thessalonians 5:17). At the same time, prayer is more than a command. Prayer is a privilege and a blessing. Through prayer, God interacts with His people. He hears their praise, accepts their thanksgiving, and responds to their pleas. Because Christians pray, God steps into time and changes the course of history. The child who might have died without prayer lives because someone prayed. Still, God's response to prayer is not automatic. He does not respond every time a lever is pulled. Because men do not see as God sees, divine response to prayer can be confusing. Job was confused and angry because he could not understand why God had allowed him to be overcome with pain. Many others like Job have stumbled in faith when prayers seemed to go unanswered. Prayer is faith because in prayer the believer comes to God knowing that He sees beyond what we can see. The believer asks and trusts the Lord to answer in the light of His omniscience.

Questions

1. Who did an unnamed disciple of Jesus say had taught his disciples how to pray?
2. To what family member are Christians to liken God when they address Him in prayer?
3. What is the kingdom for which Jesus told His disciples to pray?
4. In what context did Jesus share with His disciples the model prayer?
5. What, other than petition, does the model prayer teach Christians to do in prayer?
6. How did Jesus say that God will respond to the disciple who prays?
7. What illustration did Jesus use to help His disciples understand the way God responds to prayer?
8. What summary statement did Jesus offer for the substance of what God taught through the Law and the Prophets?
9. For whom did Paul tell Timothy that Christians ought especially to pray?
10. Why should Christians pray on behalf of family, friends, fellow Christians and all men?

Discussion Starters

1. How are faith and prayer closely related? Why is faith a prerequisite for prayer that is pleasing to God?
2. How is a Christian to maintain faith in God's hearing and answering prayers when the things he prays for often do not come about?
3. Using the model prayer as a guide, what are some of the things a believer ought to do in prayer?
4. In what way is prayer both a command and a privilege? Is God satisfied with those who pray only out a sense of duty? Explain.

Prayer, Part 2

Matthew 26:36-46

36 Then Jesus came with them to a place called Gethsemane, and said to the disciples, "Sit here while I go and pray over there."

37 And He took with Him Peter and the two sons of Zebedee, and He began to be sorrowful and deeply distressed.

38 Then He said to them, "My soul is exceedingly sorrowful, even to death. Stay here and watch with Me."

39 He went a little farther and fell on His face, and prayed, saying, "O My Father, if it is possible, let this cup pass from Me; nevertheless, not as I will, but as You will."

40 Then He came to the disciples and found them sleeping, and said to Peter, "What! Could you not watch with Me one hour?

41 "Watch and pray, lest you enter into temptation. The spirit indeed is willing, but the flesh is weak."

42 Again, a second time, He went away and prayed, saying, "O My Father, if this cup cannot pass away from Me unless I drink it, Your will be done."

43 And He came and found them asleep again, for their eyes were heavy.

44 So He left them, went away again, and prayed the third time, saying the same words.

45 Then He came to His disciples and said to them, "Are you still sleeping and resting? Behold, the hour is at hand, and the Son of Man is being betrayed into the hands of sinners.

46 "Rise, let us be going. See, My betrayer is at hand."

Ephesians 6:17-20

17 And take the helmet of salvation, and the sword of the Spirit, which is the word of God;

18 praying always with all prayer and supplication in the Spirit, being watchful to this end with all perseverance and supplication for all the saints –

19 and for me, that utterance may be given to me, that I may open my mouth boldly to make known the mystery of the gospel,

20 for which I am an ambassador in chains; that in it I may speak boldly, as I ought to speak.

1 Peter 3:8-12

8 Finally, all of you be of one mind, having compassion for one another; love as brothers, be tenderhearted, be courteous;

9 not returning evil for evil or reviling for reviling, but on the contrary blessing, knowing that you were called to this, that you may inherit a blessing.

10 For "He who would love life And see good days, Let him refrain his tongue from evil, And his lips from speaking deceit.

11 "Let him turn away from evil and do good; Let him seek peace and pursue it.

12 "For the eyes of the LORD are on the righteous, And His ears are open to their prayers; But the face of the LORD is against those who do evil."

Introduction

In prayer, people approach God in their brokenness. "All have sinned and fall short of the glory of God," Paul wrote (Romans 3:23). On top of sin is piled ignorance, helplessness and uncertainty. Status and power conveyed by human conventions are altogether out of place when a man or woman talks with God in prayer. Jesus told a parable about a group of people who "trusted in themselves that they were righteous, and despised others" (Luke 18:9). One of them stood in the temple and "prayed thus with himself" (v. 11). He thanked God that he was head and shoulders above the sinners who surrounded him. Jesus concluded the parable by saying, "Everyone who exalts himself will be humbled" (v. 14). God hears prayers offered from contrite hearts. Bowed heads and awareness of sin befit those who pray.

Before prayer is petition, thanksgiving or confession, it is worship. Ideally, people will learn to pray in such a way that their prayers bring glory to God. For that to be possible, they must let Him teach them how to pray. Those who equate prayer with an emotional cleansing or a psychological state make people the subject of prayer. The worth of prayer is measured by the honor it brings to God. The psalms in the Old Testament are more than songs for special occasions. They are also prayers, meditations, confessions, laments, petitions and worship. Both in the psalms and in the prayers of the New Testament, worshipers learn about the content and manner of prayer. Both are important. Prayer is not an appendage to a life of faith; prayer is the heart and soul of such a life. Faith without prayer is like a heart without a beat or a song without a melody.

Fervent Prayer (Matthew 26:36-46)

Depending on the circumstances, the emotional intensity of prayer will vary. At the end of a routine day, a Christian may read from the Bible and bow his head for a moment of thanksgiving. Prayer may bring healing and calmness to a person who is struggling with anxiety about a marriage or a child trying to find his or her place in the world. The worth of prayer is not measured by wringing hands and emotional fervor, though prayer is for life's intense struggles. A young man with a family who counts on him may lose his job.

A young wife may discover that her husband wants a divorce. The death of a child or parent, disease and helplessness – in countless ways people discover and deal with life's uncertainties. During periods of emotional turmoil, God offers Himself through prayer as a resource for coping and healing.

How Jesus was divine and human at the same time is a mystery that eludes finite minds; however, we may say with confidence that, in His flesh, Jesus experienced the same kinds of emotions that are common to the human family. "Jesus wept" when His friend Lazarus died (John 11:35). When teaching about the kingdom of God and healing the sick attracted conniving men whose sole purpose was to catch Him in some technical glitch, Jesus became angry (Mark 3:5). Being "in all points tempted as we are" (Hebrews 4:15) surely means that Jesus experienced the full range of human emotions. With the disciples shortly before He was crucified, Jesus faced an ordeal of such intensity that He was goaded to fervent prayer of a sort surpassing our understanding.

After meeting with His disciples to observe Passover the night before He was crucified, the company walked eastward from the temple mount. They crossed the Kidron Valley and ascended partway up the slope of the Mount of Olives. In a garden called Gethsemane, meaning "olive press," the Lord paused to pray. The weight of the horrible ordeal, torture, unbearable pain, humiliation and death bore on Him. In addition to the physical ordeal in front of Him, Jesus was aware that He would bear in His sinless self the sins of humankind. The burden of the cross quickly escapes our ability to conceive of it. He and an inner circle of three disciples advanced a little distance from the others. In short order, the intensity of His turmoil surfaced. Jesus confided with them, "My soul is exceedingly sorrowful, even to death" (Matthew 26:38). He asked them to wait and to pray with Him while He went a little farther to pray alone.

The intensity and fervor of Jesus' prayer in Gethsemane are unmatched. The ordeal demonstrates to His followers that the Lord experienced the kind of sorrows they face. No loss is so deep, no pain, so intense, that the Lord cannot identify. The prayer of Jesus in the garden gives substance to Peter's promise that the Lord ever cares about what happens in the lives of His people (1 Peter 5:7).

Continual Prayer (Ephesians 6:17-20)

Politicians sometimes land in hot water because a telephone line or a microphone near them was open when they thought it was turned off. Most of us say words and think thoughts that we had rather others not know. It is sobering to realize that the line between our minds and God is always open. Jesus warned, "For there is nothing hidden which will not be revealed, nor has anything been kept secret but that it should come to light" (Mark 4:22). The blessing of being able to talk with God at will, whenever we wish, is accompanied with the responsibility to marshal our hearts and minds in the way of righteousness.

The certainty that God knows our inmost ways does not mean that prayer is constant. In order to pray, one must consciously address the Father. When

Paul admonished Ephesian Christians to be "praying always with all prayer and supplication" (Ephesians 6:18), he was urging them to adopt a prayerful mindset. At any time of the day or night, God is available. He will listen to our confessions of sin, our intercession for loved ones, and our petitions for relief from distress. Ought Christians to build prayer into a daily routine by setting aside certain times for prayer? The Law of Moses specified no daily regimen of prayer, but by the time of Jesus, the Jews had developed traditions about times of prayer. Peter and John went to the temple "at the hour of prayer" (Acts 3:1).

In the interest of continual prayer, Christians do well to set aside times – perhaps at the beginning of day, before meals, or at the end of the day when they regularly read from the Bible and meditate on its message. Those who set aside a time for family worship testify to its benefit. All these matters fall under the general heading of "Christian liberty." Regimented times when all Christians drop what they are doing, spread prayer shawls, and pray together hardly fall within the scope of Paul's plea for continual prayer. However, Christians who fail to set aside certain times in the day for prayer often find that they forget. Some combination of set times for prayer and a constant awareness of God and spontaneously talking with Him has served devout Christians well.

God-Centered Prayer (1 Peter 3:8-12)

Essential as prayer is to Christian living, false notions about prayer can and do compromise the church in the eyes of the world. Prayer is no substitute for godly, obedient living. A person who abuses those around him – who lies, steals and gives himself over to worldly passions – does not make everything all right with occasional prayers – at least not if he continues in that way of life. In 1 Peter 3:12, Peter cited Psalm 34:15, which says, "The eyes of the LORD are on the righteous, and His ears are open to their cry" (1 Peter 3:12). One should notice that righteous living has something to do with the way God hears. Before Peter cited the Psalm, he reminded his readers that they were to have compassion for one another, to love as brothers, and to be tenderhearted and courteous (v. 8). God-centered prayer follows a God-oriented life.

God-centered prayer cannot be considered in the absence of God-centered repentance. Sin is no barrier to approaching God as long as the sinner finds in himself the "godly sorrow" that leads to repentance (2 Corinthians 7:10). As for the sinner who has no serious intent to change his life, a blind man healed by Jesus appears to have spoken the truth: "Now we know that God does not hear sinners; but if anyone is a worshiper of God and does His will, He hears him" (John 9:31).

Conclusion

For the one who is lost in sin and who wants his life to be right with God, the first step is repentance. When the Jews who heard Peter on Pentecost wanted to know what to do to be saved, Peter did not tell them to drop to their knees and offer some version of the "sinner's prayer." He told them to repent and be baptized (Acts 2:38). God is not honored and no one can be saved unless he or she confesses sin and believes that Jesus Christ is God's Son; no prayer and no confession leads to the forgiveness of sins in the absence of repentance and baptism. Lives must be changed. John the Baptist refused to allow those who came to hear him to lean on Abraham or Moses. He demanded that they repent (Matthew 3:2). Prayer, when rightly done, is worship, but in order to be worship, prayer must follow the path of obedience to the commandments of God.

Questions

1. With what kind of disposition ought we approach God in prayer?
2. Why are people unworthy to approach God in prayer?
3. In which parable of Jesus did He tell about a man who stood and prayed to himself?
4. Name the garden where Jesus prayed the night before He was crucified.
5. Which three of His disciples were with Jesus as He prayed in the garden?
6. What did the disciples do while Jesus prayed?
7. In what context did Paul admonish the Ephesian believers to pray at all times?
8. What did Paul request Ephesian Christians to pray for on his behalf?
9. What kind of life did Peter tell Christians to live, which would lead to God being open to their prayers?
10. What scripture did Peter cite in his letter?

Discussion Starters

1. Why is emotional intensity alone poor evidence that one has prayed in such a way to please God?
2. How is the emotional intensity of Jesus' prayer in the garden a comfort to Christians who face trying times in their lives?
3. What can Christians do to ensure that prayer is built into the daily routine of their lives?
4. Why is a repentant frame of mind necessary if one is to please God through prayer?

The Lord's Supper, Part 1

Isaiah 53:3-6

3 He is despised and rejected by men, A Man of sorrows and acquainted with grief. And we hid, as it were, our faces from Him; He was despised, and we did not esteem Him.

4 Surely He has borne our griefs And carried our sorrows; Yet we esteemed Him stricken, Smitten by God, and afflicted.

5 But He was wounded for our transgressions, He was bruised for our iniquities; The chastisement for our peace was upon Him, And by His stripes we are healed.

6 All we like sheep have gone astray; We have turned, every one, to his own way; And the LORD has laid on Him the iniquity of us all.

Matthew 26:26-30

26 And as they were eating, Jesus took bread, blessed and broke it, and gave it to the disciples and said, "Take, eat; this is My body."

27 Then He took the cup, and gave thanks, and gave it to them, saying, "Drink from it, all of you.

28 "For this is My blood of the new covenant, which is shed for many for the remission of sins.

29 "But I say to you, I will not drink of this fruit of the vine from now on until that day when I drink it new with you in My Father's kingdom."

30 And when they had sung a hymn, they went out to the Mount of Olives.

1 Peter 1:17-21

17 And if you call on the Father, who without partiality judges according to each one's work, conduct yourselves throughout the time of your stay here in fear;

18 knowing that you were not redeemed with corruptible things, like silver or gold, from your aimless conduct received by tradition from your fathers,

19 but with the precious blood of Christ, as of a lamb without blemish and without spot.

20 He indeed was foreordained before the foundation of the world, but was manifest in these last times for you

21 who through Him believe in God, who raised Him from the dead and gave Him glory, so that your faith and hope are in God.

Introduction

When the church assembles on the first day of the week, Christians break bread and take of the cup. They observe the Lord's Supper. In an important way, the Lord's Supper is different from other things Christians do when they assemble for worship. Christians pray together, but believers also pray in private. They enter into their rooms and talk to the Lord in secret (Matthew 6:6). The assembly sings, but individuals may lift up voices in song wherever they are, anytime they choose. Studying and giving are for the church in assembly, but one ought to study Scripture and give individually. In contrast to all these, the Lord's Supper is essentially a community event. The Lord's Supper is an event for the first day of the week, the Lord's Day. It is an observance for the gathered church.

The Lord's Supper is no more or less important than any other act of worship offered by the assembled church. Believers sometimes say, "The Lord's Supper is the most important part of Christian worship," but the Bible makes no such claim. The church in the New Testament assembled to break bread on the first day of the week (Acts 20:7), but the same verse says that Paul preached to the assembly until midnight. Christians in the New Testament also assembled to sing and to pray. Scripture authorizes no elevation of one act of worship over another. All the church does in worship when it assembles is for God's glory.

Elevating the Lord's Supper to the most important part of worship may betray a misunderstanding of the purpose of assembly on the Lord's Day. On the supposition that the Lord's Supper is more important than other act of worship, Christians sometimes sit on the back pew and slip out the door after they have taken the Lord's Supper. When unavoidable hindrances keep a Christian from the assembly, missing the Lord's Supper is no more important than missing the singing or the praying. Nowhere does the Bible suggest that the Lord's Supper ought to be weighed against other acts of Christian worship and prioritized. Collective worship is God's way for the church to express its adoration and thanksgiving (Acts 2:42; Ephesians 5:19-20). All the church does to worship needs to be elevated to the same level of importance as the Lord's Supper.

The Sacrifice (Isaiah 53:3-6)

The distinctive place of the Lord's Supper follows from the way it focuses the attention of the church on the central event of Christian redemption: the death of Christ on the cross (1 Corinthians 15:3). The Lord's Supper is about the vicarious atonement of Christ. The phrase "vicarious atonement" is not in the Bible. Atonement itself is largely an Old Testament word, but the concept of vicarious atonement is foundational to New Testament doctrine. To say that Christ suffered vicariously means that His suffering and death were not for His own guilt. On the cross, He suffered for the sins of humankind (John 3:16). To say that He atoned for human sin means that His suffering and death broke down barriers between God and men. He reconciled lost humanity to God by taking the guilt for men's sins on Himself. Peter said it like this: "For Christ also suffered once for sins, the just for the unjust, that He might bring us to God" (1 Peter 3:18).

Perhaps the prophet Isaiah gave the world the most eloquent expression of the vicarious atonement of Christ some 700 years before the Lord's birth. That God planned to send an extraordinary Messenger to His chosen people runs deeply in the Old Testament. Through Abraham's seed, all nations of the earth were to be blessed (Genesis 12:3; Galatians 3:8). God promised to send a prophet like Moses (Deuteronomy 18:18; Acts 3:22). The offspring of David would reign forever (2 Samuel 7:12-13; Acts 13:23). A priest like Melchizedek would serve in righteousness (Psalm 110:4; Hebrews 7:11). Israel looked for one who would be prophet, priest and king, but until Isaiah came, the picture was partial. The coming One, Isaiah said, was also to be a suffering servant, acquainted with grief, despised, carrying our sorrows (Isaiah 53:3-4).

From the earliest days of the church, some have been unable to reconcile the reign of Christ as King with His suffering on the cross. The contemporaries of Jesus wanted to plant Him on a throne (John 6:15). Pilate mocked the Jews with the sign he placed above the cross: "THIS IS JESUS THE KING OF THE JEWS" (Matthew 27:37). The Ethiopian eunuch puzzled over the words of Isaiah (Acts 8:32-33). When Paul preached that Jesus of Nazareth was the promised Christ, he had two burdens. First, he had to establish that it was necessary for the Christ to suffer. Isaiah 53 supplemented by Psalm 22 provided the evidence. Second, he demonstrated that Jesus was the Christ (Acts 17:3). Jesus is King, Prophet and Priest, but it was His suffering that qualified Him for all three functions. It is His suffering in our place, His vicarious suffering, that is the plea of the redeemed; salvation has appeared among men, not on the basis of human merit but, by God's grace. The Lord's Supper is the week by week proclamation and confession by the church that Jesus was our suffering Savior.

The Remembrance (Matthew 26:26-30)

Four times the New Testament tells the story of the final observance of the Passover by Jesus in company with His disciples (Matthew 26:26-30; Mark 14:22-26; Luke 22:14-20; 1 Corinthians 11:23-29). The records differ in minor ways. In Luke, it was only after the breaking of the bread that Jesus said, "Do this in remembrance of Me" (22:19). In 1 Corinthians, He repeated the phrase after the bread and the cup (11:24-25). Remembrance is inherent in all four accounts.

Remembrance is essential for the spiritual, emotional and physical well-being of the human family. Monuments recall events and people that have shaped history. Governments maintain archives of documents that make us the people we are. It is hardly a surprise when people of faith remember pivotal events that define them. The Israelites set up monuments in their land to commemorate God's work among them (Joshua 4:7). Feast days called to mind God's deliverance of Israel from Egypt (Exodus 12:14), the wandering in the wilderness, and the inheritance of Canaan. The Lord's Supper stirs the minds of God's people so that they may confess their mutual faith and remember together the love that compelled God to send His Son to die for human sin. The Lord's Day is the weekly reminder that God raised Jesus from the dead. The Lord's Supper is the weekly reminder that Christ's death brought reconciliation with God, the gift of God's love (2 Corinthians 5:21).

The Redemption (1 Peter 1:17-21)

The Lord's Supper is about redemption. The sinless death of Jesus on the cross brought about a fundamental change in the relationship between God and humankind. When Adam and Eve ate the fruit, they set the tone for all subsequent history. Following their example, all their descendants have figuratively eaten the fruit (Romans 5:12); they have all sinned. "There is none righteous, no, not one," Paul wrote (3:10). Sin drove a wedge between God and His creation; enmity was the result. By means of His death, Jesus took away the enmity (Ephesians 2:14-16). He bought a people to wear His name with the purchase price of His blood. His purchased people share as siblings in the inheritance of life.

When the assembled church breaks bread and drinks of the cup together, they share faith that the Son of God has redeemed them from sin. The purchase price for the redemption of the church collectively and for Christians individually was of greater value than the gold that came from the tomb of Pharaoh Tutankhamun or, for that matter, all the wealth in the treasure stores of nations ancient and modern. Peter said the redemption price for the souls of men was "the precious blood of Christ, as of a lamb without blemish and without spot" (1 Peter 1:19). The symbolism of the Lord's Supper is interwoven intricately into the community life of the church. The brotherhood of believers – their collective hope, mutual love and support – grow out of their sharing in the table of faith.

Conclusion

The Law taught Israel to observe three great feasts: Passover, Pentecost and the Feast of Tabernacles (cf. Leviticus 23). Each commemorated foundational events in God's fashioning the nation into the people He wanted them to be. In the New Testament too, God has given three memorial events. (1) After a sinner has believed that Jesus is the Christ, he is to repent of his sins, publicly confess Jesus, and be baptized into Christ for the remission of sins (Acts 2:38). By being buried with Christ in baptism, one observes a memorial of the death, burial and resurrection of Jesus (Romans 6:4). (2) Christians assemble in local churches week by week. The day is a memorial of the tomb the disciples found to be empty on the third day. (3) When Christians assemble, they break a common bread and drink a common cup. The Lord's Supper is a memorial of the crucifixion of Christ. By His suffering, Jesus paid the price for sin. Through the memorials of baptism, assembly on the Lord's Day, and the Lord's Supper, Christians draw strength to live holy, blameless lives throughout the time of their sojourn on earth (1 Peter 1:17).

Questions

1. What makes the Lord's supper unique as compared to the other acts of worship?
2. How did Isaiah say men would receive the suffering Servant of God?
3. Who bore the chastisement that was destined for sinners?
4. How did God's Servant bear the griefs and sorrows of men and women?
5. How many times in the New Testament was the story told of how Jesus instituted the Lord's Supper? Where are they?
6. What phrase common to Luke and Paul gives voice to an important purpose for observing the Lord's Supper?
7. Why did Jesus say His blood shed?
8. When did Jesus say He would drink the cup new with the disciples?
9. How did Peter say God will judge the works of each?
10. What did Jesus give that was more precious than silver or gold?

Discussion Starters

1. Is the Lord's Supper the most important thing Christians do when they assemble for worship? Why do some people say that it is? Explain your personal viewpoint.
2. Drawing on Old Testament teaching, what did Jews of the New Testament think the Christ was to be and do? How does that perception differ from what He was and did?
3. What does the phrase "vicarious atonement" mean? Is it a biblical phrase? Why is the phrase useful for Christians?
4. What three memorials did God give to believers to call to their minds the reason for their salvation? Why are physical things important for remembrance?

The Lord's Supper, Part 2

1 Corinthians 10:14-22

14 Therefore, my beloved, flee from idolatry.

15 I speak as to wise men; judge for yourselves what I say.

16 The cup of blessing which we bless, is it not the communion of the blood of Christ? The bread which we break, is it not the communion of the body of Christ?

17 For we, though many, are one bread and one body; for we all partake of that one bread.

18 Observe Israel after the flesh: Are not those who eat of the sacrifices partakers of the altar?

19 What am I saying then? That an idol is anything, or what is offered to idols is anything?

20 Rather, that the things which the Gentiles sacrifice they sacrifice to demons and not to God, and I do not want you to have fellowship with demons.

21 You cannot drink the cup of the Lord and the cup of demons; you cannot partake of the Lord's table and of the table of demons.

22 Or do we provoke the Lord to jealousy? Are we stronger than He?

1 Corinthians 11:23-30

23 For I received from the Lord that which I also delivered to you: that the Lord Jesus on the same night in which He was betrayed took bread;

24 and when He had given thanks, He broke it and said, "Take, eat; this is My body which is broken for you; do this in remembrance of Me."

25 In the same manner He also took the cup after supper, saying, "This cup is the new covenant in My blood. This do, as often as you drink it, in remembrance of Me."

26 For as often as you eat this bread and drink this cup, you proclaim the Lord's death till He comes.

27 Therefore whoever eats this bread or drinks this cup of the Lord in an unworthy manner will be guilty of the body and blood of the Lord.

28 But let a man examine himself, and so let him eat of the bread and drink of the cup.

29 For he who eats and drinks in an unworthy manner eats and drinks judgment to himself, not discerning the Lord's body.

30 For this reason many are weak and sick among you, and many sleep.

Introduction

The Lord's Supper is a time for remembrance. Ideally it is a sacred time when believers allow their minds to go back 2,000 years to the cross where the innocent Son of God died for their guilt. With the distractions of the world crowding in, remembrance is sometimes difficult. A mother struggles with a child. A fellow two pews over clips his fingernails. Closer by, two 10-year-old girls try to stifle giggles. For those who can shut out distractions, a bowed head and closed eyes help concentration, but even under the best of circumstances, minds wander.

Focusing the mind on the event that is central to Christian faith calls for an effort, but remembrance is only part of what the Lord's Supper is about. When a believer is baptized into Christ or when he or she breaks the bread, he confesses faith by a visual, bodily act. The Lord's Supper testifies to a living faith. Not only has Christ died for sins, God has raised Him from the dead. From His seat at the right hand of God, Jesus looks down on the lives of His people. He sees their struggles and hears their cries. The Lord's Supper proclaims the church's confidence that the same Lord who died on the cross is going to come again. Those who pierced Him (Revelation 1:7), those who have ignored Him, those who used His name as a curse – all will stand before Him to be judged. The world is purposeful. It is going somewhere.

The Lord's Supper is past, present and future. In the bread and cup, Christians remember a past event. More than 2,000 years have passed since the sky darkened and the graves were opened (Matthew 27:45, 52), but His people still remember the day, the wounded face and the flowing blood. The Lord's Supper is about the present. Somewhere out in the Pacific, after every seventh day, a new week begins. As the first day of the week dawns, worshipers go to places of assembly. Some walk, some ride, and some are carried. Many are poor; education is meager. A few are wealthy and learned, but wealth and learning by themselves count nothing in this company. In a thousand languages, they speak of His death; they break the bread and share the cup. They are united in a great universal confession that He is the Christ. He died for our sins. He is coming again. The Lord's Supper is about the living, dynamic faith of the church.

Communion (1 Corinthians 10:14-22)

The Greek word the New King James Version translated "the communion" in 1 Corinthians 10:16 is rendered "a sharing in" by the New American Standard Bible. The Greek word calls to mind common participation in an event. To "commune" is to share in or to communicate. Paul reminded his readers that when idolaters gathered to share in food that had been sacrificed to one of their gods, they all shared in the idolatry. He argued that the same was true when the people of Israel brought sacrifices to the temple in Jerusalem. Worshipers feasted on the sacrificial offerings, and in the eating all shared in the worship offered to God. To share in the table of idols was shameful; to share in the table of the Lord was a privilege. Paul urged Christians to "flee from idolatry" (v. 14). The worship of pagan gods was demon-inspired. To recent converts tempted to compromise with paganism, the apostle wrote, "You cannot drink the cup of the Lord and the cup of demons; you cannot partake of the Lord's table and of the table of demons" (v. 21).

Paul's reasoning has profound implications for Christians when they partake of the Lord's Supper. Breaking the bread and drinking the cup are remembrance, but they are more. They are also sharing. Christians share with one another in the bread and the cup, and collectively, they share with the Lord. What does the sharing entail? What does it mean? In the bread and the cup, for a few minutes on the Lord's Day, barriers between people break down. The young couple who believe that the old gentleman who sits behind them is too narrow-minded, the middle-aged businessman who has trouble getting his mind off a risky move he has to make at work, a single mom who dreads an upcoming visit to a social worker to qualify for food stamps – they and scores of others are caught up in oneness as they break bread and drink the cup. Jesus died for them all. The Lord's Supper is communion; it is sharing.

As Christians share in the faith of one another, they also share in Christ. Jesus said that the cup was "the new covenant in My blood" (1 Corinthians 11:25). As God acts through the obedience of a believer when he is baptized and takes away sin (Acts 22:16), so God acts through the Lord's Supper to empower the believer in the living of the new covenant. God and believers interact with one another, i.e., they commune when believers break the bread and drink the cup. The Lord's Supper is about a past event, but it is also about an ongoing realization of the kingdom of God among men.

Proclamation (1 Corinthians 11:23-26)

Confession, testimony and proclamation are interrelated. After Peter announced the terms of salvation on Pentecost, "With many other words he testified" (Acts 2:40). Paul wanted to finish the race God had set before him and "to testify to the gospel of the grace of God" (20:24). The nuance of testimony and confession is not quite the same as proclamation, but the thought is similar. John wrote, "Whoever confesses that Jesus is the Son of God, God abides in him, and he in God" (1 John 4:15). Paul added, "If you confess with your mouth the Lord Jesus and believe in your heart that God has raised Him from the dead, you will be saved" (Romans 10:9).

Proclamation may be with words spoken by the mouth, but one may symbolically proclaim the Lordship of Christ by how he lives. Paul said that when Christians break the bread of the Lord's Supper they make a proclamation. They proclaim that He died on the cross in order to atone for sins. They proclaim that God declared Him to be His Son by raising Him from the dead. They proclaim that He reigns over the kingdom of heaven from God's right hand (Hebrews 8:1). He listens to the cries of His people; He answers their prayers. Jesus is no passive observer of the human scene. His hand is in every heartbeat. The Lord's Supper, in addition to remembrance and communion, is the Christian's proclamation that Jesus will come a second time (Hebrews

173

9:28; 1 Thessalonians 4:16). The Lord's Supper is a proclamation that the world is not limping along to fizzle out. Its end will not be internal collapse from human decadence nor from natural disaster. The people of this planet are heading toward the time when Jesus Christ will cause all to stand before Him. Humankind will be divided like a shepherd separates sheep from goats (Matthew 25:32), and each person will "receive the things done in the body" (2 Corinthians 5:10). The Lord's Supper is proclamation.

Self-Examination (1 Corinthians 11:27-30)

When Paul wrote to the Corinthians about the Lord's Supper it was in the context of a rebuke for divisive behavior (1 Corinthians 11:18). The Lord's Supper ought to be an event that proclaims the unity of a congregation. The Corinthians had observed it with practices that drove wedges between Christians. Paul's brief remarks leave us as third party readers a little unclear about what they were doing, but this much is certain: The Lord's Supper was being combined with an ordinary meal and those who had more were separating themselves from those who had less. The result had been bitterness and confusion in the church.

In the context of division, Paul revisited the time when Jesus had instituted the Supper. After that he said, "Therefore whoever eats this bread or drinks this cup of the Lord in an unworthy manner will be guilty of the body and blood of the Lord" (1 Corinthians 11:27). Corinthian Christians were taking the Lord's Supper in an "unworthy manner" because they were making distinctions and causing divisions in the body of Christ, not because their minds wandered while the Supper was being observed. The apostle was making no reference to idolatry or immorality. The unworthy manner at issue was the divisions going on in the process of taking the Lord's Supper. The very worship the Lord had intended to proclaim the unity of the body, Corinthians were using to promote factions. Such was unworthy of Christians. Christians at Corinth were to examine themselves as they considered the consequences of their behavior for the body. Those who failed to consider the Lord's body, that is, His church, were eating and drinking condemnation on themselves by their behavior.

Conclusion

Self-examination in a general sense is always appropriate for believers. It is a first step in repentance and reformed lives. While taking the Lord's Supper, it is in order for believers to reflect on their sins, to repent and to determine to live godly lives. Because the Lord's Supper is remembrance, one does well to reflect on the crucified body of the Lord when he breaks bread and drinks the cup, but no one takes the Lord's Supper in a "worthy manner" in an absolute sense. No one is free from sin; no one can guarantee the purity of his thoughts. The "unworthy manner" Paul mentioned in 1 Corinthians 11:27 has to do with causing division in the church by observing the Lord's Supper in a divisive way. The "body" the Corinthians were failing to discern was not the literal body of Christ on the cross but Christ's body, the church (10:17; 12:12).

Questions

1. What did Paul mean when he said that the Lord's Supper was communion?
2. What pagan practice did Paul urge believers to flee?
3. With what did Christians commune when they shared in the "cup of blessing" (1 Corinthians 10:16)?
4. With what do believers commune when they break the bread?
5. With what did Christians have fellowship when they participated in idolatry?
6. What did Paul say that he had received from the Lord and delivered to the Corinthians?
7. What did Jesus say after He had given thanks and broken the bread?
8. How long are Christians to proclaim the Lord's death through observing the Lord's Supper?
9. What had Paul chastised Corinthian Christians for doing before he warned them of taking the Lord's Supper in an unworthy manner?
10. What is a person guilty of when he takes the Lord's Supper in an unworthy manner?

Discussion Starters

1. In addition to remembrance, what else do Christians do when they observe the Lord's Supper?
2. What were the Corinthians doing that resulted in taking the Supper unworthily? What might modern Christians do that would cause them to need Paul's warning?
3. In what way were Corinthian Christians failing to discern the body (1 Corinthians 11:29)? What from the context helps to define what "body" Paul had in mind?
4. How were the Corinthians observing the Lord's Supper so that it caused divisions among them? Why is the unity of the body of such great importance?

Singing, Part 1

Psalm 66:1-4

1 Make a joyful shout to God, all the earth!

2 Sing out the honor of His name; Make His praise glorious.

3 Say to God, "How awesome are Your works! Through the greatness of Your power Your enemies shall submit themselves to You.

4 All the earth shall worship You And sing praises to You; They shall sing praises to Your name." Selah.

Psalm 95:1-5

1 Oh come, let us sing to the LORD! Let us shout joyfully to the Rock of our salvation.

2 Let us come before His presence with thanksgiving; Let us shout joyfully to Him with psalms.

3 For the LORD is the great God, And the great King above all gods.

4 In His hand are the deep places of the earth; The heights of the hills are His also.

5 The sea is His, for He made it; And His hands formed the dry land.

Mark 14:26

26 And when they had sung a hymn, they went out to the Mount of Olives.

Acts 16:25

25 But at midnight Paul and Silas were praying and singing hymns to God, and the prisoners were listening to them.

Colossians 3:16-17

16 Let the word of Christ dwell in you richly in all wisdom, teaching and admonishing one another in psalms and hymns and spiritual songs, singing with grace in your hearts to the Lord.

17 And whatever you do in word or deed, do all in the name of the Lord Jesus, giving thanks to God the Father through Him.

Introduction

Whatever else singing may be, it is poetry set to music. Theorists will say that it is much more. They will point to its complexity and qualify definitions a thousand times over, but singing is at least some combination of words and music. Its power is in its combining of the two. Whether there are words or not, music communicates. Music by itself can be joyous, mournful, lustful or worshipful. It plumbs the range of emotions. Poetry, like music, commonly has a beat pattern, but poetry entails the use of words. The domain of words includes reason, data, precision – the kinds of things featured only slightly if at all in music.

The appeal of singing is in its combination of the beat pattern of music and the power of words. When the appeal of the words and the appeal of the music go in the same direction, their combined ability to influence how people think and what they do is staggering. Nations use songs to inspire patriotism. Hedonists use it to urge those caught up in its spell to follow the impulse of the moment. Napoleon Bonaparte is said to have remarked, "Music is the voice that tells us that the human race is greater than it knows." The general might have added that it is also the voice that tells us humanity is more decadent than it can imagine.

Often the Bible associates music, singing and dancing with joy and celebration. Laban had wanted to send Jacob away "with joy and songs, with timbrel and harp" (Genesis 31:27). Women went out of the cities of Israel "singing and dancing, to meet King Saul, with tambourines, with joy, and with musical instruments" (1 Samuel 18:6). The dark side of music was evident to Moses and Joshua. Joshua heard the raucous sounds of the camp and remarked, "The sound of singing I hear" (Exodus 32:18). Singing, dancing and instruments of music are not always innocent fun; much less are they always heartfelt worship.

For Joy (Psalm 66:1-4; 95:1-5)

When tragedy strikes, when an individual, a family or a church is overwhelmed by grief and a sense of helplessness, few need to be urged to turn to God. Prayer and supplication tend to be close companions. It is easier to forget God when larders are full than when hunger gnaws at the spine. Those who relegate worship to desperation and need rob themselves of their birthright. When tranquility reigns, when prayer has been answered and deliverance has come, Christians do well to lift their voices in song. Worship encompasses times of joy. Why should believers find themselves more commonly weeping with those who weep than rejoicing with those who rejoice (Romans 12:15)? Why should those who have been blessed with God's providential care resort to a dirge for worship when the occasion calls for a song of joy?

Some of the Psalms give voice to those on the edge of despair, but others find time and means for worship in joy and singing. Joy is the result when drought, plague or siege has threatened the life of the community, then deliverance comes. Rains turn the earth green, children regain their health, enemies retreat to their homeland, and God's people turn to Him with thanksgiving and songs of joy. "How awesome are Your works!" the psalmist sings, "All the earth shall worship you" (Psalm 66:3-4). Thanksgiving and joy are partners. The joyful shout is a friend of gratitude in the heart, but joyful worship is hardly relegated to the lifting of burdens. The breeze of a warm summer day, the hugs and smiles of family life, the quietness of a cup of coffee at the start of day – a thousand small satisfactions accumulate, and joy calls for expression. The author of Psalm 95 shouts "joyfully to the Rock of our salvation" in response to the Lord's reign over the deep places of the earth, the hills, the sea and dry land.

Shouts and laughter may accompany joy, but they are not essential for it. The God-centeredness of worshiping in song declines when joy evolves into having fun, when the hard beat of sensuality grinds gratitude out of the heart. Joy is not to be confused with the standup comic and the random noise of the crowd. The noise of the people Joshua heard in the camp of Israel (Exodus 32:18) and the antics of David when he brought the ark to Jerusalem (2 Samuel 6:20) are reminders that joy is artificial when it evolves into mayhem and lawlessness.

For Compassion (Mark 14:26; Acts 16:25)

Singing gives expression to a holy joy that is an important component of Christian worship, but the range of emotions issuing forth in song are more complex and varied than joy. The night before His crucifixion was one of subdued joy at best. Jesus was facing one of the most excruciating ordeals of torture that men have ever devised. The Lord and His disciples met in an upper room in Jerusalem to observe the Passover. In the course of the meal, Jesus and His followers observed the Lord's Supper, and the Lord commanded the church in ages that followed to keep the Supper in the same way.

As the company readied themselves to leave the room and to walk the short distance to the Mount of Olives where Jesus would be arrested, the Bible says that they sang a hymn. It makes no mention of what the song was about. Perhaps they chanted words in unison; perhaps they appealed to God above for protection and guidance. For whatever reason they sang a hymn, likely it was meant to comfort the Lord in His coming ordeal. Compassion called forth a song.

In another isolated, almost miscellaneous reference to singing for the comfort it can bring, Acts records the imprisonment of Paul and Silas at Philippi. The pair had been publicly stripped and beaten with rods in the city square after the Roman fashion. They had no chance to explain themselves and no opportunity for self-defense. After the beating, bruised and bloody, they were thrown into the stench of the town's city prison, their feet fastened in stocks, and in the care of the jailer. Instead of licking their wounds and feeling sorry for themselves, the duo counted themselves blessed to be able to suffer for the name of Jesus (James 1:2; 1 Peter 4:14). They lifted their voices in song and prayer. As events unfolded, God responded to their prayers and songs by delivering them and by granting salvation to the jailer who watched over them.

For Teaching (Colossians 3:16-17)

Paul told Christians at Colossae that when they worshiped, the Word of Christ was to dwell richly in them "in all wisdom, teaching and admonishing one another in psalms and hymns and spiritual songs" (Colossians 3:16). A single Christian may lift up his voice in a song of praise to God, but in this passage the apostle admonished the assembled church. Assembled believers were to teach and admonish one another. It was part of the community worship. When believers "consider one another in order to stir up love and good works" (Hebrews 10:24), songs come to mind. Songs not only teach the doctrines of Christ; they inspire hope and motivate obedience.

What do Christians teach when they sing? They tell one another of Christ's love as He hung dying for our sins. They teach that He rose from the dead and that He lives at God's right hand. They call on one another to be faithful to the Lord until He comes again. The entire range of the faithfulness, the grace and the love of God are appropriate for the teaching mission of song.

Conclusion

Perhaps no expression of Christian worship has the flexibility of songs, with a myriad of purposes. Jews and Christians set Psalms of the Old Testament into compositions suitable for the synagogue or the church to sing. The Psalms cover a wide range of praise and lament. With their songs, Christians express hope; they teach one another; they comfort; they praise God; they reflect on the mighty deeds of God – on His love, His compassion and mercy. Songs are cherished by the church for the same reasons that parables and other types of figurative language are cherished. In song, believers express what is best about their faith. They give common expression to a shared hope. In their songs, they rise above the sin and sorrow of the world. Their singing not only gives voice to their most noble longings and ideals, but it also allows them to listen to one another and to know that they are a people united in the love of God.

Questions

1. What do words contribute to singing that music without words lacks?
2. What is the purpose of singing in the remarks of Laban to Jacob?
3. When Joshua and Moses heard noise in the camp of Israel when they came down from Sinai, what kind of activity did Joshua associate with it?
4. For what purpose did the Psalmist say that the earth ought to raise a shout to the Lord?
5. Why are thanksgiving and joy often combined in the praise of song?
6. What are some of the reasons for Christians to express joy in worship because of the ordinary, daily happenings of life?
7. What had Jesus and His disciples been doing immediately before they sang a hymn and went to the Mount of Olives?
8. What happened to Paul and Silas before their singing and praying in prison?
9. What did Paul say was to dwell richly in Christians as they taught and admonished one another in song?
10. After encouraging Christians to do all in the name of the Lord Jesus, what did Paul say they ought to give to God the Father?

Discussion Starters

1. Why do people sing? What is the universal appeal of music and song that make them appropriate for worship?
2. Considering sinful practices that are encouraged by music, why does the church use it for worship? Why not discard it with other things used for evil purposes?
3. What are some of the occasions of joy in the life of the church and the lives of individual believers where they might express worship with song?

Singing, Part 2

Ephesians 5:15-21

15 See then that you walk circumspectly, not as fools but as wise,

16 redeeming the time, because the days are evil.

17 Therefore do not be unwise, but understand what the will of the Lord is.

18 And do not be drunk with wine, in which is dissipation; but be filled with the Spirit,

19 speaking to one another in psalms and hymns and spiritual songs, singing and making melody in your heart to the Lord,

20 giving thanks always for all things to God the Father in the name of our Lord Jesus Christ,

21 submitting to one another in the fear of God.

1 Corinthians 14:15

15 What is the conclusion then? I will pray with the spirit, and I will also pray with the understanding. I will sing with the spirit, and I will also sing with the understanding.

Hebrews 13:15-16

15 Therefore by Him let us continually offer the sacrifice of praise to God, that is, the fruit of our lips, giving thanks to His name.

16 But do not forget to do good and to share, for with such sacrifices God is well pleased.

Introduction

Assembly on the Lord's Day is for worship. Few will argue with that, but when questions arise about how the assembled church is to worship and why it worships, disagreements abound. The short answers to the questions are simple. The church is to worship as God directs. It worships in order to give Him the praise and the homage of which He is worthy. The church worships God because worship pleases Him. Why God wants worship from the church is more difficult. Is He an egomaniac in the sky who never gets enough adoration? How is God's glory enhanced when people worship Him? What could people possibly do that would add to His greatness?

In the Old Testament, worship centered in the rites of priests, sacrifices and feast days, but God was displeased when Israel became caught up in the *forms* of worship, as if the ritual were all that mattered. The Law of Moses, for example, commanded animal sacrifices and specified the procedure for their slaughter in painstaking detail, but God disdained sacrifices when they became ends in themselves. It must have come as a shock to Israel when they heard God say, "I do not delight in the blood of bulls, or of lambs or goats" (Isaiah 1:11). When the people congratulated themselves on their generosity in giving, God said, "For every beast of the forest is Mine, and the cattle on a thousand hills" (Psalm 50:10). "If I were hungry, I would not tell you; for the world is Mine, and all its fullness" (v. 12).

It is difficult to understand how the homage of humankind adds anything to God's power or glory. God has no need of our worship, but we need to worship Him. People are blessed by worship, not God. The doors God opens so that we may worship is His gift to us. The form and ritual of worship please Him only when they are the foundation upon which holy lives are built. Israel misunderstood worship when they supposed ritual to be its end. God's praise entailed more than the priestly slaughter of animals. "Learn to do good," God said, "Seek justice, rebuke the oppressor; defend the fatherless, plead for the widow" (Isaiah 1:17).

Speaking to One Another
(Ephesians 5:15-21)

Singing stands out in the assembly as the only manner of worship where all the church is invited to verbal participation. All worship is shared, but not all is shared verbally. Ideally, when the church sings, all believers add their voices, but all do not have the same gifts. Some Christians have physical problems that prevent them from singing. Some are mute from birth. Disease takes the voice of others. A raspy throat or laryngitis may prevent one from singing for a short time. The words and music may be strange to yet others. Sometimes a Christian sits silently and listens for a few minutes while the church edifies him or her.

Some Christians are blessed with musical talent, good voices and a sense for the rhythm inherent in song. If they are not careful they can be intolerant of others who are less talented. Not everyone has the same desire and talent for public speaking, and not everyone has the same inclination and talent for song. As those who have poor muscular coordination may lack the enthusiasm for sports seen in those with skills to display, similarly those with few musical talents may display less excitement for singing than the gifted. All do well to celebrate the talents of others and to sympathize with deficiencies. It is hardly a surprise that all Christians do not have the same desire or capacity for singing, but all can add a voice to the collective praise of the church. The desire of the heart and the love for the Savior allow even the most subdued voices to join in the adoration of God offered by the collective church. No one needs to apologize for a voice that is less than virtuoso quality.

Uplifting and vital as song can be in the worship of the church, Paul warned that music can be adapted for purposes against God's glory and praise. He preceded his admonition to sing with exhortations for holy and thoughtful living. Those who share in the kingdom of God, he said, are to "walk circumspectly, not as fools but as wise" (Ephesians 5:15). He added, "Therefore do not be unwise, but understand what the will of the Lord is" (v. 17). Drunkenness and dissipation accompanied by music of various sorts are often part of what the world equates with having a good time. Music in the medium of song is the domain of the people of God, but music can be put to ungodly purposes. When Christians worship they "speak to one another in psalms and hymns and spiritual songs singing and making melody in your heart to the Lord" (v. 19). Christians blending voices together in song are instruments for thanksgiving and praise. The music of the church is the one item of its praise that has the potential to evolve until it becomes an end in itself, sensual in its appeal, loosely attached to praise, if attached at all. Paul is careful to say that the praise Christians offer to God is with voices singing.

Spirit and Understanding (1 Corinthians 14:15)

The church in the New Testament came together on the first day of the week for worship. That much is clear (e.g., Acts 20:7), but it describes the worship of the assembly only in broad outline. The church prayed, sang, gave, observed the Lord's Supper and exhorted one another from the Scripture, but the New Testament describes practices in more detail only when problems arose. The first letter to Corinth is an example. When the church came together (1 Corinthians 14:26), believers were competing for who could stir the most commotion. Paul said the assembly ought to be decent and orderly (v. 40). When some maintained that they followed the impulses of the spirit, Paul responded, "And the spirits of the prophets are subject to the prophets" (v. 32).

Disorder in the assembly of the Corinthian church was the result of competition among those whom the Spirit had gifted to speak in languages other than the one native to them. The gift of tongues comes up a few times in Acts, but it finds no mention elsewhere except in 1 Corinthians. In the context of his plea for sensible order in the assembly, the apostle said a few words about prayer and singing. One may imagine a scene where some were speaking in an assortment of languages; others were trying to sing; and still others were talking to God in prayer. Paul knew that little praise could be rendered to God in such pandemonium. He told Christians they needed to engage their minds in worship as well as their hearts. The apostle summed up his case by writing, "I will pray with the spirit, and I will also pray with the understanding. I will sing with the spirit, and I will also sing with the understanding" (1 Corinthians 14:15). Whether various languages were involved in the prayer and song or not, the mind, Paul said, ought to be engaged. A snappy tune with a pat of the foot is not enough. Songs ought to express praise or hope or encouragement that arouse the collective "amen" of the church.

The Fruit of Our Lips (Hebrews 13:15-16)

The Greek word translated "to sacrifice" is *thuo*. The word for the sacrifice itself is *thusia*. Both words suggest the slaughter of an animal, rending it into parts and burning it on an altar. By the time the New Testament was translated into English, such offerings were not being made. English speakers had no need for such a word. As a result, translators turned to a word of Latin origin, "sacrifice," a sacred gift. It was a good choice. The author of Hebrews looks to prayer and song, sacrifices of praise that God's people offer to the Almighty. It is unfortunate that "sacrifice" has come to be used for self-denial. Sacrifices are sacred gifts offered by the church. "The fruit of our lips" (Hebrews 13:15), combined with doing good and sharing, please the Father in heaven. Giving to Him requires no denial of good things for the self. Instead, it requires that those who hear the gospel confess their sins, acknowledge His Lordship and obey His commands. His commands are not grievous burdens. Worship, along with other matters of obedience, is possible because God has been mindful of us. He has set us on the path of life (Deuteronomy 30:19; John 10:10).

Conclusion

Christian worship is both God's gift to His people and His people's gift to Him. God opens the door by revealing to Christians what they may do in order to have an ongoing relationship with Him. Worship is His gift. Christians offer to God the praise and worship they want to express to the One who has reached out to save humanity even when they had turned their backs. Worship is their sacrifice, their sacred gift to Him. People and God may have a relationship with each other in a context of giving and receiving. How could God and His people share a relationship of trust and love in the absence of giving to one another? God gives, and He has made provision for His people to give to Him the sacrifice of praise and the doing of good.

Questions

1. What was involved in the worship God prescribed for Israel?
2. What did Israel do that caused God to be displeased with its worship?
3. What does the word "circumspectly" mean (Ephesians 5:15)? What kind of life has one lived who lives "circumspectly"?
4. What did Paul want the Ephesian Christians to understand?
5. Instead of being filled with wine, what did Paul want believers to be filled with?
6. What three terms did Paul used for the songs that Christians were to sing?
7. Where was the melody to be as Christians offered songs to God?
8. What was the cause for disorderly conduct in the assembly of the church at Corinth?
9. With what mental disposition did Paul say that the Corinthians ought to offer their songs and prayers?
10. What word did the author of Hebrews use for the "fruit of our lips" (Hebrews 13:15) that believers were to give to God?

Discussion Starters

1. In what sense is worship both God's gift to His people and the gift His people offer to God?
2. Why is it more important for Christians to take care about the way they offer their music to God than it might be for other forms of worship?
3. What does the word "sacrifice" mean? How are the sacrifices that Christians offer different from Old Testament sacrifices? How are they similar?
4. What should modern Christians learn from Paul's admonition that the worship of the church is to be offered decently and in an orderly manner?

The Instrumental Question

Matthew 28:18

18 And Jesus came and spoke to them, saying, "All authority has been given to Me in heaven and on earth.

Colossians 3:17

17 And whatever you do in word or deed, do all in the name of the Lord Jesus, giving thanks to God the Father through Him.

Ephesians 5:19

19 ... speaking to one another in psalms and hymns and spiritual songs, singing and making melody in your heart to the Lord.

Acts 15:24

24 Since we have heard that some who went out from us have troubled you with words, unsettling your souls, saying, "You must be circumcised and keep the law" – to whom we gave no such commandment ...

1 Corinthians 4:6

6 Now these things, brethren, I have figuratively transferred to myself and Apollos for your sakes, that you may learn in us not to think beyond what is written, that none of you may be puffed up on behalf of one against the other.

2 John 9

9 Whoever transgresses and does not abide in the doctrine of Christ does not have God. He who abides in the doctrine of Christ has both the Father and the Son.

Revelation 22:18-19

18 For I testify to everyone who hears the words of the prophecy of this book: If anyone adds to these things, God will add to him the plagues that are written in this book;

19 and if anyone takes away from the words of the book of this prophecy, God shall take away his part from the Book of Life, from the holy city, and from the things which are written in this book.

Introduction

When people unacquainted with churches of Christ visit an assembly, the first thing they are likely to notice is that the singing is a cappella. Having been used to pianos and organs, guitars and drums, some find singing without them to be dull or boring. Others find it refreshing to contribute to the singing and to hear others sing without the distraction of instruments. Perhaps most consider a cappella singing to be a novelty, something to smile about and comment on. Many find it incredibly narrow that anyone should think it wrong to worship in song to the accompaniment of instruments. They find a cappella singing to be fine as long as it is only a matter of preference, an odd quirk for those who don't like music or at least much music. They cannot understand why anyone would think singing with or without instrumental accompaniment to be a matter of faith.

Members of modern denominations are likely to have little awareness that controversy about the use of musical instruments in the assembly of Christians has been around for nearly two millennia. Some early Christian thinkers were adamantly opposed to instruments in Christian assemblies not only because the New Testament did not authorize them but also because of sensual practices associated with them. Little by little, over the centuries Catholic churches accepted instruments. The Greek Orthodox church continues to spurn them. In the modern Protestant era, many denominations had adherents among them who rejected instruments in worship. Rejection was not billed as preference. Passages from the Bible and careful reasoning called the use of instruments into question. In the end, the use or non-use of instruments in worship was and continues to be rooted in the question of authority. Are Christians to worship in ways that God has specifically authorized or are they free to follow their personal preferences as long as the Bible does not forbid a practice? Churches of Christ, along with many others, have maintained that the Bible directs Christians in worship that is acceptable to God. That the New Testament tells Christians how to worship without the mention of instruments of music amounts to a prohibition. The following passages support that reasoning.

By What Authority? (Matthew 28:18; Colossians 3:17; Acts 15:24)

Shortly before His death, Jesus went into the temple at Jerusalem, overturned the tables of money changers and drove merchants from the area (Matthew 21:12). In short order, temple officials challenged Him with the question, "By what authority are You doing these things? And who gave You this authority?" (v. 23). The chief priests and elders who put the questions to Jesus supposed that God had delegated to them authority over what took place in the temple precincts. Jesus challenged them. He acted on His own authority.

Authority is the right to speak and to be obeyed. In earthly affairs it may be exercised by physical strength, by the control of armies, by election to a government post, by the control of resources or in a host of other ways. God's authority over the universe and the affairs of men is a result of who He is. By virtue of His being Creator and Sovereign Judge, God rules the universe. He is authoritative because He is Sovereign. Jesus partakes of the Divinity of God (John 1:1; Colossians 2:9). He speaks with the authority of God. Men obey Him as they obey God.

After Jesus had been crucified, He met with the disciples on a mountain in Galilee and declared, "All authority has been given to Me in heaven and on earth" (Matthew 28:18). To act in Jesus' name is to act by His authority. Paul wrote, "And whatever you do in word or deed, do all in the name of the Lord Jesus" (Colossians 3:17). After His death, Jesus sent the Holy Spirit to convey to His apostles authority to speak and write in His name (John 14:26; 16:13; 1 Corinthians 2:13). When the Jerusalem church, guided by the apostles, wrote to Gentile believers, they made it clear that they acted and gave command by the authority of Christ (Acts 15:24).

What this implies is that all the church teaches and does should proceed from the authority of Christ and His apostles. The church's mission, its message, its commands, its worship, its governance and all it does derives from the authority of Christ. Because the New Testament does not forbid the church to tell the lost to speak in tongues or to pray and fast three days before requesting baptism means the church has no authority to do it. Silence does not give authority anywhere. A motorist, for example, would not likely convince a judge he was innocent by pleading that no law forbade him from driving 100 miles per hour when the signs said the speed limit was 55. God authorizes the church to act with commands and examples approved by apostolic authority. Silence does not authorize.

Melody in the Heart (Ephesians 5:19)

Music is a broad term. Had the New Testament authorized the church to worship with music and left the matter there, whatever type of music the church offered in praise would have been acceptable. Paul did not instruct churches to offer music. He told them the kind of music they were to offer. The church was to speak "to one another in psalms and hymns and spiritual songs" (Ephesians 5:19). In the modern era some have argued that the Greek words translated "psalms" and "making melody" suggest singing with instrumental accompaniment. It is noteworthy that the Greek Orthodox denomination, who continues to use the spoken language, does not argue that way. They insist that singing is to be unaccompanied. The Greek word "psalm" has been studied exhaustively, and the consensus is that in the New Testament period it was used for vocal singing of one of the psalms of the Old Testament or a song modeled after the psalms.

The phrase "making melody" in Ephesians 5:19 is a verb that literally means the singing of a psalm. If we grant that the word "psalm" implies singing with an instrument (which we do not), Paul clarified the matter when he said that such singing was to issue forth from the heart. Any reference Paul may have had to instrumentation he relegates to the heart. Figuratively, the heart accompanies singing for the church as instruments may have accompanied singing in the secular sphere. The arguments of those who claim authority to sing with instruments by delving into the words translated "psalm" and "making melody" fail on two grounds. First, the evidence demonstrates that in the New Testament period no implication concerning instruments accompanied the use of the word "psalm." Second, even if such an implication were granted, Paul makes it clear that accompaniment to singing was to be with the heart, not with instruments.

Do Not Go Beyond
(1 Corinthians 4:6; 2 John 9)

That the practice of the church is to proceed from what God authorizes and not implied from silence is explicit in the New Testament. When Paul exhorted the church at Corinth to unity, he appealed to authority. He urged the church, as rendered by the New King James Version, that it not "think beyond what is written" (1 Corinthians 4:6). The Greek Paul wrote does not supply a verb. The American Standard Version has: "not to go beyond the things which are written." The New American Standard Bible has: "not to exceed what is written." All the translations make it clear that Paul expected the church to follow written instruction. Perhaps he had summarized his teaching in a written document he left with them. "Things written" likely included 1 Corinthians itself. Perhaps it included other letters he had written (see 1 Corinthians 5:9).

Whatever Paul referred to by "things written," he hardly could have meant the Old Testament. Neither the church at Corinth nor the modern church is to go beyond written instruction rooted in the authority of Christ for moral behavior, for confession and obedience to God. The mission, doctrine and worship of the church find authority in things that are written. John warned that those who do not follow in "the doctrine of Christ" do not have God (2 John 9). The use or non-use of instruments with singing is not a trivial matter to be dismissed lightly.

Do Not Add or Subtract
(Revelation 22:18-19)

John ended Revelation by warning his readers that they were not to add to or subtract "from the words of the book of this prophecy" (Revelation 22:19). No doubt he meant that they were not to add to or subtract from the book of Revelation itself, but the principle surely extends beyond any one book of the Bible. If no one was to add to or subtract from Revelation, would it be acceptable to add to or subtract from other books? Authority for the church is encompassed within the revealed message of Scripture. The worship of the church, including the music it offers in praise, ought to be limited to what God has authorized.

Conclusion

For many in the denominational world, whether the church sings with or without the accompaniment of instruments of music is a non-question. The significance of the question was widely discussed at one point, but today few care. For those who insist that New Testament authorization is fundamental for the offering of praise pleasing to God, the question of singing with instrumental accompaniment remains a vital one. Worship in prayer or by partaking of the Lord's Supper, exhortation from Scripture or giving liberally are not susceptible to the same temptation to resort to sensual appeal as is music. The church needs particularly to listen to the authorization of Scripture as it offers praise to God in song.

Questions

1. Why did some early believers object to the church's singing to instrumental accompaniment?
2. Why are objections of some early Christians to instruments in worship still relevant for the modern church?
3. What did Jesus tell His disciples on a mountain in Galilee about His authority?
4. In whose name did Paul urge Colossian Christians to do everything?
5. What does a person acknowledge when he acts in the name of Christ?
6. Who is the "we" in Acts 15:24 who had authority to command?
7. What have some argued that the Greek word for "psalm" or "to sing a psalm" implies?
8. Where did Paul say that any "instruments" accompanying Christian worship were to be located?
9. What were the things written that Christians were not to go beyond? What writing did Paul have in mind?
10. What did John say that his readers were not to add to nor subtract from?

Discussion Starters

1. How do people react when they discover that churches of Christ sing without the use of instruments? Why do many think there is no question to settle?
2. What special considerations are brought to singing that require Christians to be especially vigilant in praising Him as He directs?
3. Why is the silence of Scripture important when one asks how God is to be praised when the church assembles?
4. What did Jesus promise the apostles that He would do so that they could speak and write with authority? Why is it important to look to Christ for authority?

Giving, Part 1

Hebrews 11:4

4 By faith Abel offered to God a more excellent sacrifice than Cain, through which he obtained witness that he was righteous, God testifying of his gifts; and through it he being dead still speaks.

Leviticus 27:30-33

30 " 'And all the tithe of the land, whether of the seed of the land or of the fruit of the tree, is the LORD's. It is holy to the LORD.

31 'If a man wants at all to redeem any of his tithes, he shall add one-fifth to it.

32 'And concerning the tithe of the herd or the flock, of whatever passes under the rod, the tenth one shall be holy to the LORD.

33 'He shall not inquire whether it is good or bad, nor shall he exchange it; and if he exchanges it at all, then both it and the one exchanged for it shall be holy; it shall not be redeemed.' "

2 Chronicles 31:5-12

5 As soon as the commandment was circulated, the children of Israel brought in abundance the firstfruits of grain and wine, oil and honey, and of all the produce of the field; and they brought in abundantly the tithe of everything.

6 And the children of Israel and Judah, who dwelt in the cities of Judah, brought the tithe of oxen and sheep; also the tithe of holy things which were consecrated to the LORD their God they laid in heaps.

7 In the third month they began laying them in heaps, and they finished in the seventh month.

8 And when Hezekiah and the leaders came and saw the heaps, they blessed the LORD and His people Israel.

9 Then Hezekiah questioned the priests and the Levites concerning the heaps.

10 And Azariah the chief priest, from the house of Zadok, answered him and said, "Since the people began to bring the offerings into the house of the LORD, we have had enough to eat and have plenty left, for the LORD has blessed His people; and what is left is this great abundance."

11 Now Hezekiah commanded them to prepare rooms in the house of the LORD, and they prepared them.

12 Then they faithfully brought in the offerings, the tithes, and the dedicated things; Cononiah the Levite had charge of them, and Shimei his brother was the next.

Malachi 3:8-10

8 "Will a man rob God? Yet you have robbed Me! But you say, 'In what way have we robbed You?' In tithes and offerings.

9 "You are cursed with a curse, For you have robbed Me, Even this whole nation.

10 "Bring all the tithes into the storehouse, That there may be food in My house, And try Me now in this," Says the LORD of hosts, "If I will not open for you the windows of heaven And pour out for you such blessing That there will not be room enough to receive it."

Introduction

Giving for a Christian is more complex than writing a check to drop into the collection plate on Sunday morning. Faith, love, hope – the great concepts of the Christian faith are about relationships. Giving is an expression of faith, love and hope. Being a Christian is more than a mechanical routine, so giving is more than budgeting a dollar amount into family expenses. The beginning point for Christian giving is not like receiving a statement for a utility bill. A gift to God is not a payment for services rendered. Giving is worship; what Christians give are their sacred offerings to God. They give their sacrifices (Hebrews 13:15). Before a person offers his money to God, the Lord wants his heart (2 Corinthians 8:5). If one's heart belongs to the Lord, he or she wants to give to Him. Giving is not limited to what one puts into the collection plate. Contributing regularly to the ongoing needs of the church is only one way believers give to the Lord. They give God the fruit of their lips, their praise, their good deeds, their sharing with the needy.

In order to be a cheerful and generous giver, formidable fleshly desires have to be held in check. Ancient Romans used to say that money was like sea water, the more one drank the more he craved. Increasingly the world insists that the worth of a person is a measure of his bank account. The world believes that the poor are that way because they want to be or because they are lazy. Darwinian economics says that in the world of humans, as in the world of insects, the strong survive and the weak perish. All such thinking stirs the fear that we will run out of money, and if we do we may become parasites, turning to welfare, taking the hard-earned money of those who are more worthy. Little wonder that ordinary people drawing ordinary wages are sometimes afraid to give.

The love of money is no invention of the modern world. Readers of the Bible may overlook the sheer volume of teachings about possessions. Among the parables are the rich fool (Luke 12:13-21), the dishonest steward (16:1-15), and the rich man and Lazarus (vv. 19-31), but many others relate to giving in one way or another. A rich young man came to Jesus and asked what he needed to do to have eternal life. Jesus responded that he would do well to sell all he had and give it to the poor (Matthew 19:21). The Lord commended a poor widow who gave all her living as a gift for God (Mark 12:41-44). The book of Acts and the epistles have much to say about the love of money and the attendant spiritual dangers. To be a Christian, among other things, is to learn to worship by giving.

God's Expectations
(Hebrews 11:4; Leviticus 27:30-33)

God's expectation for generosity from His people does not begin with the passing of a collection basket. It begins with an attitude of mind. Hebrews 11 is about faith, but the author hardly begins writing about faith before he comes to giving. The subject is Abel, son of Adam and Eve (Genesis 4:1-2). After an attempt at abstract definition, the author of Hebrews described faith in terms of behavior. Abel was a man of faith who expressed his faith by giving. "By faith Abel offered to God a more excellent sacrifice than Cain" (Hebrews 11:4). God testified to Abel's faith by accepting his gifts. As the centuries have passed, the gifts of Abel have continued to proclaim his faith and to inspire others to live by the same kind of faith. Giving was not an addendum to the faith of Abel. His gifts were of the same stuff as his faith.

For those who lived under the Law of Moses, giving was inflexible. If a vine produced ten grapes, one of them belonged to God. A shepherd passed his sheep under a rod so that he could keep careful count. Every tenth one, whatever its condition, was the Lord's (Leviticus 27:32). The first mention of giving a tithe was by Jacob (Genesis 28:22); years later the Law of Moses built it into the economy of Israel. In the New Testament, Christians are admonished to give generously, but there is no mention of their giving a tithe. The two mites given by the poor widow (Mark 12:41-42) may have been more or less than a tenth of her income; she gave generously whatever the percentage was. One person who gives a tenth may be doing so at incredible self-sacrifice; for another a tithe might be a pittance.

Neither Jesus nor the apostles set a percentage on generosity. Instead of counting out every tenth dollar and giving it to the Lord, Jesus has given His people a more difficult task. He wants those who own His name to search their hearts, to read their Bibles, and to give as they determine a generous person ought to give. Under the Law of Moses, God expected a tenth; under the new covenant God expects generous, selfless giving. Some ought to put less than a tenth of their income into the collection plate. Putting food on the table and clothes on the backs of children is a more urgent demand for them (1 Timothy 5:8). Others ought to give more than a tenth and some considerably more. When the heart belongs to the Lord, one gives without being urged, without grudging and without regret.

God's Approval (2 Chronicles 31:5-12)

When Hezekiah became king in Jerusalem, the spiritual state of Judah was in a deplorable condition. In Jerusalem and the surrounding villages, shrines to the fertility gods of Canaan were in abundant supply. Descendants of Abraham and Jacob frequented the high places and consorted with "holy women" among whom were their own daughters (Hosea 4:12-13). They bowed down before images of stone and wood, symbols of the male god Baal and his consort Asherah.

Judah was at a low point when the king led the land in a great reform. Hezekiah banished the high places; priests and Levites resumed obedience to the Law of Moses. Isaiah was prophet and adviser to the king when Hezekiah put legitimate priests in place and ordered them to celebrate the feast days, to offer morning and evening sacrifices, and to see to the upkeep of the temple built by Solomon.

The people of Judah responded generously to Hezekiah's call. God blessed the land. The rains came on time and fields produced abundant crops. Of the produce and livestock, the tithe was devoted to God. From the ingathering of firstfruits until the great harvest festival in the seventh month, tithes poured into the temple precincts. God registered His approval of the reform and the generosity of the people by multiplying the abundance of the land. Azariah the chief priest said to the king, "Since the people began to bring the offerings into the house of the LORD, we have had enough to eat and have plenty left, for the LORD has blessed His people" (2 Chronicles 31:10). God approved the generous giving of the people and poured out His blessings in response.

God's Challenge (Malachi 3:8-10)

A great deal of excitement and zeal accompanied the initial return of Jews from Babylonian captivity to rebuild Jerusalem under the leadership of Jeshua and Zerubbabel (Ezra 1:1, ca. 539 B.C.). Priests had been careful to follow the Law when they resumed sacrifices at the temple, but in time religious leaders had become lax. Malachi's book is a series of hypothetical but realistic dialogues between God and the returnees. The dialogues manifest God's displeasure followed by the people's defense and their complaint against God. Of His people, for example, God said, "I have loved you" (Malachi 1:2). The people wondered if God loved them why they were weak and miserable? Where was the evidence of God's love? God takes it from there. A series of six such complaints and responses make up most of Malachi's book.

Two of God's indictments concerned the failure of the people to offer acceptable gifts to God. Sometimes they offered diseased, worthless animals as sacrifices. God demanded their best (Leviticus 22:22; Malachi 1:8), but the problem went deeper. For some, tithes were a thing of the past. They gave little or nothing. With indignation the Lord asked, "Will a man rob God?" (3:8). The tithe belonged to God; to keep it back was to rob Him of His due. Because they had withheld tithes, God had withheld His blessings from the land. They were hungry and weak because they failed to give. God challenged the Jews to test Him. If they gave generously as Moses had directed, God promised to open "the windows of heaven" (v. 10) and pour out blessings. Storehouses would be too small to contain all He would give them.

Conclusion

In God's relationship with Israel, He often laid down strict rules. Paul said that Israel's obedience was often on the order of a slave's, but in Christ God's people had become free (Galatians 4:7). The giving of a tithe was part of Israel's worship. The tenth is not enjoined in the New Testament, but God manifested

His will for Israel when they gave their gifts in ways that are instructive for Christians. First, obedient and generous giving is as essential for faithfulness to God as any other matter, being honest in business, for example, or speaking the truth or observing the Lord's Day, or being baptized for the remission of sins. Second, generous giving is a manifestation of faith. The good works that James understood to be part and parcel with faith (James 2:20) include the offering of gifts to God. Third, God responds to generosity with generosity. He pours out His blessings on those who manifest their trust and faithfulness to Him by giving.

Questions

1. What should Christians give to God first before they consider what generous giving means for them?
2. What are some of the parables that in one way or another address the tendency of people to love material things?
3. Who did the author of Hebrews say offered a more excellent sacrifice than his brother?
4. In what way does Abel still speak?
5. How much of the increase of the crops and herds were the Israelites to give to the Lord?
6. How does the widow whom Jesus commended for giving two mites instruct Christians on the way they are to give?
7. What king instituted religious reform that encouraged the people of Judah to give generously?
8. What did the chief priest tell the king that God had done as a result of the generosity of the people?
9. When did Malachi live?
10. How did God invite the returned exiles to put Him to the test?

Discussion Starters

1. In what ways do anxiety for material things and selfishness influence the way people give? What is the solution to material anxiety and selfishness?
2. Is the giving of a tenth commanded for Christians? How do God's commands to Israel about giving instruct Christians about they way they ought to give?
3. Does God always give material prosperity in return for generosity? Do material prosperity and generosity sometimes go hand in hand? Explain.
4. Is the tithe a model for Christians? Is it the base giving rate, or ought some people to give less than a tithe and some more? Explain what should guide giving.

Giving, Part 2

Acts 2:44-45

44 Now all who believed were together, and had all things in common,

45 and sold their possessions and goods, and divided them among all, as anyone had need.

Acts 4:32-37

32 Now the multitude of those who believed were of one heart and one soul; neither did anyone say that any of the things he possessed was his own, but they had all things in common.

33 And with great power the apostles gave witness to the resurrection of the Lord Jesus. And great grace was upon them all.

34 Nor was there anyone among them who lacked; for all who were possessors of lands or houses sold them, and brought the proceeds of the things that were sold,

35 and laid them at the apostles' feet; and they distributed to each as anyone had need.

36 And Joses, who was also named Barnabas by the apostles (which is translated Son of Encouragement), a Levite of the country of Cyprus,

37 having land, sold it, and brought the money and laid it at the apostles' feet.

1 Corinthians 16:1-2

1 Now concerning the collection for the saints, as I have given orders to the churches of Galatia, so you must do also:

2 On the first day of the week let each one of you lay something aside, storing up as he may prosper, that there be no collections when I come.

2 Corinthians 8:1-4

1 Moreover, brethren, we make known to you the grace of God bestowed on the churches of Macedonia:

2 that in a great trial of affliction the abundance of their joy and their deep poverty abounded in the riches of their liberality.

3 For I bear witness that according to their ability, yes, and beyond their ability, they were freely willing,

4 imploring us with much urgency that we would receive the gift and the fellowship of the ministering to the saints.

1 Timothy 6:6-10

6 Now godliness with contentment is great gain.

7 For we brought nothing into this world, and it is certain we can carry nothing out.

8 And having food and clothing, with these we shall be content.

9 But those who desire to be rich fall into temptation and a snare, and into many foolish and harmful lusts which drown men in destruction and perdition.

10 For the love of money is a root of all kinds of evil, for which some have strayed from the faith in their greediness, and pierced themselves through with many sorrows.

Introduction

When a Christian gives in response to God's command, when he gives because he loves the Lord and wants to please Him, it is an act of worship. Believers give God material things as they give Him prayers and songs. Giving is homage and praise. The two mites the widow placed in the treasury (Mark 12:43) probably did not make a lot of difference to those who kept up with the resources for the temple, but it made a difference to God. No one would have blamed the widow had she kept the two small copper coins for herself. She did not give out of compulsion; it was not to buy a little insurance for the judgment day. It never seemed to occur to her that others were more able to give than she was. The more practical sorts would have argued that she would have done better to buy a loaf of bread than to put her mites in the treasury. Officials would spend far more than her two mites for haircuts, but it made no difference to her. She worshiped by giving. In our relationships with one another and our relationship to God, we express our devotion, our commitment and our love when we give.

God does not become more powerful or more whole because Christians give. Whatever spiritual benefit follows from giving accrues to the giver. In a sense, God has given to His people by opening for them a door of praise through giving. What are the benefits when Christians give to God? First, generous giving molds and forms one's character. A giving person is one who can look further than his own pocketbook. Second, a generous giver makes a statement to the world that he or she refuses to accept that material things alone matter. Third, the church becomes a stronger, more close-knit community of people, and brotherly love multiplies (John 13:34) when God's people give sacrificially for the building up of the church.

Early Christians Gave (Acts 2:44-45; 4:32-37)

The description of the early church in Acts is important because it was under the direct authority and supervision of the apostles. Christians during those early days were plagued with the same kinds of weaknesses and sins the modern church faces. The early Jerusalem church has inspired subsequent generations of Christians not only because of its faith and brotherly love but also because of the way it handled problems. For example, persecutions came down on believers. The response of the church was to meet behind closed doors and to entrust their well-being to God (Acts 4:29; 5:42). Suffering from poverty may have resulted in some measure from persecution. The church responded to their poor by pooling resources and distributing to each according to need (2:45).

Many of the early Christians in Jerusalem gave from a meager store of goods, but a few of them were fairly wealthy. Among those with more resources than average was a Levite who had migrated to Jerusalem from the island of Cyprus. When he first appeared in Acts, he was already a Christian. His parents had given him the name Joses, but in time the apostles nicknamed him Barnabas, meaning "Son of Encouragement" (Acts 4:36). Joses may have sold property on Cyprus and used the money to buy land in Judea. When he saw the poverty of his brothers and sisters in Christ, he sold some portion of his land and brought it to the apostles to distribute to the needy. Barnabas is specifically named because of the leadership he would provide for Gentile Christianity in the years that followed, but others also likely gave generously to provide for the poor.

Barnabas and many others, some with more resources and some with fewer, gave generously to meet the needs of the church. Therein, by their generosity, Jerusalem Christians provided a model for the church in all ages, but their pooling of resources and the distribution to the needy require no universal imitation. The need and the response to the need were peculiar to the Jerusalem church. The New Testament offers no evidence that the pooling of resources was practiced elsewhere. Some of the Christians at Antioch of Syria, Corinth or Ephesus were extremely poor. Individual believers gave to help the less fortunate, but the Bible offers no evidence that Christians routinely sold property and placed the funds in a common pool for distribution. The model the Jerusalem church offers for imitation is one of selfless giving so that the work of the Lord might be carried out. It offers no model for Christians sharing in communal property.

Gave Willingly (2 Corinthians 8:1-4)

After Paul and Barnabas began to open the floodgates for masses of Gentiles who became Christians (Acts 11:26), they faced fierce opposition from a considerable number of Judean believers. The two of them in company with Titus went to Jerusalem to consult with the apostles about the matter (Galatians 2:1-2). Among other things, they took with them an offering for the poor from the largely Gentile church in Antioch of Syria (Acts 11:29). The apostles at Jerusalem found themselves in full agreement with Paul and Barnabas in the matter of preaching to Gentiles, but they also agreed that Christians ought to give to ease the burdens of the poor (Galatians 2:10). Paul's admonitions in 2 Corinthians 8-9 are an extension of their common understanding.

For some years before Paul wrote 2 Corinthians, he had been making plans to gather a large contribution from Gentile churches to help the poor in Jerusalem. The importance of the contribution was not only for the relief it would give to the poor. It was also a token of the unity behind the expanding Gentile church and the church in Judea (Romans 15:26-27). Paul explained in 2 Corinthians that he planned to pass through Corinth after spending time in Macedonia. He hoped the Corinthian church would be as generous as the

Macedonians had been. The apostle said that God had bestowed grace on the Macedonians by challenging them to give. Christians in Macedonia had suffered persecutions and trials. They were poor themselves, but they had reached deep into the meager resources they had, and they had given beyond their means. Paul hoped the generosity of the Macedonians would be repeated at Corinth. Such generosity is worthy of imitation.

Gave Regularly (1 Corinthians 16:1-2)

The exact amount of time that passed between the writing of Paul's first and second letter to Corinth is uncertain, but it could not have been more than a few years. Already in 1 Corinthians, Paul was laying the groundwork for the contribution he would describe in more detail in 2 Corinthians 8-9. The apostle's concern in the first letter was that Christians in the city might put off their giving or fail to give in a purposeful and planned manner. Because the church assembled on the first day of the week, it was an opportune time for them to set aside gifts on a regular basis. They could add to the accumulated store week after week until Paul arrived to make arrangements for all of it to go to help the poor of Judea.

Churches in every place do well to follow the pattern Paul established at Corinth. Across time and space, the needs of churches will change. Money will be needed for relief for the poor, for buildings and paying utilities for a place of worship, for the support of missionaries and for the support of local preaching. The needs will change, but the orderly practice of giving generously, laying "something aside" week by week when the church comes together (1 Corinthians 16:2), is a pattern worthy of imitation by all churches. Giving is one of the ways God has chosen for Christians to worship Him.

Sought Contentment (1 Timothy 6:6-10)

Generous giving begins with the spiritual discernment to place material, temporal things in the perspective of eternity. It is foolish and hurtful to exchange contentment for possessions. Contentment is the product of peace with God and with one's self. It comes to those who value friendships and family closeness more than a growing bank account. The apostle reminds his readers that we brought nothing into the world and we will take nothing out. For those who live as though money is the answer to every need, Paul insists that love for money is the "root of all kinds of evil." Those who seek it with all their energies pierce "themselves through with many sorrows" (1 Timothy 1:10). The route to contentment is not at the end of a life of hoarding. It is the product of generous giving.

Conclusion

The inspiring example of the Jerusalem church or Macedonian churches moves Christians in other times and places to be generous, but motivation for generous giving likely lies closer to hand. Many Christians have benefitted from loving families that have given to them. Perhaps a friend or relative showed confidence in a young person and risked, maybe lost, a considerable sum of money to help. We all have benefitted, some more, some less, from the gifts of others, but in the end inspiration for generosity comes from the Lord Himself. Here is the way Paul put it, "For you know the grace of our Lord Jesus Christ, that though He was rich, yet for your sakes He became poor, that you through His poverty might become rich" (2 Corinthians 8:9). God has given life and breath, food for our tables and clothes for our backs. Whatever believers give to honor and praise Him can hardly compare to the gifts they receive from Him.

Questions

1. Who benefits most when a person gives generously to the Lord?
2. Why do modern Christians profit by examining the generosity of the apostolic church in Jerusalem?
3. How did the Jerusalem church meet the needs of its poor during the first few years of its existence?
4. By what criterion were resources distributed to the poor of the Jerusalem church?
5. What other churches does Acts describe in addition to Jerusalem who pooled resources for distribution to the poor? What are the implications?
6. Of whom did Paul say the Jerusalem church wanted Barnabas and himself to be mindful?
7. Where were the churches whom Paul held up before the Corinthians as a model for generous giving?
8. How had these churches (in question #7) given that caused Paul to commend them?
9. In his first Corinthian letter, when did Paul tell the church to lay aside funds for the needs of the poor in Judea?
10. What did Paul tell Timothy provided great gain for those who found it?

Discussion Starters

1. If the giving of Christians does not add to God's glory, who are the beneficiaries of generous giving? What kinds of benefits follow from generosity?
2. Why do modern churches not follow the example of the Jerusalem church and pool resources for distribution according to need?
3. What circumstances led Paul to take up a collection from Gentile churches for the relief of Judean Christians? At what point in his life did the collection take place?
4. Why did Paul find it expedient to remind Timothy and others that material resources offer no long-term guarantee for contentment?

Reverence in Worship

Hebrews 12:18-29

18 For you have not come to the mountain that may be touched and that burned with fire, and to blackness and darkness and tempest,

19 and the sound of a trumpet and the voice of words, so that those who heard it begged that the word should not be spoken to them anymore.

20 (For they could not endure what was commanded: "And if so much as a beast touches the mountain, it shall be stoned or shot with an arrow."

21 And so terrifying was the sight that Moses said, "I am exceedingly afraid and trembling.")

22 But you have come to Mount Zion and to the city of the living God, the heavenly Jerusalem, to an innumerable company of angels,

23 to the general assembly and church of the firstborn who are registered in heaven, to God the Judge of all, to the spirits of just men made perfect,

24 to Jesus the Mediator of the new covenant, and to the blood of sprinkling that speaks better things than that of Abel.

25 See that you do not refuse Him who speaks. For if they did not escape who refused Him who spoke on earth, much more shall we not escape if we turn away from Him who speaks from heaven,

26 whose voice then shook the earth; but now He has promised, saying, "Yet once more I shake not only the earth, but also heaven."

27 Now this, "Yet once more," indicates the removal of those things that are being shaken, as of things that are made, that the things which cannot be shaken may remain.

28 Therefore, since we are receiving a kingdom which cannot be shaken, let us have grace, by which we may serve God acceptably with reverence and godly fear.

29 For our God is a consuming fire.

Jude 20-25

20 But you, beloved, building yourselves up on your most holy faith, praying in the Holy Spirit,

21 keep yourselves in the love of God, looking for the mercy of our Lord Jesus Christ unto eternal life.

22 And on some have compassion, making a distinction;

23 but others save with fear, pulling them out of the fire, hating even the garment defiled by the flesh.

24 Now to Him who is able to keep you from stumbling, And to present you faultless before the presence of His glory with exceeding joy,

25 To God our Savior, Who alone is wise, Be glory and majesty, Dominion and power, Both now and forever. Amen.

Introduction

Reverence is both the frame of mind with which one approaches God and overt behavior during worship. Whether in private or in company with others, worship begins with a consideration of the One into whose presence the worshiper comes. On the one hand, God is approachable. He is the heavenly Father who wants His children to commune with Him. On the other hand, He is the Almighty, altogether removed in glory and power from humankind. God is not a mailed fist ready to hammer offending souls, but neither is He a doting grandfather before whom his precious babies can do no wrong. He is a God in whom love and justice combine in mysterious ways beyond human comprehension. To be reverent is to keep in mind both His love and His holiness.

Reverence requires no walking on eggshells in His presence. Job was bold enough to charge God with treating him unjustly. The patriarch said of God, "For He crushes me with a tempest, and multiplies my wounds without cause" (Job 9:17), and adds, "It is all one thing; Therefore I say, 'He destroys the blameless and the wicked'" (v. 22). Even if Job crossed a line in the criticism he brought (38:2-3), God seemed to respect him for his candor (42:7). He charged Job with no irreverence, but when priests presumed to offer "profane fire before the LORD" (Leviticus 10:1) or a king paid no mind to His instruction (1 Samuel 15:22-23), God was severe.

Moses, Elijah and Isaiah remind Christians that it is no routine encounter to be in the presence of God. God hid Moses in a cleft of the rock on Sinai while He passed by (Exodus 33:21-22; cf. 34:6-8). Years later Elijah encountered God on the same mountain. A great wind "broke the rocks in pieces" (1 Kings 19:11). Earthquake and fire followed, but the prophet found God in "a still small voice" (v. 12). The sheer awe of being in the presence of God is perhaps best expressed by Isaiah. The prophet's vision came in the year that King Uzziah died (also called Azariah, 2 Kings 14:21), about 740 B.C. He saw God seated on a throne in the temple. Above Him were seraphim, some type of angelic creatures who appear nowhere else in the Bible. Isaiah was stricken with terror at being in the presence of the Lord. "Woe is me," he said, "for I am undone! Because I am a man of unclean lips, and I dwell in the midst of a people of unclean lips; for my eyes have seen the King, The LORD of hosts" (Isaiah 6:5).

Whatever else we may say of God, His ways are beyond ours. He is Judge and Creator. To speak to Him is to be in the presence of the Holy One (Revelation 4:11). The essence of reverence is the realization that the God who is near (Acts 17:27) is also far removed from us in might and glory. His presence calls for awe and respect.

You Have Come to Mount Zion
(Hebrews 12:18-24)

Technically Zion is the ridge of land that descends southward from the temple mount in Jerusalem. To its east is the Kidron Valley and to its west the Central Valley, popularly called the Tyropoeon Valley. Zion and Bethlehem wear the name, "city of David" (Luke 2:4). The king conquered the ridge from the Jebusites some 1,000 years before the birth of Christ (2 Samuel 5:6-7). He recognized the natural fortification of the city and made it his capital. As centuries passed, the city spread northward to the temple mount and then westward. By the time of Christ it was a large city. Herod the Great (Matthew 2:3) had fortified it well and refurbished the temple. The Jerusalem Jesus knew was one of the most powerful, most renowned cities of the East. It was the holy city for Jews scattered throughout the Roman world. For centuries before Christ, the name Zion, using a figure of speech called synecdoche, designated the temple mount or even the whole city of Jerusalem (e.g., Psalm 9:11; 48:2).

In order to impress on his readers the magnitude of the blessings they shared in Christ, the author of Hebrews reasoned from the lesser to the greater, a method of argumentation he used frequently. The lesser privilege had belonged to Israel when they were at Sinai receiving the Law of God. The events described in Exodus 19 were unparalleled. God told the hordes of Israel that if they would obey Him, they would be "a special treasure to Me above all people" (Exodus 19:5) and "a kingdom of priests and a holy nation" (v. 6). The Lord manifested His glory to the tribes with thunder and lightning, with a thick cloud and the sound of a trumpet (v. 16). If so much as an animal touched the mountain it was to die (vv. 12-13). Such were the events that attended the giving of the Law; such was the reverential awe inspired in Israel at Sinai.

Wonderful and fear-inspiring as the events at Sinai had been, they paled in comparison to blessings enjoyed by Christians. Israel had stood before God at Sinai; those washed in the blood of the Lamb will stand in His presence on Mount Zion, the place Paul called "the Jerusalem above" (Galatians 4:26). The author of Hebrews heaps up the words to impress on his readers the blessings reserved for those who partake of the kingdom of God. The church is "the city of the living God, the heavenly Jerusalem" (Hebrews 12:22). To be among "the general assembly and church of the firstborn" is to have one's name "registered in heaven" (v. 23). In the end, the new Jerusalem will come down out of heaven "as a bride adorned for her husband" (Revelation 21:2). Thanksgiving attended by reverence and wonder befit those who belong to God by virtue of "the Mediator of the new covenant" whose sprinkled blood "speaks better things than that of Abel" (Hebrews 12:24; cf. 11:4).

Serve God With Reverence
(Hebrews 12:25-29)

The author continued his reasoning from the lesser to the greater. Included in the comparison of the Law of Moses and the new covenant were serious warnings. Israel had been unfaithful to God's covenant, and the disobedient had suffered the consequences. The record of Judges and Kings described the ambassadors God sent to warn and the failure of the nation to listen. They did not escape God's anger when they refused to repent and obey. The author brings it all home with the warning, "Much more shall we not escape if we turn away from Him who speaks from heaven" (Hebrews 12:25).

Integral to the message of the New Testament is that the Lord who appeared as Redeemer and Savior will appear a second time for judgment (Hebrews 9:28). His first coming was marked by His death on the cross; His second will mean the end of time and salvation for those who wait for Him. God's judgments have come in the past, but He has promised to shake the earth one more time. If reverent obedience was God's demand for those who lived under the old covenant, how much more essential is it for those who live under the new? Those who were disobedient to the law given through Moses faced the chastisement of God. How much greater will be the chastisement for those who turn their backs on the Son of God?

Building Yourselves Up (Jude 20-25)

To worship God, to be obedient to His Word, and to be reverent in His presence result both in the praise of God and the spiritual growth of those who worship. For the most part, Jude's letter describes and refutes those "who turn the grace of our God into lewdness and deny the only Lord God and our Lord Jesus Christ" (Jude 4). Dealing with dissension that arises within the ranks of believers can be discouraging (Acts 20:30). Near the end of his short letter, Jude encourages his readers not to become obsessed with discord and heretics. Christians need to seek out those things that build them up in the faith.

Believers become stronger in Christ when they pray in the Holy Spirit, that is, when they pray with reverence and faith. Reverence in worship includes the keeping of oneself in the love of God and looking for the mercy of Christ, but it also includes love extended to brothers and sisters. Modern Christians often distinguish between the love they are to display to the sinner and the hatred they have for the sin itself. Jude gives expression to the same sentiment. The brother of James (Jude 1) and of the Lord finishes his letter with a doxology brimming over with reverence toward the Lord.

Conclusion

Important as it is for Christians to worship God in the ways that He has specified, worship that mechanically and mindlessly goes through the motions is neither satisfying nor edifying. Worse than that, such worship gives God no praise, no glory. Christians will find themselves built up in Christ, anxious to obey Him in all things, when they first purify their hearts and worship with mind and soul. Reverence in worship means that one listens to the words of public prayer. It means that believers join in the words to songs they have repeated hundreds of times. Words of exhortation from preachers or elders can and ought to be personally applied. Reverence in worship means joining in the breaking of the bread and drinking of the cup. It means remembrance of the cross, but it also means reflection on the living Lord who reigns at God's right hand. It further means that worshipers hope for His return, repent of their sins and wait anxiously for Him. Worship is according to the will of God, and it is from hearts of love and devotion, thankful for His gifts and His care.

Questions

1. What Old Testament figure challenged God, claiming that He was indifferent in the doling out of grief and joy?
2. Which prophet was called by God during a vision he saw in the temple?
3. What was the mountain where Israel had come that burned with fire?
4. Which king of Israel conquered Jerusalem and made it his capital?
5. What was the name of the ridge that extended south from the temple mount and west of the Kidron Valley?
6. How did Moses react as God made known His presence when the Law was given to Israel?
7. What is the "heavenly Jerusalem" referred to by the author of Hebrews?
8. Who did the author of Hebrews say was mediator of a "new covenant"?
9. What is the shaking that God has promised to bring to earth and heaven?
10. In what did Jude tell his readers that they were to build themselves up?

Discussion Starters

1. How are Christians to express reverence for God when the church assembles? Are worshipers always to be quiet and still? What are the signs of reverence?
2. In what way do the experiences of Moses, Elijah and Isaiah illustrate the reverence due God when people stand in the presence of His august might and holiness?
3. In what way does earthly Jerusalem, the temple and the priesthood help Christians understand the reverence due to God because of His holiness?
4. What bearing do the words of Jude have on the need for Christians to hate the sin they see in the world but to love the sinners? What does that expression mean?

This We Recognize
Summer Quarter

These lessons will focus on fellowship, preaching, teaching and serving; at the same time, we must understand church structure; anticipate the return of Jesus; and give serious thought to judgment, heaven and hell. These we recognize.

Lesson 1 • Week of June 7, 2015
The Organization of the Church

Matthew 28:18
18 And Jesus came and spoke to them, saying, "All authority has been given to Me in heaven and on earth."

John 16:13
13 However, when He, the Spirit of truth, has come, He will guide you into all truth; for He will not speak on His own authority, but whatever He hears He will speak; and He will tell you things to come.

Acts 14:23
23 So when they had appointed elders in every church, and prayed with fasting, they commended them to the Lord in whom they had believed.

Acts 20:28
28 Therefore take heed to yourselves and to all the flock, among which the Holy Spirit has made you overseers, to shepherd the church of God which He purchased with His own blood.

1 Corinthians 1:1-2
1 Paul, called to be an apostle of Jesus Christ through the will of God, and Sosthenes our brother,

2 To the church of God which is at Corinth, to those who are sanctified in Christ Jesus, called to be saints, with all who in every place call on the name of Jesus Christ our Lord, both theirs and ours.

Philippians 1:1
1 Paul and Timothy, bondservants of Jesus Christ, To all the saints in Christ Jesus who are in Philippi, with the bishops and deacons.

2 Timothy 2:2

2 And the things that you have heard from me among many witnesses, commit these to faithful men who will be able to teach others also.

Introduction

Authority for the governance of the church of Christ rests in Jesus Christ Himself. That is true even though Jesus left nothing that He personally wrote. The exercise of Christ's authority has been realized because of His promise to send a second Comforter, the Holy Spirit. The Spirit, Jesus said, would inspire His apostles so that they could write truth that had its source in Him. The early church accepted the authoritative Word revealed through the apostles because the apostles were with Christ throughout His ministry, because they received the promise of the Spirit from Him, and because of the miraculous powers given to them by the Spirit. The passing of centuries has reinforced the faith of the early church. When the church models its organization on the pattern of New Testament churches, it recognizes the authority of Christ.

Christ is the fountainhead for the church's doctrine and way of life, but individual congregations and individual people encounter myriads of situations in which human wisdom must be used in the day-to-day application of Christian doctrine and morality. The physical ways that people live – their social patterns, moral issues and a host of such things – are considerably different depending on their place and time. Churches have to make decisions about where they will assemble, how they will help the needy or preach the gospel, which missionary efforts they will support, and similar matters – all of which call for wise, well-considered judgments. Christ made provisions for the organization of the church so that the day-to-day demands of carrying out His will could be executed. Although the New Testament does not devote itself in any one place to a description of the church's organization, a careful reading of its entire contents uncovers the apostolic plan for the way the church was to be governed.

The Authority of Jesus
(Matthew 28:18; John 16:13)

When Jesus met with the apostles in Galilee after His resurrection from the dead, He asserted the universal authority given to Him by the Father (Matthew 28:18). Before this meeting, He had reassured them that He would send the Spirit of truth, whose inspiration would be evident in that the Spirit would give them miraculous recall of all that Jesus willed for them to write (John 16:13). For the organization of the church, as in all other matters of doctrine and practice, Christ is the source of authority. In theory, the denominational world is united in the assertion that Christ is the source of authority; it is divided on the type of church organization Christ has authorized for carrying out His will.

Among denominations, the term used for governance is "church polity." Many denominations have a so-called episcopal-type organization. The classic example of such a structure is Roman Catholicism, but many other denominations have a similar type of governance. Day-to-day matters are in the hands of bishops, who control the appointment of clergy to serve individual churches. In some cases, bishops hold title to assets such as land or buildings. Some denominations (e.g., Roman Catholicism) understand bishops to be successors to the apostles in the New Testament. Ordinary members have little say in how the denomination spends its money or how priests are to perform. Certainly they have no voice in doctrinal matters. Numbered among denominations with episcopal governments are the Episcopal Church; many Methodist and Lutheran churches; and, in their own peculiar way, the Mormons.

A second common type of church polity among denominations is the Presbyterian model. Presbyterian denominations and Reformed churches with national roots (e.g., Dutch Reformed) have this type of governance. Elders are elected, often to three-year terms, by members of each congregation. The preacher, often called the "teaching elder," is one of the governing board of elders. Congregations send delegates to an overseeing body called a "presbytery," and people, from there, go to a still-larger organization called a "synod." Some denominations have a hybrid governing structure consisting of elements drawn from episcopal and Presbyterian models.

In addition to these two common types of church polity, some denominations have more or less local congregational governments. Increasingly, denominations consist of one congregation governed by one person, typically its founder. They go under a wide variety of names, often with a word like "community" or "fellowship" attached. The "ruling pastor" of such denominations is often a charismatic person who rules by virtue of a personal following. Members who disagree with him will be asked to leave in short order. The pattern the apostles used for the organization of churches in the New Testament was unlike the episcopal, Presbyterian or individual model.

Those Chosen to Lead
(Acts 14:23; 20:28; Philippians 1:1)

When Paul and Barnabas were traveling from city to city on their first missionary journey, they left behind them fledgling churches. Much of the Old Testament would have been useful to the churches for guidance in morality and reverence toward God, but the teachings of the missionaries would have been their sole source for the Christian message. The pair of Christian ambassadors established churches in cities located in the southern part of the Roman province of Galatia. Specifically mentioned are Antioch near Pisidia, Derbe, Lystra and Iconium. Several months later, Jews who professed faith in Christ but who were zealous for the Law followed Paul and Barnabas through the churches and taught that Gentiles had to submit to circumcision and other ordinances of the Law in order to be saved (cf. Acts 15:1). The resulting crisis led Paul to write the Galatian letter.

In anticipation of needs Galatian churches would have for faithful and strong leaders, Paul and Barnabas made a second visit to them before they returned to their base in Antioch of Syria. Although none of the churches had believers who had been Christians for long (cf. 1 Timothy 3:6), the missionary pair appointed elders in every church. Appointing elders for churches was Paul's regular practice. For example, although neither Acts nor Ephesians says anything about the appointment of elders at Ephesus, elders surfaced at a meeting with Paul while he was en route to Jerusalem (Acts 20:17). Philippians, another of Paul's letters, was specifically addressed to church leaders – its bishops and deacons.

Those with leadership responsibilities in local churches (1 Thessalonians 5:12-13; Hebrews 13:17) were variously called "elders," "bishops," "overseers" or "pastors" in Acts and the letters of the New Testament. The same Greek word (*presbyteroi*) is sometimes translated "elder" or "presbyter." Another word (*episkopoi*) is variously translated "bishop" or "overseer." Yet a third word (*poimenes*) is translated "pastor" or "shepherd," but all three Greek words refer to the same office. Paul told the elders at Ephesus to oversee the church (Acts 20:28). The word translated "oversee" is a verb form of the word rendered "bishops" by the New King James Version in Philippians 1:1. "Bishop" itself is a rough English transliteration of the Greek word meaning "overseer." In the same verse (Acts 20:28), Paul told the overseers or elders at Ephesus to shepherd or serve as pastors for the church of God. All three terms – "elder," "pastor" and "bishop" – were used of the same office (cf. 1 Peter 5:1-2). To serve as a pastor, evangelist or teacher in the New Testament church was to serve in different capacities (Ephesians 4:11). A pastor was an elder, not an evangelist.

Continuity
(1 Corinthians 1:1-2; 2 Timothy 2:2)

For the most part, the letters of the New Testament are occasion specific; that is, they were written to address needs and situations in individual churches. Still, authors of the letters were aware that what they wrote applied to other churches. The letters have a universal element in them. For example, after addressing the church at Corinth, Paul added that the letter was for "all who in every place call on the name of Jesus Christ" (1 Corinthians 1:2). The apostle intended that, in organization and other matters, the precedents he set forth for Corinth would guide churches in other places and times. The pattern in the New Testament for the governance of the church in the first century is authoritative for the governance of the modern church.

Paul's concern that the message revealed to him by the Spirit (1 Corinthians 2:13) be passed to subsequent generations is clear in his letters to Timothy. He instructed his younger co-worker to commit what he had "heard from [Paul] among many witnesses" to faithful men who would pass it on to others (2 Timothy 2:2). The conclusion is evident: Although the books of the New Testament address specific people and churches, they were also intended to be authoritative sources for the doctrine and practice of the church until the Lord's return.

Conclusion

Few things are as vital for the well-being of churches, for their faithfulness in doctrine and practice, than that they be served by knowledgeable, sincere and godly leaders. Those who serve as elders have a particular responsibility for leading well, but evangelists, deacons and teachers also serve in leadership capacities. In matters of judgment, all members of a congregation ought to respect and follow the direction of their elders, even when they differ with decisions made (Hebrews 13:17). The New Testament gives no indication that church leaders – variously called elders, overseers or pastors – served more than one congregation at a time. It does indicate that no one serves a nobler task than the person who aspires to a leadership role in the church. Leading in the Lord's church is not a matter of personal acclaim; it is a matter of serving the Lord and His people.

Questions

1. How does Christ speak with authority to the modern church?
2. To whom did God give all authority in heaven and on earth?
3. Whom did Jesus promise to send to the apostles to guide them and to call to their remembrance all that He had said?
4. What are some modern denominations with so-called episcopal governments?
5. What are some modern denominations governed by a so-called Presbyterian model?
6. When Paul and Barnabas made a second visit to the churches they had established on their first missionary journey, what office did they appoint Christians to?
7. Which of Paul's letters did he address to the elders and deacons of the church?
8. In addition to "elders," what were those who had spiritual leadership in churches called?
9. What did Paul write in the opening verses of 1 Corinthians to indicate that he expected the letter to be read for guidance of churches in other places?
10. To whom did Paul instruct Timothy to pass the Christian message?

Discussion Starters

1. What kinds of questions come up in the day-to-day life of a congregation, which require human judgments to be made?
2. How should matters of opinion in churches be handled (cf. Hebrews 13:17)?
3. Why is it important to follow the biblical model for church organization? What problems might arise from following man-made models?
4. What are three names the New Testament gives to those who lead churches? How do those titles describe their function?

Aids to Christian Fellowship

Mark 10:29-30

29 So Jesus answered and said, "Assuredly, I say to you, there is no one who has left house or brothers or sisters or father or mother or wife or children or lands, for My sake and the gospel's,

30 "who shall not receive a hundredfold now in this time – houses and brothers and sisters and mothers and children and lands, with persecutions – and in the age to come, eternal life."

John 13:34-35

34 A new commandment I give to you, that you love one another; as I have loved you, that you also love one another.

35 By this all will know that you are My disciples, if you have love for one another.

John 17:20-23

20 I do not pray for these alone, but also for those who will believe in Me through their word;

21 that they all may be one, as You, Father, are in Me, and I in You; that they also may be one in Us, that the world may believe that You sent Me.

22 And the glory which You gave Me I have given them, that they may be one just as We are one:

23 I in them, and You in Me; that they may be made perfect in one, and that the world may know that You have sent Me, and have loved them as You have loved Me.

Galatians 6:1-2

1 Brethren, if a man is overtaken in any trespass, you who are spiritual restore such a one in a spirit of gentleness, considering yourself lest you also be tempted.

2 Bear one another's burdens, and so fulfill the law of Christ.

1 John 1:7

7 But if we walk in the light as He is in the light, we have fellowship with one another, and the blood of Jesus Christ His Son cleanses us from all sin.

Introduction

The New Testament contains a considerable amount of teaching on the movement of this present age toward a climactic conclusion. A day of judgment is on the horizon, but knowledge of the end time is more than idle curiosity. The confidence that human history is advancing to a purposeful conclusion is an incentive for Christians to live godly, noble lives in this age. After Peter spoke of the last day, he concluded, "Therefore, since all these things will be dissolved, what manner of persons ought you to be in holy conduct and godliness ... ?" (2 Peter 3:11). It is that way all through the New Testament (cf. Matthew 24:44-51). That this age is moving toward an end is no invitation to speculate about a rapture or a 1000-year reign of Christ on earth. Rather, it is a call for believers to examine themselves and to live as Jesus taught and modeled.

For Christians to know that Christ will return and that His return will be followed by judgment and eternity is enough. Neither Jesus nor the apostles gave believers reason for fixation on heaven or hell. Where in the Bible is the blueprint for the corridors of heaven? Preachers are sometimes faulted for not preaching more on hell, but interest in the subject may spring more from human curiosity than biblical teaching. The Lord will return and judge the living and the dead (2 Corinthians 5:10). Life in heaven will follow for the saved, and eternal destruction in hell will follow for the lost. Having said that, it is time to turn attention to the way people ought to live this life in order to be among the saved. Until the Lord returns, the decisions and behavior of the present time matter.

In a sense, heaven has already begun for those who have turned their lives over to the Lord who is reigning at God's right hand. Of course, pain and suffering have not come to an end, and the kingdom of God has yet to be fully realized (1 Corinthians 15:50). But already God is a refuge and source of strength (Hebrews 13:5-6); already Christians share the fellowship of those whose ideals are brotherly love, compassion and goodness. With the presence of Jesus, Christians partake of the kingdom of God (Colossians 1:13). For them, life in the church, the body of Christ, is a foretaste of eternal glory.

With One Another
(Mark 10:29-30; John 13:34-35)

Near the end of His ministry, Jesus traveled to Jerusalem for the Feast of the Passover. Shortly before He began the final leg of His journey, a young man approached Him. He genuinely wanted to follow a godly life, but he had great riches. Jesus told him to sell all he had and give to the poor and to lay up for himself treasures in heaven. It was too much for the wealthy young man. He turned his back on Jesus (Mark 10:21-22). During the conversation between Jesus and His disciples that followed, Jesus warned of the deceitfulness of riches. In this context, Peter spoke up. He and the other apostles had done what the rich ruler had been unwilling to do. They had left family and abandoned possessions to follow Jesus. Peter likely was speaking for all of them when he asked, "What are we going to get from it?" (cf. Matthew 19:27). It is a question many believers have asked. Is being a Christian worth the effort?

The response of Jesus to Peter betrayed no anger or disappointment, but He gave the apostle's question a 180-degree turn. Peter had been thinking about material things. The answer of Jesus focused on fellowship (Mark 10:29-30). Life is richer, Jesus maintained, when one relates to others guided by affection, respect and brotherhood. Life is dismal when one's relationships are defined by power, whether it be the power of a club or the power of a checkbook. Whatever trappings of material success the rich young ruler would have left behind, the fellowship of good people in the kingdom of God would have been worth infinitely more. The same was true for Peter and the other disciples.

Whatever values and habits disciples strip off for the sake of Christ will be scant loss. The new life in which they clothe themselves will be more satisfying and joyous than anything the world can offer. In the kingdom of God, Christians will find blessings attendant to fellowship with the Lord and His people – blessings that will be shaken together, pressed down and running over (Luke 6:38). Should privation, persecution, pain or suffering – or anything else the world can hurl – attend the Christian way, the love and joy of Christian fellowship will not be dampened. To be in Christ is not only to hope for a blissful life in the age to come, but also to bask in the blessings of Christ in this present age.

With Jesus (John 17:20-23; 1 John 1:7)

The Greek word translated "fellowship" suggests people who share in matters of common interest. The bonds of Christian fellowship unite believers with the Lord. Sinners become believers after they encounter the man from Nazareth who so loved them that He laid down His life to atone for their sins. Faith issuing forth in obedience results in bonds of fellowship between believers and the risen Lord. Commonly bound to the Lord, they commune with one another and jointly partake of the body of Christ. Inherent in fellowship with Christ is fellowship with His people (1 John 1:3).

The unity and joy of Christian living find their source in Christ. To the extent that churches follow Christ and revel in the fruit of the Spirit (Galatians 5:22-23), the kingdom of God has been realized. During the last Passover Jesus observed with His disciples and immediately before He led them out of Jerusalem across the Kidron Valley to a garden on the slope of the Mount of Olives, He paused to pray. The prayer in John 17 looked toward the cross, but the heart of Jesus was with the disciples He would leave behind. He prayed that the immediate disciples would bear up under the ordeal of His death, and He prayed for the well-being of disciples who would follow as centuries unfolded. He knew that the community of the saints, the church that would come into being, would face trials from without and false teachers from within. Jesus prayed that His disciples would grow in faith and unity. His will was that Christians have the same oneness among themselves that united Father and Son. Fellowship among believers requires that they first put themselves in the hands of the Lord. When believers walk in the light, the blood of Christ cleanses them from sin (1 John 1:7). They stand righteous before God and share fellowship with the redeemed.

Helping One Another (Galatians 6:1-2)

In the centuries that followed the death of Christ, untold thousands heard the gospel and were baptized into Christ. Their changed lives made an impression on nonbelievers. Pagans who had no good will for Christians nevertheless commented on the love they had for one another. Not only did they give to the poor of their own number, but they also reached out with helping hands to all (Galatians 6:10). During the first few years after the establishment of the church, Christians contributed to a common purse, and from it, distribution was made according to need (Acts 2:44-45; 4:33-34). When Barnabas and Paul conferred with the apostles and elders in Jerusalem, all agreed that providing for the poor was to be a top priority (Galatians 2:10). Paul demonstrated his commitment to the ideal that Christians ought to help one another on his third missionary journey. He spearheaded the taking up of a sizable contribution from Gentile churches for the relief of poor Christians in Judea (2 Corinthians 9:12; Romans 15:26). That Christian fellowship includes helping with the material and spiritual needs of brothers and sisters has been evident from the earliest days of the church.

Although Christian fellowship includes helping one another in material ways, Paul stressed that spiritual needs were of first importance. When a Christian allows himself to become ensnared in sin, he tends to put distance between himself and those of the faith. No one sees him when the church assembles. He needs encouragement to repent. A spirit of gentleness is more likely to result in spiritual restoration than are harsh words and accusations. The mutual sharing of burdens goes beyond relief for the poor.

Conclusion

Many of the songs Christians sing herald the beauty and joy to be realized in the age to come. When life is hard and material resources are in short supply, believers tend to turn attention to heaven. Jesus hardly discouraged His disciples from reflecting on the afterlife (John 5:28-29; 14:1-3), yet following Christ does not require a fixation on the blessings of heaven. Whatever blessings Christians will enjoy in the age to come will be ready-made. The task the Lord has left with His people is the working out of goodness and holiness in this present, evil age. He has charged His followers with being lamps and salt in the world (Matthew 5:13-14). When Christ adds the obedient to His church, eternal life has begun. Only a willful turning back to worldliness breaks the bonds of fellowship between Christ and His people (1 John 2:19; 2 Peter 2:22).

Faithfulness to Christ requires active involvement with His people, "for we are members of one another" (Ephesians 4:25). Life in the world to come, in many ways, will be an extension of life in the church, but without its sins and shortcomings.

Questions

1. What practical results follow when Christians reflect on the world to come?
2. What question did a wealthy young ruler ask Jesus?
3. What question did Peter ask after he said, "See, we have left all and followed You" (Matthew 19:27)?
4. What did Jesus say is in store for those who leave family and possessions in order to follow Him?

5. What new commandment did Jesus give to His disciples? In what sense was it new?

6. At what point in His life did Jesus offer the prayer recorded in John 17?

7. In addition to His immediate disciples, for whom did Jesus pray?

8. What results for Christians who walk in the light with the Lord?

9. When a Christian is overcome in a trespass, how are his fellow believers to respond?

10. What do Christians do when they bear one another's burdens?

Discussion Starters

1. Why are believers sometimes more interested in the coming age than they are with godly living in the current time? What do you think believers should focus on more?

2. Is it true that heavenly blessings begin in this life? What does fellowship with the people of God have to do with heavenly blessings?

3. How is the common bond Christians share with Christ the basis for the fellowship they enjoy with one another?

4. Why does faithfulness to Christ require Christians to be active participants in the body of Christ? What does it mean to be an "active participant"?

Hindrances to Christian Fellowship

John 7:16-18

16 Jesus answered them and said, "My doctrine is not Mine, but His who sent Me.

17 "If anyone wills to do His will, he shall know concerning the doctrine, whether it is from God or whether I speak on My own authority.

18 "He who speaks from himself seeks his own glory; but He who seeks the glory of the One who sent Him is true, and no unrighteousness is in Him."

Romans 16:17

17 Now I urge you, brethren, note those who cause divisions and offenses, contrary to the doctrine which you learned, and avoid them.

1 Corinthians 1:10-12

10 Now I plead with you, brethren, by the name of our Lord Jesus Christ, that you all speak the same thing, and that there be no divisions among you, but that you be perfectly joined together in the same mind and in the same judgment.

11 For it has been declared to me concerning you, my brethren, by those of Chloe's household, that there are contentions among you.

12 Now I say this, that each of you says, "I am of Paul," or "I am of Apollos," or "I am of Cephas," or "I am of Christ."

2 Corinthians 6:14

14 Do not be unequally yoked together with unbelievers. For what fellowship has righteousness with lawlessness? And what communion has light with darkness?

Ephesians 5:11

11 And have no fellowship with the unfruitful works of darkness, but rather expose them.

2 John 9-10

9 Whoever transgresses and does not abide in the doctrine of Christ does not have God. He who abides in the doctrine of Christ has both the Father and the Son.

10 If anyone comes to you and does not bring this doctrine, do not receive him into your house nor greet him.

Introduction

Christian fellowship grows out of and is dependent upon the bonds believers share with Christ. It follows that whatever weakens or destroys fellowship with God has the same effect on inter-Christian fellowship. Being a member of the church of Christ is to be organically bound to fellow believers (1 Corinthians 12:18). The vital life force of the church as an organism is the Spirit of Christ. Personal habits and conscious choices that strengthen ties between a Christian and the Savior at the same time bind believers more tightly to one another, and the converse is true. Whatever hinders one's fellowship with Christ hinders Christian fellowship.

Becoming a Christian is not the same as joining a civic club; it is not like being a Rotarian or a Civitan. The roots of Christian fellowship sink into soil having to do with much more than association with a nice group of people. The assembly is to worship God. Smiles, handshakes and pleasant banter about the garden and the grandchildren are benefits of the church, not its reason for existence. The church of Christ is a community of faith – a people who share a common confession and a common commitment to values and goals taught by their Lord. Christians love one another, forgive one another, and help one another along in this pilgrimage through life because they have an example in the life and deeds of Jesus of Nazareth. Some give more, some need more, but all draw lifeblood from Him who reigns at God's right hand.

The bonds of Christian fellowship are not based in merit any more than the forgiveness of sins is based in merit. The bonds that bind believers together are those that bind them to Christ. The loosening of bonds with Christ spells the dissolving of bonds within His body, the church. Hindrances to Christian fellowship are about those things that portend a believer's falling from grace (Galatians 5:4).

Division in the Church (1 Corinthians 1:10-12)

Both Jesus and the apostles who followed Him impressed on believers the importance of presenting a united front before the world. Jesus wanted His followers to be one in doctrine and purpose, but He also wanted them to be one in brotherly love and mutual respect. He wanted them to forgive offenses and to bear with one another's weaknesses (Ephesians 4:1-3).

From the earliest days of the church, disciples have struggled with maintaining "the unity of the Spirit and the bond of peace" (Ephesians 4:3). Sometimes wedges are driven between believers by those who are willing to compromise Christian doctrine. False teachers who abandoned the core teachings of the faith plagued the first-century church, and they have plagued the church in every age that has followed (Acts 20:30; 1 John 4:1). Christians are not to purchase unity at the cost of New Testament doctrine (Galatians 1:8), but not all division finds its source in doctrinal matters. Pettiness and self-willed determination to dominate even in matters of opinion can be and often are causes for congregational discord. All the division in the church at Corinth did not come about because false teachers had compromised the apostolic message. A sizable portion of it amounted to partisan bickering over personal preferences.

Several years passed between Paul's initial stay at Corinth and his writing of the first letter to the church. After he left the city, he came, by a circuitous route, to Ephesus, a city about 200 miles northeast across the Aegean Sea from Corinth. In Ephesus, the apostle somehow came to know associates of a lady named Chloe. She may have owned ships that helped carry brisk sea traffic between the two great commercial cities. The New King James Version has "Chloe's *household*," with the latter word in italics. The Greek hardly demands that Paul talked with Chloe's family. It was likely from sailors or dockhands, Chloe's employees, that the apostle kept up with the church at Corinth. He learned that bitterness and discord had grown rampant. Christians had divided into sides, depending on their preferred teacher. Paul and Apollos were principal candidates (Acts 18:24-28; 1 Corinthians 1:12). The two had no major doctrinal differences (3:6); neither of them had encouraged division. Divisions at Corinth, like divisions in many modern churches, sprang from partisan bickering. Unity was the casualty. Fellowship among believers was likely strained and forced.

Divisive Individuals
(Romans 16:17; 2 Corinthians 6:14)

As Paul was rounding off the Roman letter, in the midst of greetings and exhortations, he warned of those who divided churches by introducing doctrines contrary to what the Holy Spirit had revealed. Sometimes divisions result because Christians fail to bear with one another; doctrinal differences are hardly in evidence. At other times, churches divide because false teachers have compromised or otherwise changed New Testament teachings. When faced with a choice of either being faithful to biblical teaching or embracing and practicing false doctrine, adherence to the Christian confession of faith must be of first importance. The price for unity ought not to be the neglect of doctrine. Paul told Roman Christians to take notice of those who advocated doctrines contrary to those they had learned from the apostles and to oppose them. The sin of division lies at the feet of those who insist on departures from New Testament doctrine, not at the feet of those who resist them.

Those who embrace the kingdom of God are soon aware that what they do individually determines the way non-Christians view the whole church. Being a Christian is about more than "allowing Jesus to become your personal Savior"; it is also about being added by the Lord to His church. To be a Christian is to be part of a people. Paul told the Corinthians, "If one member suffers, all the members suffer with it"; then he added, "Now you are the body of Christ, and members individually" (1 Corinthians 12:26-27). In his second letter to Corinth, the message was the same: "We give no offense in anything, that our ministry may not be blamed. But in all things we commend ourselves as ministers of God" (6:3-4).

Among other things, the apostle urged Corinthian Christians to be careful about alliances they made and company they kept with the ungodly. When Paul urged the faithful "not to be unequally yoked together with unbelievers"

(2 Corinthians 6:14), the context makes it clear that he was thinking in terms broader than a Christian marrying a non-Christian. In circumstances where a believer puts his arms around and embraces people whose way of life or whose public profession undermines the lordship of Jesus Christ, the church suffers. The church cannot tolerate or embrace one who turns aside from biblical teaching.

Divisive Doctrines (John 7:16-18; Ephesians 5:11; 2 John 9-10)

In the larger megachurch, denominational scene, the word "doctrine" is taboo. For some, it conjures images of people sitting around a table, arguing and red-faced. Instead of doctrine, professed believers say they want love – although they may have little knowledge of what either doctrine or love is about. The mark of many modern churches is hands raised in the air keeping time to a hard beat provided by a band on stage. Emotions and good times crowd out thought, resolve and commitment.

Instead of advocating divisive doctrines, the expressed goal of some is to downplay doctrine or to dismiss it altogether. But insistence that doctrine be relegated to a sidebar is itself a doctrine. When Jesus said "My doctrine is not mine" (John 7:16 NKJV), the literal meaning of the Greek word is "teaching." Doctrine is nothing more or less than teaching. In John 7:16-17, Jesus used a form of the same Greek word He used when He charged His disciples to teach all nations (Matthew 28:20). If the church of Christ has any teaching, it has doctrine. Without its doctrine, the church has no affirmation to make and nothing to teach the world.

In the New Testament period, false teachers insisted that Gentile Christians embrace circumcision and other ceremonial aspects of the Law (Galatians 5:4). Others denied that Jesus had come in the flesh (2 John 7). In more recent times, men have insisted that a Christian cannot fall from grace and that obedience to Christ has nothing to do with salvation by faith. False teachings are so numerous that no one can put a number on them, but Paul urged believers to "have no fellowship with the unfruitful works of darkness" (Ephesians 5:11). John said that to greet and encourage a false teacher is to share in his evil deeds (2 John 10-11).

Conclusion

Fellowship is a warm, encouraging word, but like other Christian blessings, it calls on believers to act with discernment. One may extend friendship and maintain a certain distance, but fellowship implies approval. Friendship is acceptance of the total worth of a person, but fellowship is more specific. Two people may share fellowship in goals at work, for example, but have little else in common (1 Corinthians 5:9-10). Neighbors may share in efforts to raise money for surgery needed by a child but have decided differences in religious convictions. In whatever matter one extends fellowship, he declares his approval. Christians who offer fellowship to false teachers in such a way that they approve doctrine contrary to New Testament teaching partake in the evil deeds of the false teachers.

Questions

1. What division in the church at Corinth resulted from personal preferences?
2. Where was Paul when he wrote 1 Corinthians?
3. From whom did Paul learn about internal problems in the church at Corinth?
4. Around whom had parties formed at Corinth?
5. Whom did Paul urge Roman Christians to take notice of?
6. With whom did Paul tell the Corinthians they should not be yoked?
7. What point did Paul make to the Corinthians by comparing light and darkness?
8. With whose doctrine did Jesus equate His own?
9. What does the word "doctrine" mean?
10. What did John say Christians do when they receive those whose doctrine is contrary to Christ?

Discussion Starters

1. Why do doctrines or deeds that make barriers between Christians and Christ also make barriers between fellow Christians?
2. What should Christians do when tempted to choose unity by compromising biblical doctrine? Give examples of how such temptations might arise.
3. How are being a friend and extending fellowship similar, and how are they different? Give an example of when extending fellowship implies approval of sin.
4. What is the source of the tendency among believers to make light of doctrinal differences? What is the danger of the idea that doctrine is unimportant?

Preaching and Teaching God's Word

Matthew 28:18-20

18 And Jesus came and spoke to them, saying, "All authority has been given to Me in heaven and on earth.

19 "Go therefore and make disciples of all the nations, baptizing them in the name of the Father and of the Son and of the Holy Spirit,

20 "teaching them to observe all things that I have commanded you; and lo, I am with you always, even to the end of the age." Amen.

Romans 10:13-15

13 For "whoever calls on the name of the Lord shall be saved."

14 How then shall they call on Him in whom they have not believed? And how shall they believe in Him of whom they have not heard? And how shall they hear without a preacher?

15 And how shall they preach unless they are sent? As it is written: "How beautiful are the feet of those who preach the gospel of peace, Who bring glad tidings of good things!"

1 Corinthians 9:16-18

16 For if I preach the gospel, I have nothing to boast of, for necessity is laid upon me; yes, woe is me if I do not preach the gospel!

17 For if I do this willingly, I have a reward; but if against my will, I have been entrusted with a stewardship.

18 What is my reward then? That when I preach the gospel, I may present the gospel of Christ without charge, that I may not abuse my authority in the gospel.

2 Corinthians 11:5-9

5 For I consider that I am not at all inferior to the most eminent apostles.

6 Even though I am untrained in speech, yet I am not in knowledge. But we have been thoroughly manifested among you in all things.

7 Did I commit sin in humbling myself that you might be exalted, because I preached the gospel of God to you free of charge?

8 I robbed other churches, taking wages from them to minister to you.

9 And when I was present with you, and in need, I was a burden to no one, for what I lacked the brethren who came from Macedonia supplied. And in everything I kept myself from being burdensome to you, and so I will keep myself.

Introduction

It is more than a truism to say that Christianity is a taught religion. Not all religions are. Some are self-justified religions of conquest. In the seventh and eighth centuries, Islam spread from Arabia. It reached into Egypt, across North Africa, into Spain and eventually into Eastern Europe. The self-justification for conquest was the expansion of the religion of Muhammad. Hundreds of thousands died to the cry "Allah is God, and Muhammad is his prophet." By contrast, Christ and His apostles conquered by persuasion. In a few instances, misguided rulers have forcibly baptized pagans, but churches of all stripes have condemned the practice. Few things have been more universally recognized across denominational lines than that persuasion is the key to Christian expansion. Conversion matters only when minds, hearts and wills have been given to the Lord. Baptism alone saves no more than faith alone.

Christianity is a missionary religion. After the death and resurrection of Christ and the establishment of His church, only a few decades passed before missionaries fanned out across the Roman Empire. A few of their names are preserved in the book of Acts, but there must have been hundreds of others. Paul of Tarsus, Barnabas from the nearby island of Cyprus, John Mark and Silas from Jerusalem left churches behind them from Spain to Antioch in Syria. Greek- and Latin-speaking Jews and Gentiles listened to persuasive reasoning and turned in faith and obedience to Christ. Within a bare 30 years after Pentecost (Acts 2), Paul said the gospel had been "preached to every creature under heaven" (Colossians 1:23). No doubt the apostle used conscious exaggeration (hyperbole) to impress on his readers the rapid expansion of the church (cf. Romans 10:18). Although we know little of their effort, in short order missionaries were speaking of Christ in North Africa, Alexandria, Cyrene, Mesopotamia and the East.

Before many years had passed, missionaries were moving further east and west into the known world. As the centuries have passed, Christianity has flourished where men and women have been able to speak the truth, where they have been able to reason together. The church of Christ in ancient and modern times, by its nature, is a missionary – that is, a preaching and teaching – enterprise. Should it fail in its commission to preach, it would cease to be the church described in the New Testament.

Why Preach and Teach? (Matthew 28:18-20)

The short answer to the question "Why preach and teach?" is that Christ commanded it. The church is a preaching and teaching enterprise because Christ wants it to be, and the commission Jesus gave His disciples has at least three important implications. (1) It says that for people to be saved, they must hear, understand and place their faith in God. Teaching implies learning. Jesus wants His followers to implant faith in the hearts of sinners by way of the mind. The pathway to faith and salvation is not praying and waiting for the Holy Spirit to bring about an emotional experience. No supernatural infusion of faith from outside a person's mind results in salvation from sin. No one is saved because God has predestined him to be one of the elect. The first step to becoming a child of God is to hear the gospel preached.

(2) The message is easy to understand. Although it is true that the ways of God transcend human understanding (Isaiah 55:8-9), the message of the cross begins with concepts that are easily understood because they find support in universal human experience. Paul proclaimed that sin is universal (Romans 3:23). Through his own sins, a person knows why the cross was necessary. Justice requires a payment for wrongdoing. The sinless Son of God died in order to pay the price for sinners to be saved. Because no one merits salvation, the way for forgiveness and reconciliation with God is by means of faith. A corollary of faith is obedience. When the sinner confesses faith in Christ, repents of sins, and is baptized for the remission of sins, he stands justified and forgiven before God. The saved need to grow in faith (Hebrews 6:1); the message of the cross is not difficult.

(3) Those who hear the gospel have a decision to make. The followers of Jesus were to make disciples by presenting sinners with a choice (cf. Joshua 24:15). God chose to send His Son to die for human sins. When those who are lost in sin hear the gospel, it is time for them to choose. Those who choose faith in Christ and respond with obedience will be saved. Christians preach in order to glorify God and turn sinners to life (James 5:20).

The Preacher's Motivation (1 Corinthians 9:16-18)

A preacher finds himself in the position where he is answerable to someone other than those who write his weekly or monthly check. A preacher works for Christ. When he is faithful, he teaches what Christ has told him; he behaves as the Lord has directed. His answerability to Christ does not mean that he pays no mind to the Christians among whom he works. Within the bounds of good judgment, he will visit in homes, spend time in his study, and preach on biblical matters to address congregational needs. What the preacher will not do is proclaim a different doctrine or compromise demands for godly living in order to gain the approval of men. A preacher must be true to his commitment to Christ. He is not a hireling who can compromise in order to please those who hear him. He is not paid to preach what people think to be expedient. Instead, godly men and women provide him with support so he can give his full-time energies to serving Christ.

Paul never explained why he would not accept material support from the church at Corinth. Perhaps someone accused him of exploiting people for his own profit. The apostle did accept support from churches in order to preach full time (Philippians 4:15). At Corinth he even defended his right to receive assistance from the church, although he refused to accept it (1 Corinthians 9:14). Preaching for Paul was not a matter of receiving a salary. He was going to preach Christ. The apostle was consumed with the conviction that the God of creation and the God of Abraham and Moses were the same. The one God who chose Israel according to His eternal purpose sent His Son as a Savior. Paul's love for God and for God's creation compelled him to preach (v. 16). The preacher's motivation is the salvation of men and women from sin. He does what he does because he has responded to the love of God (v. 18).

The Support of the Preacher (Romans 10:13-15; 2 Corinthians 11:5-9)

Missionaries and preachers have this in common: Both have devoted their lives to the study and teaching of Scripture. Both proclaim the message of Christ revealed in Scripture to the lost. Both have a passion for leading those lost in sin to a loving, gracious Savior who wants to redeem them for God. Missionaries are, in some sense, preachers, and preachers are missionaries. Scripture teaches that those who give their full-time efforts to teach the lost or to build up the saints ought to be supported financially. Perhaps Paul expressed it most clearly: "Even so the Lord has commanded that those who preach the gospel should live from the gospel" (1 Corinthians 9:14).

In Romans 10:13, Paul reminded his readers that those who are saved must call on the name of the Lord. He followed by asking a rhetorical question: "And how shall they preach unless they are sent?" (v. 15). Every Christian participates in the Great Commission when he supports those who go into the world with the Word of God. In 2 Corinthians 11:5-9, the apostle returned to the subject he had broached in 1 Corinthians 9. Because of peculiar circumstances at Corinth, Paul refused to accept financial support from the church in the city. His refusal was galling to some Corinthians because he had accepted support from other churches. He told them, "I robbed other churches, taking wages from them to minister to you" (2 Corinthians 11:8). In a given circumstance, a preacher may choose to refuse financial support, but Scripture is clear that under normal conditions, financial support for those who labor full time in Christ strengthens the church.

Conclusion

The Bible authorizes churches or individual Christians to support those who work for the church. Some are missionaries (Romans 10:15); some, preachers (1 Corinthians 9:14); and some, elders (1 Timothy 5:17-18). Scripture does not specify the amount they are to receive. All parties have to fall back on the good judgment of the church's spiritual leaders – its shepherds. In general, it is safe to say that the preacher should receive wages similar to others in the church who have comparable training and experience. The church should be aware of benefits that typically go with employment, such as paid vacation time, retirement planning and health insurance. Mutual respect and consideration among churches and those they support will result in a satisfying experience.

Questions

1. How did Christ authorize that the gospel spread throughout the earth?
2. How much time passed after the death of Christ before Paul said that the gospel had gone to the ends of the earth?
3. What did Jesus tell His disciples to do when He told them to fan out into all the nations of the earth?
4. What, specifically, did Jesus tell His disciples to teach?
5. To whom is a preacher of the gospel answerable?
6. What did Paul say would be the result if he failed to preach Christ?
7. What was the point of Paul's illustration concerning the law about muzzling a threshing ox (1 Corinthians 9:9)?
8. To the degree that he places his faith and love in Christ, what motivation drives a preacher to do his work?
9. What did Paul argue the church needs to do so that preachers and missionaries will take Christ to the lost?
10. From what churches had Paul received wages so that he could preach Christ at Corinth?

Discussion Starters

1. What are at least three implications inherent in the Great Commission? Why do the implications require that Christians be diligent in obeying the Lord?
2. Why do some preachers distinguish between receiving a salary from the church and receiving support? Do you think the distinction is worthwhile?
3. What circumstances might have led Paul to refuse material support from the church at Corinth? How do we know he accepted support from other churches?
4. How should a church decide how much support it will give a preacher who labors with them full time? Why is the amount of support important?

Building the Body

Acts 14:21-23

21 And when they had preached the gospel to that city and made many disciples, they returned to Lystra, Iconium, and Antioch,

22 strengthening the souls of the disciples, exhorting them to continue in the faith, and saying, "We must through many tribulations enter the kingdom of God."

23 So when they had appointed elders in every church, and prayed with fasting, they commended them to the Lord in whom they had believed.

Acts 15:36

36 Then after some days Paul said to Barnabas, "Let us now go back and visit our brethren in every city where we have preached the word of the Lord, and see how they are doing."

Romans 14:19

19 Therefore let us pursue the things which make for peace and the things by which one may edify another.

Ephesians 4:11-13

11 And He Himself gave some to be apostles, some prophets, some evangelists, and some pastors and teachers,

12 for the equipping of the saints for the work of ministry, for the edifying of the body of Christ,

13 till we all come to the unity of the faith and of the knowledge of the Son of God, to a perfect man, to the measure of the stature of the fullness of Christ.

1 Thessalonians 5:11

11 Therefore comfort each other and edify one another, just as you also are doing.

1 Timothy 4:8

8 For bodily exercise profits a little, but godliness is profitable for all things, having promise of the life that now is and of that which is to come.

Hebrews 10:24-25

24 And let us consider one another in order to stir up love and good works,

25 not forsaking the assembling of ourselves together, as is the manner of some, but exhorting one another, and so much the more as you see the Day approaching.

Introduction

In order to impress on individual Christians their responsibility to support and draw support from one another, Paul frequently resorted to the metaphor of the church as a body. It was a common trope in the Greco-Roman world, but in most cases, city officials used it in a political context. Rich citizens were urged to build temples or other public buildings at their own expense. Rulers called on ordinary people to forgo their interests for the sake of the city's beauty and fame. The community, they said, was like a body. Some members had more prominence. Each part of the body functioned in its own way for the benefit of the whole. Paul observed that what was true for the city was also true for the church.

The building up of the body of Christ happens or fails to happen at the level of the individual congregation. All benefit when godly elders oversee and serve the flock of God or when worship is carefully planned so that all can express joyous praise and thanksgiving. The body is strong when individual believers work together and respect one another for the contributions they make. The church, as a Christian community, needs a pat on the back when it feeds the hungry, offers resources to build up struggling families, or reaches out to bring lost souls into its number. Cheerful smiles and hardy handshakes go a long way to building up the body of Christ.

Projecting the reality of a saved, united people bent on reflecting the image of Christ is contagious. When Christians self-consciously love one another, the church grows, but no one should suppose the building of strong churches is only a matter of public relations. A slick advertising campaign and a winning church softball team are likely to have little long-term benefit for the health of the body. Permanent health requires growth in knowledge, faith and imitation of Christ. It is a slow, deliberate process that requires enlightened leaders and a committed membership. No easy, three-step process guarantees strong churches. Persistence that stretches across generations results in growing churches that serve the Lord with faith.

With Orderliness (Acts 14:21-23; 15:36; Ephesians 4:11-13)

Those who have studied such things say that nothing is more crucial for the success of an organization than a clear sense of purpose. A corollary is that nothing is more essential for a clear projection of purpose than effective leaders. Orderliness is dependent on good leaders; good leaders project a sense of purpose. Board members of a Christian college or university testify that the selection of a president is their most important function. Elders know that hardly anything is more important for the well-being of a church than the choosing of an effective preacher. Final responsibility for the functionality of a school rests with a board of directors, and the faithfulness of a church, with its elders. It remains true that a president in one case and a preacher in the other are public figures. Their positions give them leadership roles. Early Christian leaders used to say that elders, preachers and members do well when they work together and support one another like the strings of a harp.

After Paul and Barnabas left fledgling churches behind in the cities they visited on their first missionary journey, they realized that orderliness in the churches would be important if they were to continue being faithful to the Lord. The missionaries' purpose was not merely to baptize the lost into Christ. They wanted to leave behind them self-sustaining churches that would become centers for continued outreach. They recognized that the baptized would need to grow in knowledge and faith. Before they returned home, they circled back to teach and encourage those they had baptized (Acts 14:21-22). To promote orderliness, they appointed elders in every church (v. 23). The two missionaries were not content to baptize the lost and ride off into the sunset. After a year or more had passed, they were still talking with each other about what they might do to learn how the new converts were faring (15:36). The process of teaching and exhorting was never-ending.

Orderliness in churches was not a system invented by Paul and Barnabas. It was under God's direction that churches were organized. Paul appealed to Christ as the One who ordained that the church should be led by godly men. The Lord willed that apostles and prophets be endowed with supernatural gifts to benefit churches in every place. In local churches, Christ gave some to be evangelists and pastors. The last two words, "pastors and teachers" (Ephesians 4:11), may refer to the same people, i.e., some were to be "teaching pastors." Far from doing all the work of the church themselves, church leaders were to equip all the saints for the work of ministry.

With Worship
(Hebrews 10:24-25; 1 Timothy 4:8)

The building up of the church begins with orderliness, but worship is a key ingredient. In worship, churches express their unity, their common hope, and their common purpose. Given the importance of the assembly to modern Christians, it is surprising that the New Testament sketches what took place in the assemblies of first-century churches only in broad terms. That they sang, prayed, studied from Scripture, shared in the Lord's Supper, and gave of their means is certain, but we know little about the kinds of songs they sang or the order of events when the church assembled. From what Paul told the Corinthian church, he expected the assembly to be orderly (1 Corinthians 14:40).

The author of Hebrews told his readers that Christians should give thought to the planning of their assemblies so that worship encourages brotherly love and good works. Worship is about the glorification of God, but it is also about the building up of the people of God. Although a believer can worship in the privacy of his own home (Matthew 6:6), private worship is no substitute for public assembly. Including himself with his readers, the Hebrews author urged Christians not to forsake "the assembling of ourselves together"

(10:25). The assembly contributes to the fellowship of the people of God as they join in songs, prayer and study of Scripture. Assembled together, they encourage one another to continue steadfastly by feeding the poor, sending missionaries to teach the lost, and stimulating one another to faithfulness.

The phrase "bodily exercise" (1 Timothy 4:8) is likely to convey a different sense to modern Americans than it did for Paul. In the context, the apostle had warned his readers that false teachers would come who would equate godliness with self-denial. They would forbid marriage and the eating of foods (v. 3). Paul rejected the equation. Some small spiritual benefit may accrue to one who denies himself innocent bodily pleasures, but godliness requires more than that. The New American Standard Bible gets closer to Paul's meaning when it translates "bodily discipline." Paul was not telling his readers that physical training, like lifting weights and running marathons, is of little benefit. That was not his subject at all. He was telling them that the buffeting of the body, self-denial for its own benefit, is of little value spiritually. The building up of the church is attendant on a strong sense of partaking of a community committed to obeying Christ. Community consciousness is stronger when believers assemble and stimulate one another to brotherly love and godliness.

With Fellowship
(Romans 14:19; 1 Thessalonians 5:11)

That Western European and American culture has become individualistic to a degree that ancient people could hardly have imagined it needs little proof. Individualism is the beginning point from which sociologists reason. What is called "social media" turns out to be anything but social as people hide behind the anonymity of "devices" and "apps" to spew outrageous view-points, sometimes offensive and violent. In such an atmosphere, civic clubs, whose aim is community betterment, go begging for members, and holding a political office is often more about power than public service.

By its nature, the church is a community of believers. It is difficult in the modern era to interest people in God – to say nothing of involvement with a people. It is hardly the first time in its long history that the church has had to confront cultural trends with an alternative agenda. When describing interaction among Christians, Paul frequently used the word "edify." To edify is to build up. Stated negatively, the apostle told believers to resist whatever tendencies they had to point fingers at one another or to judge motives. Extend the benefit of the doubt, he pleaded, "with all lowliness and gentleness, with long-suffering, bearing with one another in love" (Ephesians 4:2). Fellowship in the church begins with people who are bent on encouraging one another.

Conclusion

Until the Lord returns, the body of Christ will need to be about the business of building one another up. The edification of the church follows on the heels of orderliness in organization and purpose, of thoughtful and carefully planned worship, and of the mutual support that grows from Christian fellowship. The mission Jesus gave the church was not only to make disciples of all nations, but also to teach "them to observe all things that I have commanded you" (Matthew 28:20). The subsequent history of the church, seen through the windows of Acts and the letters of the New Testament, illustrates the kinds of issues that arise as the church proceeds in the day-to-day demands for godliness and righteousness.

Questions

1. What type of unity did people in the Greco-Roman world often encourage by comparing the community to a body?
2. What cities did Paul and Barnabas circle back to in order to encourage orderly community life (Acts 14:21-22)?
3. What did Paul and Barnabas appoint in those churches (Acts 14:23)?
4. What did Paul and Barnabas tell new Christians would be necessary for entrance into the kingdom of God (Acts 14:22)?
5. For what purpose did Paul say God had set offices and responsibilities in the church?
6. From 1 Corinthians 14:40, what can Christians learn about the conduct of the assembly of the church?
7. To what end did the author of Hebrews say Christians should stir one another up?
8. What does Hebrews say Christians are not to forsake?
9. What did Paul tell Roman Christians they were to pursue?
10. What did Paul mean by the phrase "edify [one] another" (Romans 14:19)?

Discussion Starters

1. What does a church need to do in order to encourage and build up its numbers in service to Christ?
2. What ought Christians to do in order to promote and encourage orderliness? What happens when orderliness fails?
3. What type of bodily exercise did Paul say is of little profit? How does the context of Paul's statement help to define the phrase?
4. What kinds of things should Christians do in order to make the Lord's Day assembly a time for mutual edification?

Serving Those in Need

Deuteronomy 15:7-8

7 If there is among you a poor man of your brethren, within any of the gates in your land which the Lord your God is giving you, you shall not harden your heart nor shut your hand from your poor brother,

8 but you shall open your hand wide to him and willingly lend him sufficient for his need, whatever he needs.

Matthew 25:37-46

37 Then the righteous will answer Him, saying, "Lord, when did we see You hungry and feed You, or thirsty and give You drink?

38 "When did we see You a stranger and take You in, or naked and clothe You?

39 "Or when did we see You sick, or in prison, and come to You?"

40 And the King will answer and say to them, "Assuredly, I say to you, inasmuch as you did it to one of the least of these My brethren, you did it to Me."

41 Then He will also say to those on the left hand, "Depart from Me, you cursed, into the everlasting fire prepared for the devil and his angels:

42 "for I was hungry and you gave Me no food; I was thirsty and you gave Me no drink;

43 "I was a stranger and you did not take Me in, naked and you did not clothe Me, sick and in prison and you did not visit Me."

44 Then they also will answer Him, saying, "Lord, when did we see You hungry or thirsty or a stranger or naked or sick or in prison, and did not minister to You?"

45 Then He will answer them, saying, "Assuredly, I say to you, inasmuch as you did not do it to one of the least of these, you did not do it to Me."

46 And these will go away into everlasting punishment, but the righteous into eternal life.

2 Corinthians 8:13-15

13 For I do not mean that others should be eased and you burdened;

14 but by an equality, that now at this time your abundance may supply their lack, that their abundance also may supply your lack – that there may be equality.

15 As it is written, "He who gathered much had nothing left over, and he who gathered little had no lack."

Colossians 3:17

17 And whatever you do in word or deed, do all in the name of the Lord Jesus, giving thanks to God the Father through Him.

1 Timothy 6:17-19

17 Command those who are rich in this present age not to be haughty, nor to trust in uncertain riches but in the living God, who gives us richly all things to enjoy.

18 Let them do good, that they be rich in good works, ready to give, willing to share,

19 storing up for themselves a good foundation for the time to come, that they may lay hold on eternal life.

James 1:27

27 Pure and undefiled religion before God and the Father is this: to visit orphans and widows in their trouble, and to keep oneself unspotted from the world.

Introduction

Churches have the twin commitments to (1) build up Christians and equip them for service (Ephesians 4:12) and (2) reach out to serve all people, especially those who share the faith (Galatians 6:10). Either commitment can become the focus to the neglect of the other. A church that turns in on itself may provide a beautiful fellowship hall, a game room for children, and other amenities until it becomes a kind of common man's country club. Such a body wears the name of Christ with difficulty. The church of Christ is defined by the mission the Lord gave it to go beyond its doors. Its purpose is to serve humankind by extending a message of hope to the lost and a helping hand to the needy.

In recent decades, population shifts have resulted in churches that are intent on escaping their old surroundings. Affluent neighborhoods sometimes are overrun by the poor. Businesses board up their windows and move to the suburbs; churches follow shortly behind. Reasons for moving are varied; one should be slow to cast stones. Still, it hardly seems reasonable for affluent Christians to spend millions on expensive facilities for their own comfort and to allow the needy to go begging. A serving church takes risks. It touches the leper and eats with dirty hands.

Jesus challenged a rich man to invite "the poor, the maimed, the lame, the blind" to his banquet (Luke 14:13). To another, He said, "Sell all that you have and distribute to the poor" (18:22). No matter how one tries to soften the words, they sound extreme. Jesus has certainly told us this much: Serving is no shallow commitment. Christians, whether acting alone or as churches, will be more effective when they plan their service deliberately and self-sacrificially. In the course of the Bible, God has offered guidance.

Who Are the Needy?
(Deuteronomy 15:7-8; James 1:27)

Reaching out a helping hand to the poor and vulnerable had been baked into the hearts of the Israelites. When they encountered the poor, Moses said those with means were to "willingly lend [the poor man] sufficient for his need" (Deuteronomy 15:8). They were to *lend* to the poor, not *give* assistance. But before we allow the words to justify a tight-fisted response to needs, we ought to notice the context. Lending laws were liberal. First, no Israelite was to loan money to a poor brother at interest (23:19; cf. Leviticus 25:35-37). In addition, God decreed that every seventh year, all debts were to be forgiven (Deuteronomy 15:1-2). If a poor brother needed a loan and the year of release was shortly at hand, the man of means would be tempted to deny the loan. Moses essentially said, "Don't let that happen" (cf. v. 9). If a brother were poor and his needs were dire, those with resources were to loan regardless of the proximity of the year of release.

Compassion extended beyond the poor brother in need of a loan. When an Israelite farmer reaped his fields, he was to leave behind portions so the needy and the sojourner could claim them for themselves (Leviticus 19:9-10). Foreigners in a strange land are vulnerable to injustice. The Law of Moses specified that temporary residents had the same legal rights as native sons (Numbers 15:16). None of Israel's neighbors had laws for the protection of the poor that compared to God's Law. The poor were expected to do all they could for themselves, but those with means were not to indulge themselves by supposing poor people were that way because they were lazy.

Concern for the needy extends into the New Testament. Not only is the compassion of Jesus on constant display, but He demanded that His disciples be the same way (cf. Matthew 25:31ff.). The early church followed in His steps. In Jerusalem, Christians shared their resources (Acts 4:34-35), and pillars in the Jerusalem church urged Paul and Barnabas to remember the poor (Galatians 2:9-10). James was in complete accord with the Old and New Testaments when he declared that pure religion is "to visit orphans and widows in their troubles" (1:27). "Visit" is a shorthand way of saying that God is pleased when His people demonstrate compassion for the helpless and vulnerable of society.

Who Can Aid?
(2 Corinthians 8:13-15; 1 Timothy 6:17-19)

Avarice and greed tend to justify a tight-fisted approach toward the poor by dividing people into givers and takers. Those who have the means to give, so the thinking goes, are hard workers. The takers are lazy and shiftless. It is easy to forget that all of us are both givers and takers, depending on the circumstances. Some give of their wisdom and their nobility of character; others give of their time or their money. Giving is not the sole domain of the rich, nor do the poor have a monopoly on receiving.

On his third missionary journey, Paul spearheaded a drive to amass a large sum of money for the relief of poor Christians in Judea. He called on churches made up largely of Gentiles to contribute to the fund. The apostle urged Gentiles to give generously by reminding them of how much benefit they had received from the Jews. He reasoned that it was fitting for Gentile abundance to supply Jewish needs so that "their abundance also may supply your lack – so that there may be equality" (2 Corinthians 8:14). The apostle wrote about the same contribution to Roman Christians. He said that largely Gentile churches in Greece (Macedonia and Achaia) were sending an offering for "the poor among the saints who are in Jerusalem," and then he added, "For if the Gentiles have been partakers of their spiritual things, their duty is also to minister to them in material things" (Romans 15:26-27). Paul understood giving and receiving to be multidimensional. Some give in different ways than others, but all give and all receive.

Those who have large amounts of money are able to wield influence and power, which can feed arrogance. Paul urged humility on the rich, which results in generosity. In his first letter to Timothy, Paul warned those with wealth not "to trust in uncertain riches" (6:17). He reminded those with material things that they had opportunities to do good that others lacked. By being "ready to give, willing to share," they were "storing up a good foundation for the time to come" (vv. 18-19).

Why Offer Aid?
(Matthew 25:37-46; Colossians 3:17)

The story of the poor widow who dropped her mites into the collection box in the court of the Jerusalem temple is a powerful testimony to the importance God attaches to one's motive in giving (Mark 12:41-44). The three long parables in Matthew 25 are about being prepared for the Lord when He comes again. The first ends with "for you know neither the day nor the hour" (v. 13); the second, with "cast the unprofitable servant into outer darkness" (v. 30); and the third, with "these will go away into everlasting punishment, but the righteous into eternal life" (v. 46). The third parable is about offering aid with the right motives.

The righteous gave generously, whether their means were great or small. They gave with little awareness of personal sacrifice. The Lord had to remind them of their acts of compassion and generosity. They served without their right hand knowing what their left hand was doing (Matthew 6:3), i.e., with no desire for credit or acclaim. In their serving, the righteous became like the Lord. They asked no questions about the merits or the sins of those they helped. Their serving was not wrung from them by a promise of life in the age to come. Rather, they served because they wanted to be like Christ. In being like Him, they prepared themselves to rejoice in being numbered with the righteous who will enter into eternal life.

Conclusion

Paul's admonition in Colossians 3:17 offers a fitting conclusion to reflections on the church's responsibility to serve those in need. It is a passage that describes Christian service in broad outline. Specifics about how the church is to apply the message of Christ to every conceivable situation are notably absent. Jewish rabbis over centuries of time have produced the Mishnah, the Talmud and hosts of lesser-known writings. The works, found in scores of volumes in the great libraries of the world, are attempts to apply the Law of Moses to all circumstances. Christians have nothing similar.

It is enough for Christians to say that in the New Testament the Holy Spirit has left a record of Jesus, of His way of life, and of the early church. The saved are to imbibe the spirit of the biblical testimony and, with the guidance it offers, to "do all in the name of the Lord Jesus." The people who wear the name of Christ are to be servants. To serve requires that heart and motives be in the right place. After that, it is a matter of serving from love and making adjustments as needed.

Questions

1. When a rich young man asked Jesus what he had to do in order to inherit eternal life, how did the Lord respond (Luke 18:18-22)?
2. How much did the Law say those with means should be willing to lend the needy?
3. According to the Law of Moses, what happened to debts at the end of every seventh year?
4. What did James say pure and undefiled religion consists of?
5. What plan for Judea did Paul execute on his third missionary journey?
6. Why did Paul maintain that it was fitting for Gentile churches to help Judeans in their poverty?
7. What temptation did Paul seem to think the wealthy might fall into?
8. Where did Paul say the rich would store up treasure when they were generous?
9. What theme unites the three long parables recorded in Matthew 25?
10. In whose name did Paul tell the Colossians to do all words and deeds?

Discussion Starters

1. What are the twin purposes to which the church should devote itself? Give Scripture references, and explain them.
2. Does the tendency to divide people into givers and takers stifle the church's willingness to serve the needy? Support your answer with biblical reasoning.
3. Why do you think the New Testament lacks attempts to codify the ways Christians are to serve? How are believers to respond when needs surface?
4. What resulted when Paul brought funds for the poor to Judea (cf. Acts 21–22)? What should we learn about unexpected outcomes to sincere efforts to serve?

The World of Shepherds

Acts 20:28-31

28 Therefore take heed to yourselves and to all the flock, among which the Holy Spirit has made you overseers, to shepherd the church of God which He purchased with His own blood.

29 For I know this, that after my departure savage wolves will come in among you, not sparing the flock.

30 Also from among yourselves men will rise up, speaking perverse things, to draw away the disciples after themselves.

31 Therefore watch, and remember that for three years I did not cease to warn everyone night and day with tears.

1 Timothy 3:1-2

1 This is a faithful saying: If a man desires the position of a bishop, he desires a good work.

2 A bishop then must be blameless, the husband of one wife, temperate, sober-minded, of good behavior, hospitable, able to teach.

Titus 1:7-9

7 For a bishop must be blameless, as a steward of God, not self-willed, not quick-tempered, not given to wine, not violent, not greedy for money,

8 but hospitable, a lover of what is good, sober-minded, just, holy, self-controlled,

9 holding fast the faithful word as he has been taught, that he may be able, by sound doctrine, both to exhort and convict those who contradict.

1 Peter 5:1-4

1 The elders who are among you I exhort, I who am a fellow elder and a witness of the sufferings of Christ, and also a partaker of the glory that will be revealed:

2 Shepherd the flock of God which is among you, serving as overseers, not by compulsion but willingly, not for dishonest gain but eagerly;

3 nor as being lords over those entrusted to you, but being examples to the flock;

4 and when the Chief Shepherd appears, you will receive the crown of glory that does not fade away.

Introduction

Until the Lord returns, churches will need godly leaders. In the New Testament, those who guided individual congregations were variously called shepherds, overseers or elders. Temporary offices peculiar to the early church (e.g., apostles or inspired prophets) had authority from Christ wherever Christians congregated, but a shepherd's authority did not extend beyond the local church where he served. In the New Testament, churches were autonomous. They answered to Christ, not to extra-congregational councils or officials.

Shepherds exercise authority in the local church in matters of opinion, in matters where good judgment is required. They have no authority to change the teachings of Christ and His apostles. Elders serve in a variety of ways. Some decisions are routine, but someone has to make them. They promote good order in the congregation. Other matters are more substantial. Members may not see eye to eye on which preacher should work with them or which missionary to support. Differences of opinion sometimes drive wedges between believers. The church's shepherds have authority to settle questions.

That elders have authority in the churches they serve is clear (1 Thessalonians 5:12-13; Hebrews 13:17), but Christians err if they suppose elders function only as decision-makers. Shepherds oversee the teaching mission of the church. They spend long hours consulting with preachers and Bible class teachers in order to give guidance. Is the church plagued by broken homes? How can biblical teaching help? Can professional counselors help troubled homes? What can the church do? Has false doctrine made inroads in the church? What steps can be taken to reach lost souls in the community with the message of Christ? Needs and questions are never-ending. Sometimes elders acting alone or in concert with fellow elders engage those with spiritual needs one-on-one. At other times, they set policy for the church or direct financial resources to troubled areas. Churches guided by godly and wise elders are richly blessed, and their elders deserve all the support Christians can give them.

Shepherds and Character
(1 Timothy 3:1-2; Titus 1:7-9)

In the world of the first century, *episkopos* referred to an official appointed to oversee a task, perhaps the organization of a government for a conquered city or the cleaning up of a city's financial house. The office of bishop in the modern denominational scene has connotations that have little to do with the office in the New Testament church. For that reason, recent translations often have "overseer" (e.g., NASB, NIV84) where the King James Version and the New King James Version have "bishop." "Overseer" is a better translation.

Overseer is suggestive of the character of those who serve as shepherds in a church. Paul said that those who aspire to serve the church in the capacity of overseers seek to serve the Lord in a noble and self-sacrificial way. Character suggests an imprint that is etched into the mind and soul of a person, like letters chiseled into stone or an impression left in steel by a die. The character of a shepherd is to be above reproach. He has no dark secrets to hide, no private life that belies his public portrayal. Of the many traits of a good shepherd, Christians sometimes give an inordinate amount of time to his being the husband of one wife. Important as it is that shepherds be good family men, the call for a noble character is hardly exhausted by appeal to marital status. "Husband of one wife" is quantifiable (1 Timothy 3:2); it can be checked off. But other measures of good character are of equal importance.

Character is measured by a man's evenness of temper, by how he deals with difficult and frustrating situations. A temperate man is self-restrained; he does not tend to extremes when matters of judgment are in front of him. In matters of morality and Christian doctrine, right and wrong are often clearly defined, but life has a way of presenting Christians with all sorts of shades of gray. A temperate man – one who is sober-minded – offers his best judgment; then he listens to those who view the matter differently than he does. He does not demand that his opinion always prevail, nor does he quickly indict the character of those who differ from him. In the end, character is a measure of behavior as well as words. Not only is he to be honest and truthful, but an elder is also to welcome others into his home. His good example is evident to all. He loves to study and to teach the Word of God.

Shepherds and Example (1 Peter 5:1-4)

Peter began both his letters by calling attention to the authority Christ had entrusted to him as an apostle (1:1), but when he neared the end of his first letter, he appealed as "a fellow elder and a witness of the sufferings of Christ" (5:1). His work and the work of his fellow elders was to lift the lost out of sin. Peter was also "a partaker of the glory that is to be revealed." Instead of calling attention to himself and his personal relationship to Jesus, when exhorting his fellow elders, the former fisherman placed the suffering of Christ and the hope of glory at the center (cf. 3:18). The example Peter left for the church of subsequent ages is that the Christian message begins and ends with the exaltation of Christ.

Peter expected elders to be good examples for the church not only in their teaching but also in their conduct. They were to rule with no iron fist and no arrogant swagger. They were to guide the flock like shepherds. Laborers do what the foreman says because he controls the paycheck. Motorists obey a policeman because the authority of the law stands behind him. An elder has neither. He rules because of the nobility of his example. Long years of service have made him worthy of imitation. Some elders, like some preachers, are supported financially by the church so they can give themselves full time to the ministry (1 Timothy 5:17-18). Peter warned his fellow elders to take care that they yield not to the temptation to look on their ministry as a mere means of earning a living. Their labor was for an eternal crown of glory that Christ will give them when He appears at the end of time.

Peter addressed himself to men whom he called "elders," but in short order, he urged them to be shepherds or pastors of the flock. He mentioned in passing that as elders they were "serving as overseers." Elsewhere the same Greek word is translated "bishops" (e.g., 1 Timothy 3:1; Philippians 1:1). As in Acts 20, the designations "elder," "bishop," "overseer," "pastor" and "shepherd" refer to the same office. In all other cases where elders were mentioned in the New Testament, they served over a single congregation. Was Peter an elder at large, or was he an elder in the church at Jerusalem, Rome or some other place? The apostle did not explain, but he likely served as an elder in some particular church.

Shepherds and Compassion (Acts 20:28-31)

When the qualifications for elders in 1 Timothy 3 are compared with those in Titus 1, the principal difference is that, in Titus, Paul emphasized the responsibility of elders to uphold the integrity and truth of the Christian message. In Timothy, elders are to be "able to teach" (3:2), but in Titus, they are "to exhort and convict those who contradict." Paul followed by warning of rebellious deceivers "whose mouths must be stopped" (1:8-11). Elders were to see to the soundness of Christian doctrine.

When Paul called the elders at Ephesus to travel a few miles south to meet him at Miletus, as in Titus, he urged them to protect the church from "savage wolves" who would seek "to draw away the disciples after themselves" (Acts 20:29-30). The teaching ministry of the church requires the full attention of elders; however, they are to exercise that responsibility with a spirit of meekness and humility. They are to do their duty as shepherds who care for their flocks. Elders watch over the church because they know, love and appreciate every member. Jesus distinguished between the hireling who flees at the first sign of danger and the shepherd who is willing to lay down his life for the sheep (John 10:11-12). Paul wanted elders to be shepherds as Jesus was (1 Peter 2:25). He wanted compassion, resolve and knowledge to be combined in them.

Conclusion

Elders accept a great deal of responsibility. Normally they volunteer their time and talents without expectation of material gain. Long meetings, complaints and inner doubts are often their reward. Christians sometimes act as if a man has suddenly been infused with a double portion of Elijah's spirit (2 Kings 2:9) when he becomes an elder. He is not allowed to make a mistake in judgment, nor is he to overlook anyone who might be suffering, regardless of whether he has been kept informed. One is tempted to respond to 1 Timothy 3:1 by asking, why would anyone ever want the office of overseer?

Why do elders serve? Most do so because they want to serve Christ. Elders know they can go to heaven and let someone else have the headaches. They do not serve for money or for a front row ticket to the pearly gates. They serve because people they love want them to serve. Churches who want good leaders will do well to show their appreciation. An occasional "thank you" will not hurt. A special event to honor them might be helpful. All Christians ought to be grateful for those who are willing to step forward to watch for the souls of men and women.

Questions

1. How far does the ministry and authority of an elder extend?
2. What English word have some recent translations used instead of "bishop"?
3. When a man aspires to be an elder, what kind of work did Paul tell Timothy he is seeking?
4. What characteristics should a church look for in potential elders?
5. Why did Paul say elders should hold fast to the Word of God?
6. What did Peter say about himself when he addressed elders in the church?
7. What did Peter tell elders they will receive when Christ returns?
8. From what city were the elders whom Paul spoke to in Acts 20?
9. To whom did Paul tell the elders they ought to take heed?
10. Who did Paul warn would enter the flock after he left them?

Discussion Starters

1. Why do you suppose Christians who benefit from the work of elders are often slow to express appreciation? What can be done to improve this situation?
2. What are some things elders do in order to keep a congregation on a path that is doctrinally sound and encouraging to Christians?
3. Why would Peter have told elders not to lord over those entrusted to them? What does it mean to "lord over" something or someone?
4. Why do you think elders desire to serve? Why do you think elders should desire to serve?

Lesson 8 • Week of July 26, 2015

The Congregation and the Shepherds

1 Corinthians 12:12-18

12 For as the body is one and has many members, but all the members of that one body, being many, are one body, so also is Christ.

13 For by one Spirit we were all baptized into one body – whether Jews or Greeks, whether slaves or free – and have all been made to drink into one Spirit.

14 For in fact the body is not one member but many.

15 If the foot should say, "Because I am not a hand, I am not of the body," is it therefore not of the body?

16 And if the ear should say, "Because I am not an eye, I am not of the body," is it therefore not of the body?

17 If the whole body were an eye, where would be the hearing? If the whole were hearing, where would be the smelling?

18 But now God has set the members, each one of them, in the body just as He pleased.

1 Timothy 3:2-7

2 A bishop then must be blameless, the husband of one wife, temperate, sober-minded, of good behavior, hospitable, able to teach;

3 not given to wine, not violent, not greedy for money, but gentle, not quarrelsome, not covetous;

4 one who rules his own house well, having his children in submission with all reverence

5 (for if a man does not know how to rule his own house, how will he take care of the church of God?);

6 not a novice, lest being puffed up with pride he fall into the same condemnation as the devil.

7 Moreover he must have a good testimony among those who are outside, lest he fall into reproach and the snare of the devil.

Hebrews 13:7

7 Remember those who rule over you, who have spoken the word of God to you, whose faith follow, considering the outcome of their conduct.

Hebrews 13:17

17 Obey those who rule over you, and be submissive, for they watch out for your souls, as those who must give account. Let them do so

239

with joy and not with grief, for that would be unprofitable for you.

Hebrews 13:24

24 Greet all those who rule over you, and all the saints. Those from Italy greet you.

Introduction

Congregations, like individual Christians, exude a spirit. Churches have personalities. They develop over time and are hard to change. The variables that go into making a church what it is are subtle and complex. Preachers will impress their values, their knowledge of Scripture, and their love for lost souls on a church. Leadership is key, but leadership is apt to assert itself in surprising ways. One person, man or woman, may have a winsome disposition and a zeal for the Lord that spreads, osmosis-like, into the rest of the church. When kindness and brotherliness prevail, members of a church love to be together for worship, for shared meals, for vacation Bible school, for a gospel meeting, for a church workday – for anything. Love or wickedness may penetrate quietly, inexorably, into every nook and cranny of the church's life without anyone noticing where it is coming from.

The personality of a church is in a constant state of flux. Change is inevitable. A healthy, vibrant church, such as the one Paul left at Corinth within the space of a few years, can become a bickering, disgruntled mass. How a church changes, for the better or the worse, depends on nothing so crucially as its shepherds. Although they are not the sole contributors to a Christlike spirit in a congregation, their conscious efforts or their benign neglect or their dictatorial stance or their loving concern tends to spread from person to person. The relationship among Christians in the pews, the preacher and the elders tends to manifest itself in everything the church does.

The foundation is laid for a growing church when godly men seek the office of an elder. As with most things, the rewards of service are great, but the pathway is strewn with perils. It is rewarding to be a husband or a wife, but adjusting to and living with another person has its challenges. Few blessings are more satisfying than bringing a child into the world and nurturing it to maturity, but tears are likely to be shed along the way. Similarly, the shepherding of a church is both exhilarating and demanding. When a man steps forward and shoulders the responsibility for the safety and edification of a church, he embraces a special partnership with the Chief Shepherd of the souls of men and women (1 Peter 2:25; 5:4).

United (1 Corinthians 12:12-18)

The apostle Paul was fond of comparing the physical body's unity despite its diversity to the working of a congregation of the Lord's people (1 Corinthians 12:12-18). Individual members of the church function in a variety of ways for the building up of the body. Talents vary widely. One may have a beautiful singing voice; another, the knowledge and ability to teach well. Variations on talent are endless. Egos being what they are, unhealthy competition sometimes breeds suspicion among those with similar abilities. Feelings can be hurt, and the unity of the body can suffer over seemingly trivial concerns. Shepherds of the church serve in no small way when they facilitate the employment of Christians so that they serve in profitable ways that bring satisfaction. Wise shepherds plan the outreach of the church in order to use available talents. A seamstress, for example, may teach and oversee the making of quilts or clothing for the poor. A carpenter may coordinate a woodworking shop for the building and repair of furniture.

Shepherding the church is likely to include the arbitrating of disputes. An ideal family is a place of mutual acceptance and support, but ideal families are rare. Raging conflicts can develop, even in Christian families. Sermons and Bible classes can offer helpful guidance for forgiveness and support within families. In some cases, elders may sit down with a troubled family, listen to complaints, ask questions and make recommendations. If their prayers and teachings fail to help and the family cannot afford professionals, the church may supply a marriage counselor or a crisis manager. Outside the immediate family, individuals within a church will sometimes grow to dislike one another. One may believe that some-one has lied and gossiped about him or cheated him in a business transaction. Elders can facilitate unity in the church by listening and being impartial arbiters.

Christians are often thrown together in the body of Christ from all walks of life. They are apt to have different home experiences and different expectations for the church. Income levels, education and emotional dispositions are likely to vary widely. It will call for all the wisdom elders can muster to provide for unity in matters of faith and to allow for diversity in matters of opinion. Elders will need not only to speak the truth but also to speak the truth in love (Ephesians 4:15). Unity in the church is the result when shepherds hold firmly to New Testament doctrine but deal gently with new Christians to bring them to maturity in Christ.

Knowledgeable (1 Timothy 3:2-7)

Elders perform their God-given mission to the degree that they are knowl-edgeable of Scripture, of the church they serve, and of themselves. Moses impressed on the Israelites that knowledge of the Law was the foundation for their lives (Deuteronomy 6:6-9). The revelation of God's grace in Christ has not erased the need for law among His followers. James directed attention to the confluence of law and grace when he urged readers to submit to "the perfect law that gives freedom" (1:25 NIV84). Paul did not shy away from the declaration that he lived under "the law of Christ" (1 Corinthians 9:21), but with James, he understood Christ's law to be the gateway to liberty (2 Corin-thians 3:17). It is self-evident that in order to live under law, one must know it. The beginning place for the knowledge elders need to serve is the Bible.

In order to lead a church in righteousness, elders must know the church's needs, which is to say they must know its people. Not only should an elder be well-seasoned in the faith of Christ, but he must also be knowledgeable of the history of the church he serves. Does doctrinal controversy lie just beneath the surface? What marriages have been on the verge of collapse? Are there families who have bad blood between them? Who can be counted on to step forward to give time or money? Who supports and appreciates the work elders do, and who is quick to find fault? Every church is different. In order to serve well, an elder needs an intimate knowledge of the particular problems and potentials of the church he oversees.

Elders who serve well are knowledgeable of Scripture and of the Christ whom Scripture reveals. They will love and know the churches they serve, but they will also need to know themselves – their own weaknesses and strengths. In His wisdom, God decreed that one elder is not enough to guide a church. Elders always appear in the plural. No matter how wise he might be, no matter how faithful to Christ, every person in the confines of his own skin deals with sin. A plurality of elders protects a church from being susceptible to the undiluted sins of an individual. Elders need to search their own hearts and behavior and ask themselves whether they are the kinds of people Paul described in 1 Timothy 3:2-7. An elder should neither hold himself to an impossible standard of perfection, nor excuse his sins lightly. No one, for example, will judge himself to be perfectly blameless, but an elder ought to expect of himself a life that has been lived honorably in the sight of all.

Respectful (Hebrews 13:7, 17, 24)

For the sake of good order in a church, mutual respect between the church's elders and its members is essential. For various reasons, some members of a church will feel closer to some or one of the elders than others. Elders differ widely in personality traits. Some are more businesslike; some, more affable. Some shed tears as easily as they change coffee mugs; some never cry. Elders, like family members or like church members, are as varied as faces are varied. Yet superficial judgments based on appearances are enemies of goodwill and unity in a church.

The author of Hebrews urged his readers to be respectful of those who taught them and guided them as shepherds in the faith (13:17). Handshakes, smiles and hugs can be superficial. The outcome of one's faith is likely to be measured in more substantial ways. Hebrews calls on Christians to obey those who "watch out for your souls" (v. 17), not as a mere requirement but in an effort to reciprocate the blessings and goodwill.

Conclusion

Among a detachment of soldiers, leadership is assigned and mandatory. The unit functions because the order of authority is clear. A well-run business venture is similar. The brig in the one case, a paycheck in the other, ensures obedience, even if it does not guarantee respect. In few places does leadership function at a more personal level than in a congregation of the Lord's church. Leaders are liable to receive complaints when they abuse or ignore their duties, and they are vulnerable to unreasonable complaints when they are doing their best. Within the bounds of reason and good judgment, members of a church ought to honor and respect those who shoulder the responsibility of leadership. In their turn, elders ought to respect, love, teach and tend the Christians they serve.

Questions

1. Who in a church contributes to the personality or spirit of the church?
2. What group of people has the most influence in the formation of the spirit of a church?
3. What image did Paul use to illustrate the unity of a church despite the diversity of its members?
4. What have all Christians done in order to be added to the one body of Christ?
5. What body members did Paul mention in order to demonstrate how each church member functions differently yet still contributes to the whole (1 Corinthians 12:15-18)?
6. What did James say the "perfect law" gives to Christians (James 1:25)?
7. What do elders need to know about the churches they serve in order to serve them well?
8. What temptation did Paul say a novice might face if he were appointed as an elder?
9. With what kind of spirit does Hebrews say Christian leaders are to watch for the souls under their care?
10. To whom did the Hebrews author extend greetings in the last verses of the letter?

Discussion Starters

1. How can the elders of a church facilitate the use of the wide variety of talents found in a typical congregation?
2. What did the Hebrews author mean when he urged readers to remember those who ruled over them? In the context, what does it mean to remember them?
3. Why is mutual respect between elders and members of a church essential? What should each do to show respect for the others?
4. Why do elders need to be knowledgeable of the peculiarities and history of the churches where they serve?

The Return of Jesus

Matthew 24:36

36 But of that day and hour no one knows, not even the angels of heaven, but My Father only.

John 5:28-29

28 Do not marvel at this; for the hour is coming in which all who are in the graves will hear His voice

29 and come forth – those who have done good, to the resurrection of life, and those who have done evil, to the resurrection of condemnation.

1 Corinthians 15:51-53

51 Behold, I tell you a mystery: We shall not all sleep, but we shall all be changed –

52 in a moment, in the twinkling of an eye, at the last trumpet. For the trumpet will sound, and the dead will be raised incorruptible, and we shall be changed.

53 For this corruptible must put on incorruption, and this mortal must put on immortality.

1 Thessalonians 4:14-18

14 For if we believe that Jesus died and rose again, even so God will bring with Him those who sleep in Jesus.

15 For this we say to you by the word of the Lord, that we who are alive and remain until the coming of the Lord will by no means precede those who are asleep.

16 For the Lord Himself will descend from heaven with a shout, with the voice of an archangel, and with the trumpet of God. And the dead in Christ will rise first.

17 Then we who are alive and remain shall be caught up together with them in the clouds to meet the Lord in the air. And thus we shall always be with the Lord.

18 Therefore comfort one another with these words.

2 Peter 3:10-13

10 But the day of the Lord will come as a thief in the night, in which the heavens will pass away with a great noise, and the elements will melt with fervent heat; both the earth and the works that are in it will be burned up.

11 Therefore, since all these things will be dissolved, what manner of persons ought you to be in holy conduct and godliness,

12 looking for and hastening the coming of the day of God, because of which the heavens will be dissolved, being on fire, and the elements will melt with fervent heat?

13 Nevertheless we, according to His promise, look for new heavens and a new earth in which righteousness dwells.

Introduction

The dividing line between belief and non-belief is nowhere more starkly apparent than in this: Christians believe the world is going somewhere; nonbelievers trust that, in due course, it will fizzle out – it is going nowhere. Christianity is an optimistic, hope-filled faith. Although Christ taught His people not to make light of sin, God manifested His love by sending His Son to redeem us for Himself. Judgment will accompany the return of the Lord, but in Jesus, the grace of God has appeared to all men (Romans 3:24; Titus 2:11). Resurrection from the dead, which began with Jesus, will culminate at His return. Christians have every reason to hope in an age where sin, death, sorrow and tears will have passed away (Revelation 21:4). Nonbelievers, at best, hope in a grave where their memory and their name will pass into oblivion.

Intellectual nonbelievers have tried to put a courageous face on a dismal landscape. Men, they say, are noble creatures who make moral choices, who can reason, and who perform mighty deeds. They have made a name for themselves; their towers reach to the heavens (cf. Genesis 11:4). When pressed, the intellectually honest among them say that men are nevertheless no different in kind from other life forms found on planet Earth. Homo sapiens have proved to be survivors, at least to this point in geological time, like cockroaches and nematodes. That being true, morality is a survival device, nothing more. In the great order of things, the death of a child means no more than the death of an armadillo. Without God, no benchmark for morality exists.

In the end, the choice between belief and non-belief is a decision about what it means to be a human being. Christians have a great deal of support from the world around them when they assert that an orderly God created an orderly universe (Acts 14:17). In addition, God spoke – He spoke to Abraham, to Moses, to Isaiah, to Jesus, to Paul. The God who raised Jesus from the dead and who left reliable witnesses to the event will send Jesus a second time (Hebrews 9:28). The world is moving toward an end. Belief in the return of Jesus is not an appendage to Christian doctrine. It lies at its heart.

When? (Matthew 24:36; 2 Peter 3:10-13)

That God will bring events to a conclusion, that He will act in a cataclysmic way to assert His rule in earthly affairs, goes all the way back to Israel's prophets. God's messengers never pinpointed a time; rather, they guaranteed the Israelites that God watched over them. God and Israel had a covenant. Obedience would result in prosperity (Deuteronomy 28:1ff.), but disobedience would bring judgment (vv. 15ff.). The prophets warned of judgment, and it was to judgment that Israel came.

The judgment of God does not go away in the New Testament. An end day is coming in which all will stand before the judgment bar of Christ (2 Corinthians 5:10), but thanks to Christ and God's mercy, Christians will not have to stand in hopeless guilt. Through Christ, mercy has triumphed (James 2:13). Because of God's grace, a door of faith has been opened to eternal life. Until the day of His appearing, Christians live in expectant hope (Romans 8:24). They long for His return; they love His appearing (2 Timothy 4:8). Jesus promised that He would come again, but by a deliberate act, neither He nor His apostles so much as hinted at a specific time. The Christian hope would be considerably different had the Lord left some secret formula in the Bible to calculate the date of His return. As it is, faith and hope require that believers live in readiness (2 Peter 3:11).

Shortly before His death, Jesus sat with His disciples on the Mount of Olives and taught them (Matthew 24:3). Judgment, He said, was coming on Jerusalem as it had come on the city in the past. Some would associate the devastation with the end of the world and the final judgment. Jesus clarified. Signs would be abundant leading up to the fall of the city, "but of that day and hour," He said, "no one knows, not even the angels of heaven, but My Father only" (v. 36). He added, "You do not know what hour your Lord is coming" (v. 42).

Who? (John 5:28-29)

The Lord Christ who will appear in glory at the last day for judgment will be the man Jesus, who walked in Galilee. The sinless Son of God who died for our sins will divide humankind as a shepherd divides his sheep from his goats (Matthew 25:32). Because Jesus was tempted in all points as we are (Hebrews 4:15), no one will have a right to raise a voice against the fairness of His judgment.

After Jesus healed a lame man at the pool of Bethesda in Jerusalem (John 5:1-9), He got into a dispute with Jewish leaders. In the process, the Lord asserted His equality with God. It was too much for the Jews; they determined to kill Him (v. 18). Jesus did not back off from His words for an instant. Harkening back to His assurance to Nathanael (1:51), He told them that an hour was coming when all the dead would hear the voice of the Son of God (5:25). As in the great judgment scene of Matthew 25, those who came forth from tombs would be divided. The carpenter from Nazareth would judge men on the basis of their deeds. Those who had lived lives of faithful obedience would go to the resurrection of life, and those whose deeds were evil would go to a resurrection of condemnation. The merciful Savior who walked in Galilee and died in Jerusalem, at His second coming, will judge the human race.

How? (1 Corinthians 15:51-53)

When the Lord became incarnate, when He emerged from the womb of Mary, it was a spectacular event in its own way, but His first coming attracted little attention on the world stage. By contrast, the Second Coming will escape the attention of no one. Every knee will bow, and every tongue, confess (Philippians 2:10). Those who pierced Him will see His glory (Revelation 1:7), and those who ministered to Him will welcome Him with tears of joy.

His coming will be like a thief in the night (Matthew 24:43; 1 Thessalonians 5:2) in that it will be sudden and unexpected, but it will also be with the sounding of a trumpet and the resurrection of the dead (1 Corinthians 15:52).

Some will die before the Lord returns, and some will be alive to welcome Him. "We shall not all sleep," Paul said (1 Corinthians 15:51). Faithful Christians will be on hand when He comes. The Bible knows of no secret coming attended by a few. The Lord will snatch up no one in a rapture, nor will His appearance be by stages. The return of Jesus will be instantaneous, "in a moment, in the twinkling of an eye" (v. 52). For 2,000 years, people have been thinking that the evil age in which they live is surely a portent of the end of time. Speculation on when the end will come is hopeless and misguided. To live in readiness is the Christian ideal, not to second-guess God about when it will be.

Why? (1 Thessalonians 4:14-18)

The Bible is the story of interaction between God and His creation. It reports on what God has done and what He is going to do. To ask "Why?" takes us quickly into realms of mystery. At best, we know partially. It is reasonable to suppose that God created the earth and placed people on it as an expression of love – a love that is inherent in His Being. The degree to which human potential has been marred by rebellion is the backdrop for the coming of a Son and Savior, but the full meaning of the events eludes us. They stir us to thought; perhaps it is no great sin to try to understand. Still, the answers to the "Whys?" are for Him to know.

This we know: The Lord will return because it is the final act in the drama of sin. It is God's final victory over evil, the last chapter in the book. At His second coming, "the day dawns and the morning star rises in your hearts" (2 Peter 1:19). Those who are asleep in Jesus will come with Him, and the rest will be changed. "And thus we shall always be with the Lord" (1 Thessalonians 4:17). The Lord will return because God is the Ruler of all. Goodness prevails; God is and must be the Victor.

Conclusion

Expectation is in the air wherever one opens the Bible. Many preachers have observed that a fitting theme for the Old Testament is "Someone is coming." Beginning with John the Baptist, the message becomes "Someone is here." After the apostles were baptized with the Holy Spirit on the first Pentecost after the resurrection of Jesus, the theme is "Someone is coming again." After the sin of Adam and Eve (Genesis 3), the next significant event in the history of the human race was the appearance of the second Adam (Romans 5:14-15; 1 Corinthians 15:45). "For as in Adam all die, even so in Christ all shall be made alive" (v. 22). One more significant event lies in the future of humankind. The One who came the first time as Savior and Redeemer will come a second time as Judge and Lord.

Questions

1. How do nonbelievers think the world will come to an end?
2. What did prophets warn would happen to the Israelites if they turned their backs on the covenant between themselves and God?
3. Who did Jesus say knows the day and the hour of His return?
4. How did Peter illustrate the suddenness and unexpectedness of the Lord's return?
5. How did Peter say people ought to live in consideration of the end time?
6. When the Lord returns, what did Paul say will happen to Christians who are alive and waiting for Him?
7. How much time will elapse as the events of the end time are taking place?
8. When the Lord returns, what will happen to mortal bodies?
9. Who will Christ bring with Him when He returns?
10. Who did Paul say will rise first when Jesus returns?

Discussion Starters

1. Why is faith that the Lord will return and judge humankind important for the Christian's understanding of what it means to be human?
2. Is it true that without a prior belief that God exists, people have no justification to declare anything right or wrong? Defend your answer.
3. Where in Jesus' or Paul's words is there reference to a rapture or a 1,000-year reign of Christ on earth? Why do so many people believe in such things?
4. What practical differences ought the expectation of the Lord's return make in the lives of believers?

The Judgment

Matthew 25:31-33

31 When the Son of Man comes in His glory, and all the holy angels with Him, then He will sit on the throne of His glory.

32 All the nations will be gathered before Him, and He will separate them one from another, as a shepherd divides his sheep from the goats.

33 And He will set the sheep on His right hand, but the goats on the left.

John 12:48

48 He who rejects Me, and does not receive My words, has that which judges him – the word that I have spoken will judge him in the last day.

Acts 17:31

31 ... because He has appointed a day on which He will judge the world in righteousness by the Man whom He has ordained. He has given assurance of this to all by raising Him from the dead.

Romans 2:5-10

5 But in accordance with your hardness and your impenitent heart you are treasuring up for yourself wrath in the day of wrath and revelation of the righteous judgment of God,

6 who "will render to each one according to his deeds":

7 eternal life to those who by patient continuance in doing good seek for glory, honor, and immortality;

8 but to those who are self-seeking and do not obey the truth, but obey unrighteousness – indignation and wrath,

9 tribulation and anguish, on every soul of man who does evil, of the Jew first and also of the Greek;

10 but glory, honor, and peace to everyone who works what is good, to the Jew first and also to the Greek.

2 Corinthians 5:10

10 For we must all appear before the judgment seat of Christ, that each one may receive the things done in the body, according to what he has done, whether good or bad.

Introduction

In the New Testament, the second coming of Christ and a great judgment day happen simultaneously. Only those who do not know Christ, who are disobedient to the gospel, need fear that day (2 Thessalonians 1:7-9). For "those who eagerly wait for Him" (Hebrews 9:28), His second coming will be a day of salvation, a day of joy. God has revealed that justice – like truth, love and grace – is inherent in who He is. God's justice demands a day when wrongs are made right, when goodness wins the day. Even in earthly matters, evil demands a day of judgment. If world leaders, for example, had shaken hands with Hitler and his henchmen after the atrocities of Nazi Germany and said, "You lost, but no hard feelings," the world would have had no justice. Because moral beings must answer for what they do, judgment days must come.

Sin demands that a price be paid, but God's revulsion at sin has hardly been the only force operating in the divine sphere. In addition to being a God of justice, He is a God of love and grace. Judgment and grace were brought together by the incarnation of God's Son. Jesus Christ lived sinlessly and, in His innocence, paid the price to save men and women from sin. No one earns salvation with an obedient response to the teachings of Christ, but obedient faith is the response God demands when His grace is proclaimed. When sinful men and women respond to God's grace by placing faith in Him, they eagerly await His appearing. Those who wait face the judgment day with promise and hope. Eternal life in the presence of God will be the outcome of judgment for the faithful. Paul admonished, "Therefore comfort one another with these words" (1 Thessalonians 4:18).

A Final Gathering
(Matthew 25:31-33; 2 Corinthians 5:10)

Shortly before His crucifixion, Jesus met with four of His disciples on the slopes of the Mount of Olives and spoke to them about judgment (Matthew 24:3; Mark 13:3-4). Matthew 24–25, one of five long teaching sections in Matthew, is often called the "Olivet Discourse." Jesus spoke about judgment under two headings: (1) judgment on Jerusalem and (2) universal judgment at the end of time. Speaking less than 40 years before the event, Jesus said siege works would be cast against Jerusalem, and the city would be destroyed. The prophecy was fulfilled in A.D. 70 when the Romans reduced the city to rubble.

The four who listened were likely to associate judgment on Jerusalem with the end of time. Jesus corrected them. In addition to judgment on the city, the Lord would appear at the end of time for a universal judgment. They could anticipate the destruction of Jerusalem; signs would be abundant (Matthew 24:33). By contrast, "of that day and hour no one knows" (v. 36). Because no one can predict when He will come in final judgment, disciples are to live in expectation. On that day, two men will be in the field, or two women will be at the mill; one will be taken, and the other, left. Jesus told a parable about a servant who thought he had plenty of time. While he was abusing his position, the master returned, sooner than expected. The evil servant was assigned to a place of torment with the hypocrites (vv. 48-51).

Matthew 25 consists of three long parables. If the master returned sooner than the evil servant expected (24:48), the groom came later than the foolish virgins expected. The lesson is clear: The part of disciples is not to anticipate when He will come. They are to live in constant readiness. The parable of the talents continues to teach about the Lord's return, but the final parable is the conclusion of the matter. More descriptive of the final judgment scene than He had been in the other parables, Jesus said on the last day He will sit on a throne of glory surrounded by angels. He will judge humankind and separate the saved from the lost like a shepherd dividing sheep from goats. When Paul wrote of the same event decades later, he said that each would receive according to what he had done, whether it be good or evil (2 Corinthians 5:10).

To Sit for Judgment
(John 12:48; Acts 17:31)

The imprint of grace is stamped all over the ministry of Jesus in the Gospels. He showed Himself to be the Son of God with undeniable signs (John 5:36); His teaching was unlike anything the Jewish people had heard (Matthew 7:28-29). Jesus fulfilled what inspired men of God had said about the coming of the Christ (John 5:39). After spending at least three-and-a-half years teaching and doing good (Acts 10:38), He went to the cross as a payment to redeem a people for God. Of His ministry on earth, Jesus said, "I did not come to judge the world but to save the world" (John 12:47).

God manifested His grace in Jesus of Nazareth, but the death of Christ is no free pass for rebellion against God. The door for the remission of sins has been opened for all (John 3:16), but when Jesus comes a second time it will be for judgment. Jesus told His contemporaries that when the last day comes, the words He has spoken will be the standard by which God will render judgment. His words include all that He has revealed, all that is recorded in the New Testament. Words that some translations put in red letters have no higher authority for Christian living than any other words the New Testament records. Jesus promised the apostles that after He died, He would send another Comforter, who would bring His words to their remembrance and direct them into all truth (14:26; 16:13).

When Paul told the philosophers on the Areopagus that God will "judge the world in righteousness by the Man whom He has ordained," he affirmed God will judge them by the Word of Christ (Acts 17:31). John's vision on Patmos included the judgment of the last day. The beloved disciple testified that men "were judged according to their works, by the things which were written in the books" (Revelation 20:12). When Jesus sits on the throne of His glory (Matthew 25:31), the words He has revealed will be the rule by which men and women of every age and every place will be judged.

To Hear God's Word (Romans 2:5-10)

To hear God's Word entails a blessing and a responsibility. Millions have lived and died with no opportunity to know Christ. Those who wish may speculate about their status when all are gathered before Him at the last day, but no one need speculate about those who have heard the gospel. To hear is to be responsible (Luke 12:47-48). Paul told Roman Christians that stubborn unbelief and unrepentant hearts will result in the storing up of "wrath and revelation of the righteous judgment of God" (Romans 2:5). The apostle made it clear that the revelation of God's grace in Christ calls for an obedient response in this life. When the end comes, the time for repentance has past.

Belief has to do with more than mental assent to a series of propositions. The truth is that Jesus of Nazareth was God manifest in the flesh (John 1:1). To confess that His death and resurrection happened in real time is to confess the truth. The One who lived in Galilee and rose from the dead now reigns at God's right hand (Acts 2:32-33). That is the truth, but belief is not limited to what a person confesses. It is also what he does. God expects those who hear the truth to obey it. Guided by the Holy Spirit, Paul declared that those who fail to obey the truth, who choose instead to obey unrighteousness, will not escape judgment (Romans 2:3). When the last day comes, they will face God's indignation and wrath (v. 8).

Conclusion

Judgment is a theme that runs throughout the course of the Bible, but in the Old Testament, it usually has to do with God judging His people in this life. When Israel turned to idols, the people faced God's judgment. Moses reassured the Israelites that if they would obey God, He would bless them in the land to which they were going (Deuteronomy 28:1ff.). But He warned them that judgment was coming if they were to disobey (vv. 15ff.). God sent prophets to reinforce the warning Moses had given. In the wilderness, suffering and death were God's judgment in response to disobedience. The kingship faltered and ceased to be when God judged the Israelites and found them wanting.

In the New Testament, God established a spiritual kingdom, His church. God continues to act in His world. He answers prayers (James 5:16) and chastens His children (Hebrews 12:6). God continues to judge the world, but Christians anticipate a final judgment when all the wrongs of life, all the sin and greed, will be called to account. In that day, the righteous will shine like the sun (Matthew 13:43). Because of His grace in Christ, God will forgive sins. Eternal life will begin in the kingdom He has prepared for His people (25:34).

Questions

1. What two future events will happen simultaneously?
2. What two traits of God were brought together in the incarnation of His Son?
3. Of what two judgments did Jesus warn the four apostles who were with Him on the Mount of Olives?
4. Who were the four apostles to whom Jesus described God's coming judgment?
5. Who did Jesus say will be gathered before Him when He comes in glory?
6. Through whom will God judge the world in righteousness?
7. What did Paul say every soul will receive at the judgment (2 Corinthians 5:10)?

8. What did Jesus say will judge every person who rejects Him?

9. What are the similarities and differences between God's judgment in the Old Testament and His judgment in the New Testament?

10. In addition to believing the truth, how does God call on people to respond to the truth?

Discussion Starters

1. Why is it important for readers of the Bible to distinguish between God's judgment on Jerusalem and the final judgment described in Matthew 24–25?

2. Why do you think people speculate about the time when the Lord will return for judgment? What dangers attend such speculation?

3. Compare and contrast the first coming of Christ with the Second Coming.

4. What did Paul say will be the outcome for those who obey the truth compared to those who obey unrighteousness (Romans 2:7-9)? What does this passage say about accountability?

The Punishment of Hell

Matthew 5:29

29 If your right eye causes you to sin, pluck it out and cast it from you; for it is more profitable for you that one of your members perish, than for your whole body to be cast into hell.

Matthew 13:41-42

41 The Son of Man will send out His angels, and they will gather out of His kingdom all things that offend, and those who practice lawlessness, **42** and will cast them into the furnace of fire. There will be wailing and gnashing of teeth.

Matthew 25:41-46

41 Then He will also say to those on the left hand, "Depart from Me, you cursed, into the everlasting fire prepared for the devil and his angels: **42** "for I was hungry and you gave Me no food; I was thirsty and you gave Me no drink; **43** "I was a stranger and you did not take Me in, naked and you did not clothe Me, sick and in prison and you did not visit Me." **44** Then they also will answer Him, saying, Lord, when did we see You hungry or thirsty or a stranger or naked or sick or in prison, and did not minister to You?" **45** Then He will answer them, saying, "Assuredly, I say to you, inasmuch as you did not do it to one of the least of these, you did not do it to Me." **46** And these will go away into everlasting punishment, but the righteous into eternal life.

2 Thessalonians 1:6-9

6 ... since it is a righteous thing with God to repay with tribulation those who trouble you, **7** and to give you who are troubled rest with us when the Lord Jesus is revealed from heaven with His mighty angels, **8** in flaming fire taking vengeance on those who do not know God, and on those who do not obey the gospel of our Lord Jesus Christ. **9** These shall be punished with everlasting destruction from the presence of the Lord and from the glory of His power.

Revelation 20:15

15 And anyone not found written in the Book of Life was cast into the lake of fire.

Revelation 21:8

8 But the cowardly, unbelieving, abominable, murderers, sexually immoral, sorcerers, idolaters, and all liars shall have their part in the lake which burns with fire and brimstone, which is the second death.

Introduction

The Old Testament gives little attention to life after death – to either punishment or reward. The Hebrew word *Sheol*, translated "hell" in the King James Version (1611), does not necessarily refer to the place of eternal torment. Sometimes it means the grave (e.g., 1 Kings 2:6). At other times it seems to refer figuratively to a vague, shadowy world where all the dead go (e.g., Ezekiel 31:17). In Daniel 12:2 and perhaps in some of the psalms, references to life after death appear, but other Old Testament passages that are sometimes brought forward as evidence for life after death are hardly clear. They can be, and often are, interpreted otherwise.

In the Old Testament, faithfulness to God resulted in blessings for this life, but the New Testament goes further. It testifies to rewards and punishment beyond the grave, to life in the age to come. During the centuries immediately preceding Jesus' birth, the doctrine of life after death gained increasing support among Jewish sects such as the Pharisees, but not all agreed. The Sadducees, among others, maintained that God blesses the obedient in this world and nowhere else (Matthew 22:23). In this matter, Jesus cast His lot with the Pharisees. He told the Sadducees that they erred because they neither understood Scripture nor the power of God (v. 29).

Jesus and His apostles taught that after men and women exit this world, new life awaits in a world to come. Peter said that after death, people will live in a new heaven and a new earth (2 Peter 3:13). Jesus said the new age will begin when He returns to the earth in glory, when every person who has ever lived stands before the Son of Man to be judged (Matthew 25:31-32; John 5:29). The Lord warned of the consequences for those who die with the guilt of sin on them (8:24; Matthew 10:28). Hell, He taught, is a place from which there is no return. In the early 14th century, the Italian author Dante Alighieri captured something of the horror of hell with the immortal lines he placed above hell's entryway: "Abandon all hope, ye who enter here."

A Place Away From God (Matthew 25:41-46)

Jesus used extreme words to describe hell. It is a place, He said, "where their worm does not die, and the fire is not quenched" (Mark 9:48). With a single exception (2 Peter 2:4), the word "hell" in the King James Version (1611) translates two Greek words. The first is *Hades* (Matthew 16:18; Luke 16:23), which the Greeks thought of as a shadowy world, not unlike Sheol in Ezekiel 31:17.

The word Jesus more commonly used for hell was *Gehenna* (e.g., Mark 9:43). It was borrowed from the name of the deep Hinnom Valley to the south of Jerusalem. Other than Jesus, only James used the word (cf. James 3:6). In time past, the Israelites had sacrificed their children in the valley to the terrible god Molech (2 Kings 23:10). After the city had been destroyed and rebuilt, the people of Jerusalem used the valley for their garbage. Worms always worked in the filth; the fire never died out. For Jesus, it was a fitting emblem of eternal torment, of separation from God. God had prepared the place Jesus spoke of for those who would be cursed with the devil and his angels (Matthew 25:41).

Two matters should be observed concerning New Testament teaching on hell. (1) Jesus and the apostles did not fixate on the subject. The fear of hell is only one of the reasons why a person should follow Christ. The New Testament emphasizes that love, not fear, is the great motivation for Christian living (1 John 4:18). (2) The punishment of hell is not a payment God exacts for those who want to have fun in this world. The commands of God are not to keep us from having a good time. Sin is its own punishment in this world. It breeds tears, shame, misery and loneliness. In addition to what sin does to people in this age, it separates people from God eternally.

A Place of Sin (Revelation 20:15; 21:8)

Christians are used to being around people who are trustworthy, who love their spouses, who have compassion for those around them, who find joy in the simple pleasures of life. The kingdom of God, which is the church of Jesus Christ (Colossians 1:13), is a foretaste of heaven. That does not mean that Christians never fall short or that they never disappoint those who love them. The kingdom of Christ has been realized for believers (Luke 17:21), and at the same time, Christians await its full realization.

Eternal punishment means separation from God. Because it is separation from God, it is also separation from goodness. Hell is to live eternally in the company of those for whom every vile thing is normal. It is to be cut off from smiles of goodness and compassion. In his vision, the seer of Patmos (Revelation 1:9) caught symbolic glimpses of the throne room of God (4:2ff.) and of the New Jerusalem (21:2), but he also caught a glimpse of hell. In the latter was no truth, no kindness, no laughter. In a great lake of fire, the cowardly, murderers, sexually immoral, idolaters and liars bore the burden of sin – their own and their neighbors' (v. 8). Such are the denizens of the abyss.

A Place of Punishment (Matthew 5:29; 13:41-42; 2 Thessalonians 1:6-9)

Few things are more painful than a serious burn. Perhaps it is for that reason the New Testament speaks of eternal separation from God as a fiery torment. When John the Baptist foretold the manifestation of the Christ, he said He would come with His winnowing fan in His hand. He would burn up the chaff and every tree that bore no fruit with "unquenchable fire" (Matthew 3:10, 12). Jesus concluded the parable of the tares by foretelling His appearing at the end of the age. He said the Son of Man would send His angels, who would gather all who offended and were lawless and "cast them into the furnace of fire" (13:41-42).

Perhaps fire is symbolic of severe punishment as "streets of gold" are symbolic of the glories of heaven (Revelation 21:21). The word "resurrection" suggests continuity between the earthly and the immortal body, but the New Testament reveals little about the nature of the resurrected body. Paul suggested that the body that will stand before the Lord on the last day will bear likeness to the earthly body, but without its defects and weaknesses (1 Corinthians 15:42). He called the body with which the saved will be clothed a "spiritual body" (v. 44). Jesus spoke of resurrection both for those who will go to life and for those who will go to condemnation (John 5:29). The implication is that both the saved and the lost will spend eternity in bodily form.

New Testament authors do not encourage further speculation, but it is safe to say that those separated from God in hell will suffer torment in a body. Jesus indicated the severity of the punishment when He said that it would be better to go through this life without an eye or a hand than for the whole body to be cast into hell (Matthew 5:29-30). When he wrote to the Thessalonians, Paul highlighted the certainty that separation from God in hell means punishment. He said that those who do not know God and who refuse to obey the gospel will be "punished with everlasting destruction from the presence of the Lord" (2 Thessalonians 1:8-9).

Conclusion

When theologians have searched the Scriptures in order to say what is possible to say about God, they sometimes succumb to the temptation to slide from clear statements in the Bible to speculation. It is safe to say that God is holy or that He is omnipotent, but classical theologians have also asserted the impassibility of God. By that they mean God cannot be emotionally affected by anything humankind might do or fail to do. In that, they are surely mistaken. To claim the impassibility of God, many biblical passages must be ignored or explained away. The Bible speaks of God's pleasure when people do the right thing (Psalm 105:43) as well as His anger when confronted with rebellion (Exodus 4:14).

When Jesus met His friend Mary and saw her grief, He wept with her (John 11:35). When He saw the hypocrisy of the Pharisees who tried to catch Him in a trap, the Bible says He looked around "with anger" (Mark 3:5). The punishment for sinners who die in their rebellion has something to do with God's anger. When His creatures sin against Him, it is a reflection on His holiness. The punishment of hell is His vindication. He saves those who come in faith and obedience to His grace.

Questions

1. What kinds of rewards did God give the faithful in the Old Testament?
2. In addition to blessings from God in this world, what did Jesus reveal about rewards for the righteous and punishment for the wicked?
3. Which sect of the Jews maintained that God's reward and punishment were for this life alone?
4. What will the Son of Man say to the disobedient when He separates them from the righteous?

5. For whom has the place of everlasting fire been prepared?

6. What does Revelation say will happen to those whose names are not written in the Book of Life?

7. What kinds of people will have their place in "the lake which burns with fire" (Revelation 21:8)?

8. If one's eye or hand were to result in his being lost, what did Jesus say he should do?

9. Whom did Jesus say His angels will gather out of His kingdom?

10. How did the apostle Paul describe the punishment awaiting the disobedient when the Lord returns?

Discussion Starters

1. Do you believe the descriptions of heaven and hell in the Bible are literal, partially literal or figurative? Do you believe the "spiritual body" will experience pleasure and pain?

2. How do love for God and fear of God both motivate Christians to live in a way that pleases Him? Should love or fear predominate?

3. Will those eternally lost in sin spend eternity in a bodily form? Are the promises of a resurrected body the same for the lost and the saved?

4. Does God's anger have anything to do with the disobedient and ungodly spending eternity separated from Him? Explain and justify your answer.

The Reward of Heaven

John 14:1-3

1 Let not your heart be troubled; you believe in God, believe also in Me.

2 In My Father's house are many mansions; if it were not so, I would have told you. I go to prepare a place for you.

3 And if I go and prepare a place for you, I will come again and receive you to Myself; that where I am, there you may be also.

2 Corinthians 5:1

1 For we know that if our earthly house, this tent, is destroyed, we have a building from God, a house not made with hands, eternal in the heavens.

1 Peter 1:3-4

3 Blessed be the God and Father of our Lord Jesus Christ, who according to His abundant mercy has begotten us again to a living hope through the resurrection of Jesus Christ from the dead,

4 to an inheritance incorruptible and undefiled and that does not fade away, reserved in heaven for you.

Revelation 22:1-5

1 And he showed me a pure river of water of life, clear as crystal, proceeding from the throne of God and of the Lamb.

2 In the middle of its street, and on either side of the river, was the tree of life, which bore twelve fruits, each tree yielding its fruit every month. The leaves of the tree were for the healing of the nations.

3 And there shall be no more curse, but the throne of God and of the Lamb shall be in it, and His servants shall serve Him.

4 They shall see His face, and His name shall be on their foreheads.

5 There shall be no night there: They need no lamp nor light of the sun, for the Lord God gives them light. And they shall reign forever and ever.

Introduction

Just as the Old Testament has little to say about punishment for sinners in a world to come, it has little to say about the reward for the saved in heaven. Almost all that Christians know about heaven or hell is from Jesus and His apostles. The information about either place is brief; the New Testament has no extended description of the way people will live in the world to come. Even the book of Revelation is a self-acknowledged visionary, figurative portrayal with the purpose of encouraging believers who are suffering for their faith in this world. Christians need to know that all people will stand before the judgment bar of Christ when He comes again (2 Corinthians 5:10). They need to know that those Christ has saved will live eternally in a paradise God has made for them. Those who die in sin will go into outer darkness and eternal punishment. In the New Testament, references to hell or heaven are not to satisfy idle curiosity but to inspire holiness of living (2 Peter 3:11).

Having acknowledged the dearth of information the Bible provides about life in the world to come, the New Testament abounds in assurances that individual life and consciousness extend beyond the grave. Jesus died on the cross precisely because life does not end when the physical body dies. In Paul's words, "If in this life only we have hope in Christ, we are of all men most pitiable" (1 Corinthians 15:19). The certainty of life in an age to come drove the apostle to tell people about Christ. He wanted to snatch sinners from the punishment of hell. "Knowing, therefore, the terror of the Lord," he said, "we persuade men" (2 Corinthians 5:11).

As in other areas of Christian thought and practice, extremes are out of order. The believer who becomes fixated on mapping out the time when the Lord will return and judge humankind has gone too far. People write volumes about a supposed 1,000-year reign of Christ on earth, a seven-and-a-half-year rapture of the saved in the sky, a battle of Armageddon, the restoration of ethnic Jews to Canaan, the rebuilding of a temple like Solomon's on Jerusalem's temple mount, and the resumption of Old Testament sacrifices. The speculation is endless, going miles beyond what the Bible has revealed. Another extreme is to push the judgment of God from our minds. The Bible is certain about this: The Lord will come again and judge the deeds of mankind. The saved will receive a reward: eternal life in heaven. Those who do not know Christ and who disobey Him in this life will be consigned to hell for eternity. This much we need to know.

A Place Prepared
(John 14:1-3; 2 Corinthians 5:1)

All four of the records of Jesus' ministry say that the night before His crucifixion, He met with the disciples in Jerusalem to observe the Passover. In Matthew, Mark and Luke, the institution of the Lord's Supper is a highlight of the meeting, but in John, the Lord's Supper goes unmentioned. Instead, Jesus talked to the disciples at length about His coming death and the unfinished tasks that lay before them (John 13–17). He washed their feet and taught them to serve one another (13:14). He promised that the Father would send another Helper – a Comforter who would guide them into all truth (14:26). He taught them they were to draw spiritual life from Him, as branches draw life from a vine (15:4). They would need strength after the time of His departure, and that time was shortly upon them.

With a sardonic smile, people say, "The only certainties are death and taxes." A case could be made that even taxes are uncertain, but of death, there is no doubt. As Jesus observed His last Passover with the disciples, death hung in the air. Jesus reassured them that His death was not to be the tragedy they imagined. He was going to die, but He would be back. His death was necessary for Him to be our sacrifice. Following His ascension, He would prepare a place for the faithful. In the end, Jesus and His followers would be together again. They could trust His words; they were to put the same confidence in Jesus that they had in God. The word translated "mansions" in the New King James Version (John 14:2) hardly suggests opulent, multimillion-dollar castles as we see on oceanfronts and mountaintops. More simply, it refers to dwelling places (cf. NASB). Similarly, the Greek word translated "crown" means a wreath of leaves awarded to winners in games (1 Corinthians 9:25). Jeweled crowns and rich mansions have to do more with the values people attach to this world than with the promises of Christ. Victory, peace, rest and unending life with God and His people are the rewards of heaven (2 Corinthians 5:1).

A Place Reserved (1 Peter 1:3-4)

In the opening verses of his first letter, Peter drew tight the cords that unite the faith of Christians and the faith of the Old Testament. The apostle, in fact, co-opted for Christians some of the most endearing doctrines of Israel. The physical descendants of Abraham were an elect people chosen by God from all the families of the earth. Peter redefined the elect to include all who have embraced Jesus by being baptized into Him. Israel was a sanctified people, set apart by God to be holy; Christians are those who have been sanctified by the Spirit. The sprinkling of blood served as a purifying act for tabernacle and temple worship. Christians have been sprinkled by the blood of Jesus.

Peter co-opted the highest and noblest of Old Testament thought, but he went further. The message of Christ entails new concepts unparalleled in Israel. God, the Father, stands side by side with Jesus Christ, the Lord. The inheritance of Israel was the physical land of Canaan, but because of Christ and His resurrection from the dead, Christians have inherited a "living hope" (1 Peter 1:3). The hope of Christians is living because the Lord who reigns over them from God's right hand is living. Crucifixion and burial were not the end of His story. The hope of Christians is living because He is the firstfruits (1 Corinthians 15:23). Resurrection from the dead began with Him, but all the elect of God will live eternally in His presence (Romans 8:23).

No word was more important to the Israelites in the wilderness than "inheritance." It occurs some 60 times in Numbers and Deuteronomy alone (NKJV). The land of Canaan – bound by the wide Euphrates River in the north; the Brook of Egypt in the south; the great sea, the Mediterranean, on the west; and the River Jordan on the east – was Israel's inheritance. Peter said, without reservation, that those who die in Christ will have a greater inheritance. Symbolically, Christians, in death, will pass over the Jordan into the land called Beulah (Isaiah 62:4 KJV, NKJV). This land, the apostle said, is in the third heaven (2 Corinthians 12:2) in company with God and is an inheritance "incorruptible and undefiled and that does not fade away" (1 Peter 1:4). Christ has reserved a place for His people there.

A Place Described (Revelation 22:1-5)

To an earthbound people, a literal description of heaven will likely inspire little confidence. For that reason, the Holy Spirit inspired biblical authors to explore the imagination for earthly symbols that might approach the glories of heaven. Peter found heaven to be like the Promised Land for Israel, a land flowing with milk and honey, but the eternal dwelling place for the redeemed was to be infinitely more. The revelation to John went in a different direction. Instead of like Canaan, he saw heaven as if it were a glorified Jerusalem. As Peter co-opted Canaan to speak of heaven, John turned to the Jerusalem above (Revelation 21:2; cf. Galatians 4:26).

The presence of God and the Lamb adorn the city of God. The river of life and the tree of life are poetic reminders that the saved of God live eternally in His presence. "The leaves of the tree [of life]," John said, "were for the healing of the nations" (Revelation 22:2). The apostle leaned on descriptions in Ezekiel and Zechariah, but he turned to Isaiah again to highlight the wonders of a city where no sun or moon shine. God is the perpetual light of the heavenly city (Isaiah 60:19). Such poetic, figurative language is as close as God comes to describing the eternal blessings in store for those whose sins have been washed away by the blood of the Lamb.

Conclusion

After Christians have read the descriptions of heaven and listened to God's promises, questions remain. Perhaps the perpetual struggle with the shame and suffering of sin convinces us that a life of everlasting peace and joy will be without challenge. Believers wonder how they will spend their time in heaven. They wonder how they will deal with the knowledge that some whom they love will have died lost in sin.

God did not see fit to offer a detailed description of heaven. He promised that life in the age to come will know eternal goodness and joy. Believers know that He is willing and able to bring His promises to fruition. John's vision of the New Jerusalem in Revelation 21–22 reminds us that human language and human experience limit our ability to understand. Heaven, no doubt, will hold joys and blessings that cannot be compared to this life. God will strain sin and death out of nature itself (Romans 8:21); He will supply the saved with spiritual, incorruptible bodies (1 Corinthians 15:42-44); and He will dwell with them as Friend and Savior.

Questions

1. What type of language did John use in Revelation to describe heaven?
2. What important things can Christians say with confidence about life in the world to come?
3. What rationale did Jesus give His disciples for believing in Himself?
4. What did Jesus tell His disciples He was going away to do for them?
5. Where did Jesus promise His disciples they will be after He comes back for them?
6. What kind of house did Paul say the faithful will receive when the earthly house is destroyed?

7. To what did Peter say God has begotten Christians again?

8. What kind of inheritance has been provided for those begotten by God?

9. What did John see a pure river of life flowing from?

10. What did John see growing in the street of the New Jerusalem and on either side of the river of life?

Discussion Starters

1. Why do you suppose the Bible gives no extended description of what life will be like for believers in heaven? Justify your answer.

2. How does John's description of the last Passover differ from those of the other three Gospels? What are important themes in John's account of that night (cf. John 13–17)?

3. In what ways does the inheritance God promised to Christians resemble the inheritance of Israel? In what ways does it surpass the Old Testament inheritance?

4. What literal truths about heaven can Christians extract from John's figurative description of the New Jerusalem? Why did John use figurative language?

The Lord Is My Shepherd

Psalm 23:1-6

1 The Lord is my shepherd; I shall not want.

2 He makes me to lie down in green pastures; He leads me beside the still waters.

3 He restores my soul; He leads me in the paths of righteousness For His name's sake.

4 Yea, though I walk through the valley of the shadow of death, I will fear no evil; For You are with me; Your rod and Your staff, they comfort me.

5 You prepare a table before me in the presence of my enemies; You anoint my head with oil; My cup runs over.

6 Surely goodness and mercy shall follow me All the days of my life; And I will dwell in the house of the Lord Forever.

John 10:1-4

1 Most assuredly, I say to you, he who does not enter the sheepfold by the door, but climbs up some other way, the same is a thief and a robber.

2 But he who enters by the door is the shepherd of the sheep.

3 To him the doorkeeper opens, and the sheep hear his voice; and he calls his own sheep by name and leads them out.

4 And when he brings out his own sheep, he goes before them; and the sheep follow him, for they know his voice.

John 10:14-18

14 I am the good shepherd; and I know My sheep, and am known by My own.

15 As the Father knows Me, even so I know the Father; and I lay down My life for the sheep.

16 And other sheep I have which are not of this fold; them also I must bring, and they will hear My voice; and there will be one flock and one shepherd.

17 Therefore My Father loves Me, because I lay down My life that I may take it again.

18 No one takes it from Me, but I lay it down of Myself. I have power to lay it down, and I have power to take it again. This command I have received from My Father.

John 10:25-30

25 Jesus answered them, "I told you, and you do not believe. The works that I do in My Father's name, they bear witness of Me.

26 "But you do not believe, because you are not of My sheep, as I said to you.

27 "My sheep hear My voice, and I know them, and they follow Me.

28 "And I give them eternal life, and they shall never perish; neither shall anyone snatch them out of My hand.

29 "My Father, who has given them to Me, is greater than all; and no one is able to snatch them out of My Father's hand.

30 "I and My Father are one."

Introduction

For the people who lived in the biblical world, the shepherd was an iconic figure. Maybe a cowboy in the mold of Roy Rogers or Gene Autry is the nearest American idealism has to the shepherd of yore. Both the shepherd and the cowboy were tough, men of few words. Bears, rattlesnakes and bad guys were no match for them. At the same time, they were decent, handsome, thoughtful of the old, and gentle with the girls. When the occasion was right, they could pull out a guitar or a lyre, offer a psalm, or croon a ballad. Like the cowboy, the image of the shepherd was often idealized – more fictional than real. Still, the Israelites needed the shepherd, as we need the cowboy, to tell them what was strong, selfless and noble in themselves and in the world.

In the selfless care and dogged leadership of the shepherd, the Israelites came to understand what God had done for them and what He wanted from them. He was their Shepherd; they wanted only to be the sheep of His pasture. Helpful as it was for Israel to know God as a shepherd, no one figure of speech was sufficient to explain Him. The nation drew on other agricultural metaphors to help them view aspects of His care from different angles. In Isaiah 5:1-7, God was a husbandman who planted a vineyard, cared for it, and expected good fruits (cf. Matthew 21:33-44). In Mark 4:3-8, He was a sower whose seed fell on good and bad soil. No one figure of speech communicated the mystery and power of God, but taken together, they helped His people relate the Almighty to their earthbound ways.

The relationship between God and His people is more complex than any one figure of speech can capture, but the image of the ideal shepherd and the sheep under his care remains particularly colorful in its expression and profound in its description. Its appropriateness finds expression not only in the language of the wise men and prophets of Israel but also in that of Jesus and the apostles of the New Testament. By entering into the world of shepherds, Christians can grow to understand nuances of the relationship between God and His people that otherwise might elude them.

He Leads (Psalm 23; John 10:1-4)

Until Jesus returns, those who love Him must live in a fallen world – fallen because of the sin in which they partake. In this fallen world are precious few green pastures, precious few still waters. Jesus left His followers in a world of contradictions, in a world where respites from fear and suffering are in short supply. Christians long for His return; they love His appearing (2 Timothy 4:8). But in the meantime, they follow His lead. He leads "in paths of righteousness" (Psalm 23:3). Those who come to know God grow in the realization that paths of righteousness lead to green pastures and still waters. The sage who observed that God's "thou shalt not" amounts to an admonition to do yourself no harm had it right. Sin is a path to misery and shame. Those who yield to transgressions justly suffer because of them. The paths of righteousness lead to satisfying relationships with family members and friends, to hope and peace with God. In those paths is no fear. His rod and staff comfort the sorrowful and protect those who discover themselves to be in the valley of death.

To live in Christ is to live with irony. In this fallen world, the path to goodness and mercy is attended by struggles. Suffering is plentiful; death, not unknown. Jesus fed His disciples on no pablum diet; He insisted on realism. "Do not think that I came to bring peace on earth," He said. "I did not come to bring peace but a sword" (Matthew 10:34). He was in every sense Prince of Peace, but Satan would not go down without a fight. The Prince of Peace died violently on a Roman cross. Still waters and green pastures, blessings found in the paths of righteousness, were overshadowed by a cross. His people can expect nothing different. "My peace I give to you," He said. "Let not your heart be troubled" (John 14:27).

Until Jesus returns, those who love Him will listen to the voice of the Shepherd who forgives sins and leads in righteousness. The "meekness and gentleness of Christ" (2 Corinthians 10:1) inspire them. They recognize His voice when He enters by the door into His sheepfold. They recognize their names when He calls. They confess that their Shepherd knows infinitely and loves eternally. Shepherd and flock together struggle to shine the light of Christ in this troubled world. Where He leads, they will follow.

He Protects (John 10:14-18)

Not all shepherds care for and protect the flocks committed to their care. Some are hirelings who abandon their charges at the first sign of danger. Others are in the sheep business; their sole interest is to exploit the animals for profit. When Jesus said "I am the good shepherd" (John 10:11, 14), among other things, He was warning His followers that all who claim to protect and guide will not live up to the billing. In the Sermon on the Mount, Jesus said, "Beware of false prophets, who will come to you in sheep's clothing, but inwardly they are ravenous wolves" (Matthew 7:15). Speaking to Ephesian elders, Paul said, "After my departure savage wolves will come in among you, not sparing the flock" (Acts 20:29). The mantle of shepherd can be a pretext for self-aggrandizement.

Jesus based His claim to be the Good Shepherd on two considerations. (1) He would lay down His life for the sheep (John 10:11). The Lord knew the cross was before Him. Laying down His life was no mere theoretical possibility. (2) Between Jesus and His followers was a relationship of trust. He knew the sheep, and they knew Him. Before He died, before He gave His followers the commission to make disciples of all nations (Matthew 28:19-20), Jesus was already preparing them for their mission. All His sheep would not be drawn from "this fold" – that is, Jews and Gentiles would be fellow partakers of the grace of God (Galatians 3:26-29). The church of Christ would be one fold serving under one Shepherd. Jesus would lay down His life for the sheep, and He would take it back again. Death and resurrection were shortly upon Him, but the Good Shepherd did not blink an eye. Trusting the Father, He was to die on behalf of the flock.

He Rewards (John 10:25-30)

Chapter and verse divisions in the Bible are handy for quick reference, but they can obscure the continuity that flows across chapters. Jesus spoke of Himself as the Good Shepherd in the context of disputes with the Pharisees. The Lord had healed a blind man in Jerusalem (John 9:7), and the Pharisees had challenged Him (v. 16). But what could they do other than sputter and accuse? The miracle was undeniable. When Jesus pointed out their self-imposed blindness, frustration boiled over into rage (vv. 40-41). They determined to kill Him, but they needed respectability. Jesus had a sizable following. The question the Pharisees put to Jesus in John 10:24 is a continuation of their attempts to discredit Him in the aftermath of His healing of the blind man. "Why do You keep us in doubt?" they asked. "If You are the Christ, tell us plainly." It would have been difficult for them to kill Him for healing a blind man, but an open claim to being the Christ had political and religious implications. They might have parlayed that into a death sentence.

Jesus responded by developing the metaphor of the shepherd and the sheep still further. Referring to the blind man, the Lord told them that His works spoke clearly. Those who responded to His signs with faith were His sheep. The Pharisees refused to believe. Having turned their backs on the works of God, they could not be His sheep. If the Pharisees wanted an excuse to kill Him, Jesus would not withhold the truth. He openly said that He would grant the gift of God to His sheep; He would give eternal life. Did He have the authority to make such an audacious promise? Jesus followed the implications to their conclusion: "I and My Father are one," He said (John 10:25). They picked up stones to kill Him.

Conclusion

Those who are in positions of leadership in the church do well to lead on the model Jesus provided. The leadership of a shepherd is on a different order than a CEO or a construction boss. Jesus is Shepherd and Bishop (Overseer) of the souls of men (1 Peter 2:25), but Peter made it clear that, in day-today matters of church life, He delegated authority to men appointed to the task of shepherding. In the latter portion of his letter, the apostle turned to men who served as Jesus served, in the likeness of shepherds. He called them elders and identified himself as a fellow elder (5:1). For elders to serve well, a church must give them the respect and the appreciation due to them. The word "bishop" or "overseer" implies that elders have authority in the church in matters of opinion. When elders are wise, they refuse to flaunt their authority. They listen, take advice when it is fitting, and measure themselves as a shepherd measures his responsibility toward his sheep. Above all, an elder loves those committed to his charge. He stands ready to lay down his life for the sake of the people of God.

Questions

1. How did people in the biblical world view shepherds?
2. Besides shepherding, what other agricultural metaphors help people understand God and His ways?
3. In what sense does God lead His people to green pastures and quiet waters?
4. What does deliverance from the "valley of death" mean in Psalm 23?
5. By what means did Jesus say the shepherd enters the sheepfold?
6. What was Jesus warning His disciples about when He said a thief enters the fold in some other way?
7. How do the doorkeeper and the sheep react when they hear the voice of the shepherd?
8. Who were the "other sheep" Jesus said would be His – sheep not of His fold?
9. Why did Jesus say the Father loves Him?
10. Whom did Jesus indict by telling them they were not of His sheep?

Discussion Starters

1. Besides the shepherd metaphor, what other figures of speech were used in the Bible to describe God? What aspects of His character do we learn from each?
2. In what way is sin its own punishment in this life? Does obedience to God guarantee a life of tranquility and peace? What does obedience guarantee?
3. What people did Jesus contrast Himself with when He said He was the Good Shepherd? Who are the bad shepherds, the hirelings who have no concern?
4. What had happened immediately before Jesus described Himself as the Good Shepherd? How does the context help us understand what Jesus said?

Endnotes

Fall Quarter

Lesson 8

1 Gordon D. Fee and Douglas Stuart, *How to Read the Bible for All Its Worth*, 3rd ed. (Grand Rapids: Zondervan, 2003) 169.

2 F.F. Bruce, *The Epistle to the Hebrews (New International Commentary on the New Testament)* (Grand Rapids: Eerdmans, 1964) 375.

Winter Quarter

Lesson 2

1 Jack Cottrell, *Power From on High: What the Bible Says About the Holy Spirit* (Joplin: College Press, 2007) 371.

Lesson 3

1 The phrase is from John Bunyan's *The Pilgrim's Progress*, Part 1, "The First Stage."

Lesson 8

1 R.T. France, *The Gospel According to Matthew (Tyndale New Testament Commentaries)* (Grand Rapids: Eerdmans, 1985) 148.

Lesson 11

1 When a Hebrew word from the Old Testament or a Greek word from the New Testament is transliterated, it is sounded out and written in English. The English word is pronounced approximately like the word was pronounced in the original language. "Baptism," for example, is a transliteration of a Greek word pronounced roughly the same way. A word is translated when the meaning of the Hebrew or Greek word is transferred to an English word with approximately the same meaning. Had the Greek word for baptism been translated, it would have read, "immersion."

2 For further study, see Duane Warden, "Born of Water and Spirit," *Luke: A Gospel for the World (Abilene Christian University Annual Bible Lectures 1990)* (Abilene: ACU Press, 1990) 193-201.

Daily Bible Reading

This system of daily Bible reading provides six days of reading and one day a week to catch up and reflect on what has been read. By following this schedule, you will be able to read the entire Bible in a year.

SEPTEMBER

1   Genesis 1-4
2   Genesis 5-8
3   Genesis 9-12
4   Genesis 13-16
5   Genesis 17-20
6   Genesis 21-24
7   Review
8   Genesis 25-28
9   Genesis 29-32
10 Genesis 33-36
11 Genesis 37-40
12 Genesis 41-44
13 Genesis 45-50
14 Review
15 Exodus 1-4
16 Exodus 5-8
17 Exodus 9-12
18 Exodus 13-16
19 Exodus 17-20
20 Exodus 21-24
21 Review
22 Exodus 25-28
23 Exodus 29-32
24 Exodus 33-37
25 Exodus 38-40
26 Leviticus 1-4
27 Leviticus 5-8
28 Review
29 Leviticus 9-12
30 Leviticus 13-16

OCTOBER

1   Leviticus 17-20
2   Leviticus 21-24
3   Leviticus 25-27
4   Numbers 1-4
5   Review
6   Numbers 5-8
7   Numbers 9-12
8   Numbers 13-16
9   Numbers 17-20
10 Numbers 21-24
11 Numbers 25-28
12 Review
13 Numbers 29-32
14 Numbers 33-36
15 Deuteronomy 1-4
16 Deuteronomy 5-8
17 Deuteronomy 9-12
18 Deuteronomy 13-16
19 Review
20 Deuteronomy 17-20
21 Deuteronomy 21-24
22 Deuteronomy 25-28
23 Deuteronomy 29-31
24 Deuteronomy 32-34
25 Matthew 1-4
26 Review
27 Matthew 5-8
28 Matthew 9-12
29 Matthew 13-16
30 Matthew 17-20
31 Matthew 21-24

NOVEMBER

1   Matthew 25-28
2   Review
3   Mark 1-4
4   Mark 5-8
5   Mark 9-12
6   Mark 13-16
7   Luke 1-4
8   Luke 5-8
9   Review
10 Luke 9-12
11 Luke 13-16
12 Luke 17-20
13 Luke 21-24
14 John 1-4
15 John 5-10
16 Review
17 John 11-15
18 John 16-21
19 Acts 1-4
20 Acts 5-8
21 Acts 9-12
22 Acts 13-16
23 Review
24 Acts 17-20
25 Acts 21-24
26 Acts 25-28
27 Joshua 1-4
28 Joshua 5-8
29 Joshua 9-12
30 Review

DECEMBER

1   Joshua 13-16
2   Joshua 17-20
3   Joshua 21-24
4   Judges 1-3
5   Judges 4-6
6   Judges 7-9
7   Review
8   Judges 10-13
9   Judges 14-17
10 Judges 18-21
11 Ruth 1-4
12 1 Samuel 1-3
13 1 Samuel 4-7
14 Review
15 1 Samuel 8-11
16 1 Samuel 12-15
17 1 Samuel 16-19
18 1 Samuel 20-23
19 1 Samuel 24-27
20 1 Samuel 28-31
21 Review
22 2 Samuel 1-4
23 2 Samuel 5-8
24 2 Samuel 9-12
25 2 Samuel 13-16
26 2 Samuel 17-20
27 2 Samuel 21-24
28 Review

29	1 Kings 1-3	12	Job 15-18	31	Psalms 103-105
30	1 Kings 4-6	13	Job 19-22		
31	1 Kings 7-10	14	Job 23-26		

JANUARY

1	1 Kings 11-14	15	Review		**APRIL**
2	1 Kings 15-18	16	Job 27-30	1	Psalms 106-108
3	1 Kings 19-22	17	Job 31-34	2	Psalms 109-111
4	Review	18	Job 35-38	3	Psalms 112-115
5	2 Kings 1-4	19	Job 39-42	4	Psalms 116-118
6	2 Kings 5-8	20	Psalms 1-3	5	Review
7	2 Kings 9-12	21	Psalms 4-6	6	Psalm 119:1-48
8	2 Kings 13-17	22	Review	7	Psalm 119:49-96
9	2 Kings 18-22	23	Psalms 7-9	8	Psalm 119:97-136
10	2 Kings 23-25	24	Psalms 10-12	9	Psalm 119:137-176
11	Review	25	Psalms 13-15	10	Psalms 120-124

JANUARY

1. 1 Kings 11-14
2. 1 Kings 15-18
3. 1 Kings 19-22
4. Review
5. 2 Kings 1-4
6. 2 Kings 5-8
7. 2 Kings 9-12
8. 2 Kings 13-17
9. 2 Kings 18-22
10. 2 Kings 23-25
11. Review
12. 1 Chronicles 1-3
13. 1 Chronicles 4-6
14. 1 Chronicles 7-9
15. 1 Chronicles 10-13
16. 1 Chronicles 14-17
17. 1 Chronicles 18-21
18. Review
19. 1 Chronicles 22-25
20. 1 Chronicles 26-29
21. 2 Chronicles 1-6
22. 2 Chronicles 7-11
23. 2 Chronicles 12-16
24. 2 Chronicles 17-21
25. Review
26. 2 Chronicles 22-26
27. 2 Chronicles 27-31
28. 2 Chronicles 32-36
29. Ezra 1-4
30. Ezra 5-7
31. Ezra 8-10

FEBRUARY

1. Review
2. Nehemiah 1-4
3. Nehemiah 5-8
4. Nehemiah 9-13
5. Esther 1-5
6. Esther 6-10
7. Job 1-3
8. Review
9. Job 4-6
10. Job 7-10
11. Job 11-14
12. Job 15-18
13. Job 19-22
14. Job 23-26
15. Review
16. Job 27-30
17. Job 31-34
18. Job 35-38
19. Job 39-42
20. Psalms 1-3
21. Psalms 4-6
22. Review
23. Psalms 7-9
24. Psalms 10-12
25. Psalms 13-15
26. Psalms 16-18
27. Psalms 19-21
28. Psalms 22-25

MARCH

1. Review
2. Psalms 26-29
3. Psalms 30-33
4. Psalms 34-36
5. Psalms 37-39
6. Psalms 40-42
7. Psalms 43-45
8. Review
9. Psalms 46-48
10. Psalms 49-51
11. Psalms 52-54
12. Psalms 55-57
13. Psalms 58-60
14. Psalms 61-63
15. Review
16. Psalms 64-66
17. Psalms 67-68
18. Psalms 69-71
19. Psalms 72-74
20. Psalms 75-77
21. Psalms 78-80
22. Review
23. Psalms 81-83
24. Psalms 84-86
25. Psalms 87-89
26. Psalms 90-93
27. Psalms 94-96
28. Psalms 97-99
29. Review
30. Psalms 100-102
31. Psalms 103-105

APRIL

1. Psalms 106-108
2. Psalms 109-111
3. Psalms 112-115
4. Psalms 116-118
5. Review
6. Psalm 119:1-48
7. Psalm 119:49-96
8. Psalm 119:97-136
9. Psalm 119:137-176
10. Psalms 120-124
11. Psalms 125-129
12. Review
13. Psalms 130-133
14. Psalms 134-136
15. Psalms 137-139
16. Psalms 140-142
17. Psalms 143-146
18. Psalms 147-150
19. Review
20. Proverbs 1-5
21. Proverbs 6-10
22. Proverbs 11-15
23. Proverbs 16-20
24. Proverbs 21-25
25. Proverbs 26-31
26. Review
27. Ecclesiastes 1-4
28. Ecclesiastes 5-8
29. Ecclesiastes 9-12
30. Song of Solomon 1-4

MAY

1. Song of Solomon 5-8
2. Isaiah 1-5
3. Review
4. Isaiah 6-10
5. Isaiah 11-15
6. Isaiah 16-20
7. Isaiah 21-25
8. Isaiah 26-30
9. Isaiah 31-35
10. Review
11. Isaiah 36-40
12. Isaiah 41-45
13. Isaiah 46-50
14. Isaiah 51-55

15 Isaiah 56-61
16 Isaiah 62-66
17 Review
18 Jeremiah 1-5
19 Jeremiah 6-10
20 Jeremiah 11-15
21 Jeremiah 16-20
22 Jeremiah 21-25
23 Jeremiah 26-30
24 Review
25 Jeremiah 31-35
26 Jeremiah 36-40
27 Jeremiah 41-44
28 Jeremiah 45-48
29 Jeremiah 49-52
30 Lamentations 1-5
31 Review

JUNE
1 Ezekiel 1-4
2 Ezekiel 5-8
3 Ezekiel 9-12
4 Ezekiel 13-16
5 Ezekiel 17-20
6 Ezekiel 21-24
7 Review
8 Ezekiel 25-28
9 Ezekiel 29-32
10 Ezekiel 33-36
11 Ezekiel 37-40
12 Ezekiel 41-44
13 Ezekiel 45-48
14 Review
15 Daniel 1-4
16 Daniel 5-8
17 Daniel 9-12
18 Hosea 1-4
19 Hosea 5-8
20 Hosea 9-11
21 Review
22 Hosea 12-14
23 Joel 1-3
24 Amos 1-4
25 Amos 5-9
26 Obadiah 1
27 Jonah 1-4
28 Review
29 Micah 1-4
30 Micah 5-7

JULY
1 Nahum 1-3
2 Habakkuk 1-3
3 Zephaniah 1-3
4 Haggai 1-2
5 Review
6 Zechariah 1-2
7 Zechariah 3-5
8 Zechariah 6-8
9 Zechariah 9-11
10 Zechariah 12-14
11 Malachi 1-2
12 Review
13 Malachi 3-4
14 Romans 1-4
15 Romans 5-8
16 Romans 9-12
17 Romans 13-16
18 1 Corinthians 1-4
19 Review
20 1 Corinthians 5-8
21 1 Corinthians 9-12
22 1 Corinthians 13-16
23 2 Corinthians 1-5
24 2 Corinthians 6-9
25 2 Corinthians 10-13
26 Review
27 Galatians 1-3
28 Galatians 4-6
29 Ephesians 1-3
30 Ephesians 4-6
31 Philippians 1-4

AUGUST
1 Colossians 1-4
2 Review
3 1 Thessalonians 1-5
4 2 Thessalonians 1-3
5 1 Timothy 1-3
6 1 Timothy 4-6
7 2 Timothy 1-4
8 Titus 1-3; Philemon 1
9 Review
10 Hebrews 1-3
11 Hebrews 4-7
12 Hebrews 8-10
13 Hebrews 11-13
14 James 1-5
15 1 Peter 1-5

16 Review
17 2 Peter 1-3
18 1 John 1-5
19 2 John; 3 John; Jude
20 Revelation 1-3
21 Revelation 4-6
22 Revelation 7-9
23 Review
24 Revelation 10-12
25 Revelation 13-14
26 Revelation 15-17
27 Revelation 18-20
28 Revelation 21-22
29 A special OT verse
30 Review
31 A special NT verse